Gender and Mental Health

Also by Pauline M. Prior:

Mental Health and Politics in Northern Ireland

Gender and Mental Health

PAULINE M. PRIOR
Consultant Editor: Jo Campling

MACMILLAN

First published 1999 by
MACMILLAN PRESS LTD
Houndmills, Basingstoke, Hampshire RG21 6XS
and London
Companies and representatives
throughout the world

ISBN 0–333–68761–2 hardcover
ISBN 0–333–68762–0 paperback

A catalogue record for this book is available
from the British Library.

This book is printed on paper suitable for recycling and
made from fully managed and sustained forest sources.

10 9   8   7   6   5   4   3   2   1
08 07 06 05 04 03 02 01 00 99

Editing and origination by
Aardvark Editorial, Mendham, Suffolk

Typeset by T & A Typesetting Services, Rochdale

Printed in Hong Kong

Dedicated to my mother, Rita Prior

Contents

Preface and Acknowledgements

This book is intended as a critical introduction to debates on the impact of gender on mental health experiences and on mental health service use. It will be useful to students from a number of disciplinary backgrounds interested in either gender or mental health – students of sociology, social policy, gender studies, anthropology and psychology. It will also be suitable as reference and training material for professionals who encounter women and men with mental health problems – social workers, nurses, doctors, psychologists and lawyers. In addition, the author hopes that it will be of interest to members of the general public who have personal experience of the impact of mental disorder on themselves or a member of their family, as the issues raised are of such importance in the personal lives of so many people that they cannot be confined only to academic debate.

I would like to thank a number of people who have been instrumental in both the genesis and production of the final arguments that are presented in this book. On a professional level, these include Jo Campling, the consultant editor, and the anonymous referee for Macmillan Press, both of whom challenged some of my early ideas in a way that helped to clarify my thinking and greatly enhanced the final product; Professor Kathleen Jones, of York University, who is a constant inspiration to me in my work on mental health policy; Dr Bernadette C. Hayes and Dr Jim Campbell, both of Queen's University Belfast, who have collaborated with me in research that informed the debate; and staff at the Medical Library of Queen's University, who never complained about my obvious addiction to Medline and my unending demands for interlibrary loans. I would also like to formally thank Virago Press, the publishers of *The Loony Bin Trip* by Kate Millett, for permission to use extracts from this wonderful novel. On a more personal note, I would like to thank Angela and Stephanie Bourke, who made possible and enjoyable my retreat to a cottage in Kerry in the summer of 1997, and to Sarah Prior and other members of my family, who offered encouragement throughout the final writing phase. Finally, to the commissioning editor, Catherine Gray, and to the

many others too numerous to name, who have helped me both personally and professionally during the preparation of this book, may I also
say 'thank you' for your support and advice.

PAULINE M. PRIOR

1

Introduction

> Mental disorders cause an enormous amount of misery, suffering, economic loss and decreased quality of life of individuals, their families and their communities. At least 300 million people suffer from such disorders, and it is probable that one third or two fifths of all disability is caused by them. (Sartorius *et al.* 1989: 178)

The words of Sartorius and his colleagues from the World Health Organization (WHO) highlight the enormity of the cost of mental disorder to the individual and to society. The question is, who should bear the burden of this cost? Until recently, it was assumed that it would fall mainly on the public purse as services were provided primarily within national health care systems. This is no longer the case, however, as governments throughout the Western world withdraw from the direct provision of health and welfare services and as perceptions of mental disorder change.

This book is a contribution to the debate on changes both in the perceptions of mental disorder itself and in society's response to it – with a special focus on gender. It will review recent evidence of changes in gender patterns in psychiatric diagnosis and treatment, and consider these changes from a policy perspective. In addition, it will offer some explanations for the particular vulnerability of women to psychiatric diagnosis in the past through an exploration of sociological theories on mental disorder and professional responses to it. The discussion is based on epidemiological research on mental health and illness, sociological and anthropological debates on the definitions of mental disorder, legal debates on compulsory treatment, crime and dangerousness, and policy debates on models of service delivery. Data will be drawn mainly from the UK and USA, with some examples from continental Europe and other parts of the world.

Why write another book on gender and mental health?

This book is unique in what it hopes to achieve – a rounded discussion of the current debates within sociology, social policy and psychiatry in an area that is constantly changing. Existing literature in this area includes substantial work on women and mental health (Busfield 1989, 1996; Chesler 1972; Russell 1995; Showalter 1987; Ussher 1991), and on women and crime (Allen 1986; 1987; Daly 1994; Heidensohn 1996; Morris 1987; Naffine 1987). Some of this literature is based on assumptions that are now open to challenge because of new research on the experiences of mental disorder and new theorising on masculinity. One of the most basic of these assumptions is that women are more prone than men to the diagnosis of mental disorder. This viewpoint is based on evidence that they have been overrepresented in all psychiatric statistics in the UK and the USA in the nineteenth and twentieth centuries. Recent historical research suggests that the dominance of women in the public asylum system in England cannot be taken for granted and that it is probable that the gender patterns seen during the second half of the nineteenth century were more like those in Ireland, with young single men forming the largest group in asylums (Finnane 1981).

Current psychiatric research in a number of countries also points to the increasing visibility of men in psychiatric statistics in the twentieth century. For example, a study in New Zealand found a slightly higher rate of psychiatric morbidity for men than women (Thornley *et al.* 1991), in Northern Ireland young men are becoming increasingly visible in psychiatric hospital statistics (Prior and Hayes 1998), and in England hospital admission rates are changing in urban areas, with young males from ethnic minorities becoming the group most vulnerable to psychiatric admission (Payne 1995, 1996). Perhaps the most interesting finding is from the American Epidemiologic Catchment Area (ECA) study, which acknowledged that if substance dependence is included in statistics on mental disorder, men have a higher lifetime prevalence of psychiatric disorder than women (Robins and Regier 1991). The statement that women always dominate psychiatric statistics is clearly an overgeneralisation that is no longer accurate. However, gender differences continue to operate, and the search for explanations for the overrepresentation of either men or women in any particular diagnostic category must continue in order to highlight risk factors in socio-economic conditions and gender bias in approaches to diagnosis and treatment.

The decision to focus on gender, rather than on women only, was based on concerns arising from this new research. Men with mental health problems have received relatively little attention in sociological or psychiatric literature. Fortunately, in recent years, the situation has been remedied by a number of developments. Gender is now routinely included as a variable in most American and cross-national psychiatric studies, substance dependence and personality disorder (conditions associated with men) are now being recognised as mental disorders, and a number of social scientists have begun to analyse the male experience of illness in general and of stress related to male identity and sexual orientation (Barnes *et al.* 1990; Clatterbaugh 1990; Connell 1992, 1995; Gomez 1993).

The decision to include a policy perspective and chapters on law and crime in this book was based on the author's experience as a researcher and teacher – at present there are no other texts that attempt to provide this kind of overview of society's responses (through law and service structures) to mental disorder as we begin a new century. The policy perspective comes from the author's disciplinary background in social policy, with its emphasis on citizenship and rights, and on the role of government in service provision. Within social policy as a discipline, comparative research on models of social legislation and service provision has proved both interesting and enlightening in demonstrating how societies deal with specific social problems. In relation to mental health care, for example, Europe was much later than the USA in its policy of de-institutionalisation, a factor that has led to different patterns of service provision. Also, in the area of law, the issues of most concern to European users of mental health services and their families occur in relation to rights to an adequate level of treatment in the community, whereas in the USA this battle was fought (and some would say lost) during the 1980s (Wexler 1990). In the knowledge that international comparisons are difficult, they are presented here not to provide all the answers but rather to raise questions about 'taken for granted' ways of viewing mental health care (for a discussion, see Ramon 1995).

New knowledge

New knowledge also raises new questions. During the past three decades, developments in medical knowledge have given rise to an almost continuous transformation of definitions of mental illness and mental disorder. The internationally recognised classifications of mental disorder, included as part of the *International Classification of Diseases* (ICD) from the WHO, has had four revisions since 1948, and the *Diagnostic and Statistical Manual* (DSM) from the American Psychiatric Association has undergone four revisions since 1952 (for a discussion, see Chapter 2). Each revision takes into account not only scientific developments, but also changes in social attitudes. In other words, professional and lay views of what constitutes mental illness and mental disorder are constantly changing. In the knowledge that both terms are contested by health professionals, academics and the public at large, I propose to use the term 'mental illness' only when it is already in use to describe a particular situation or person. For the most part, the preferred term throughout the book will be 'mental disorder' as this is the designation most widely used in the social science and health literature. It includes all mental disturbances, even those which have not been traditionally regarded as 'illness' – substance dependence and personality disorder – in addition to all forms of mental disturbance traditionally accepted as mental illness (see Chapter 2).

Of course, changes in definition have not occurred in a vacuum. Recent large-scale studies in Europe and America have greatly enhanced our knowledge of the experience of mental disorder and the use of mental health services. The findings from these studies sometimes confirm and sometimes challenge current assumptions about gender and mental health. In the USA, the ECA, initiated in 1980 by the National Institute of Mental Health (NIMH), provided valuable information on the prevalence of mental disorder in the community and on mental health needs that were not being met. The study consisted of surveys carried out on community samples on five sites throughout the USA, comprising a total of 18,571 people. The prime objectives of the study were to estimate the prevalence of mental disorders in both treated and untreated populations and to study the factors that prevented people accessing mental health services (Regier *et al.* 1993; Robins and Regier 1991).

This was not the first large-scale study carried out in the USA, but it was designed expressly to overcome the methodological problems in earlier studies – problems that had resulted in different prevalence estimates. These well-known studies, including the Stirling County Study of 1,010 subjects, the Midtown Manhattan Study of 1,660 subjects and the Baltimore Morbidity Study of 809 subjects, were all carried out in the late 1950s and the early 1960s. The Stirling County Study found significant impairment as a result of a mental disorder in 24 per cent of participants. The Midtown Manhattan Study did not assess specific mental disorders but estimated that 81 per cent of the population had some mild degree of impairment caused by psychiatric symptoms – a finding received by the public with some scepticism. The Baltimore Study focused strictly on the DSM-I categories and estimated that a psychiatric diagnosis could be attached to only 11 per cent of the population (Robins and Regier 1991: 4–5).

The disparity in findings highlighted the problem of estimating with any certainty the levels of mental disorder in society. Although assessment procedures were different, the definitions of mental disorder used in all three surveys were the same, being based on the first edition of the *Diagnostic and Statistical Manual*, DSM-I (1952). Since then, cross-national co-operation has led to the development of standardised assessment instruments, such as the NIMH Diagnostic Interview Schedule (DIS) used in the ECA study. Because of the efforts to standardise instruments, the results of the ECA study are regarded as the best current estimates of prevalence of psychiatric disorders in the USA. The rates were higher than expected and approximated more closely to the Stirling County Study than to the other earlier large-scale studies.

The surveys found a 32 per cent lifetime prevalence and a 20 per cent annual prevalence of psychiatric disorder in the population. This means that (on the basis of self-reporting) one in five Americans had a mental disorder with at least one active symptom in the year prior to the interview, and that almost one in three had experienced one or more symptoms at some time in their lives (Robins and Regier 1991: 327–9). An interesting finding in relation to the discussion here is the fact that men had a higher *lifetime* prevalence (36 per cent) than women (30 per cent), although men and women had the same *annual* prevalence rate. Robins and Regier (1991: 332) conjecture that earlier studies often paid more attention to illnesses considered psychosomatic and less to substance dependence and personality disorders than did the ECA study, leading to evidence of a higher incidence of mental disorder among women. This is a very exciting finding as, for the first time, there is strong research evidence from a large-scale study in support of the feminist allegation of institutionalised sexism in social definitions of mental disorders.

In addition to the first wave of ECA surveys in the 1980s, there is now another major source of information in the USA – the National Comorbidity Study (NCS). Building on the work of the ECA, this study was carried out between 1990 and 1992 by the Survey Research Centre at the University of Michigan, Ann Arbor (Kessler *et al.* 1994). Using

DSM-III-R criteria, a structured psychiatric interview was administered to a representative national sample of 8,098 individuals. It was designed specifically to study the co-morbidity of substance use disorders and non-substance psychiatric disorders, an area of concern highlighted by the President's Commission on Mental Health and Illness in 1978. The NCS represents an advance on the ECA on three counts. It is based on the DSM-III-R, a later version than that used in the ECA surveys, and also includes some questions that allow for comparisons with the DSM-IV and the ICD version 10 (ICD-10), the classification used in most large-scale studies outside the USA. It was also designed to study risk factors for mental disorder as well as prevalence and incidence rates, and finally, as a nationally representative sample, it made possible the study of regional variations and urban–rural differences (Kessler *et al.* 1994: 10). This rich source of material will be used extensively in later discussions.

At the WHO, interest in subjecting national research to cross-national comparison was reflected in the work of Jablensky (1986) and Sartorius (1986). In a seminal contribution to the debate on trends in mental disorder, Sartorius and his colleagues discussed the results of a number of repeat surveys in Taiwan, Canada, Sweden, Germany, Denmark, Scotland and Iceland (Sartorius *et al.* 1989). As the purpose of each individual piece of research had been to examine changes over time in each country, it was possible to compare trends in relation to socio-economic changes in the general population. One of the most interesting findings was that, contrary to the expectations of many of the researchers, an increase in the number of mental disorders did not follow as a consequence of industrialisation and the disruption of traditional family systems. Some specific trends appeared to supersede national boundaries. For example, the incidence of schizophrenia seemed to be decreasing, while depressive disorders were on the increase. Each of these trends was found to be different in relation to men and women. The decrease in schizophrenia was greater for women than men, and the increase in depression was greater for men (particularly young men) than for women (Sartorius *et al.* 1989: 176–7; see Chapter 3 for a further discussion of these findings). In other words, the impact of both trends was to increase the proportion of men in psychiatric statistics. Another interesting prediction made by the WHO team was that there would be a decrease of organic mental disorders in the elderly population. This does not mean that the overall prevalence of mental disorder among older people will decrease but instead that most of it will be amenable to good treatment and rehabilitation, as for other age groups. As the WHO team also found that women respond more positively to care and treatment programmes, this will undoubtedly have an impact on the gender balance in mental health statistics.

In the UK, the lack of good-quality, large-scale data was acknowledged in *The Health of the Nation* (Department of Health 1992). This policy document, which aimed to set the parameters for the delivery of health care for the twenty-first century, included as one of its targets the gathering of more accurate information on health need. Spurred on by the success of the ECA studies in the USA, the Department of Health commissioned the Office of Population Censuses and Surveys (OPCS) to undertake the Surveys of Psychiatric Morbidity. The aim was to provide detailed information on the prevalence of psychiatric problems, on patterns of service use and on the impact on individuals' lives in terms of the social disability associated with mental illness. Four separate surveys of people aged 16–64 from England, Scotland and Wales were carried out in 1993 and 1994. The first study was of 10,000 adults living in private households; the second, a supplementary sample of 350 people with psychosis living in private households; the third, 1,200 people living in institutions specifically catering for people with mental illness; and the fourth, a sample of 100 homeless people living in hostels for the homeless, including some people sleeping rough (Jenkins and Meltzer 1995; Mason and Wilkinson 1996: Meltzer *et al.* 1995).

Early reports of these surveys indicate that 14 per cent of the adult population had a neurotic health problem, defined as a score of 12 or more on the Revised Clinical Interview Schedule (CIS-R). Women were much more likely than men to feature in these statistics. Within the working age population (aged 20–54 years), 22 per cent of women and 12 per cent of men achieved a score of 12. These findings are in line with those of earlier studies of minor psychiatric disorders in the community, which indicate a prevalence of between 10 and 30 per cent depending on the threshold used to determine the presence of a disorder. As expected, gender patterns for alcohol and drug dependence were the reverse of those for neurotic psychopathology. Within an overall rate of 5 per cent for alcohol dependence and a rate of 2 per cent for drug dependence, men were three times more likely than women to have alcohol dependence and twice as likely to be drug dependent. Those most at risk for substance dependence were young men aged 20–24 years, with a yearly prevalence of 18 per cent for alcohol dependence and 11 per cent for drug dependence. Although this figure decreases with age, it is clear that, if substance dependence is included as evidence of the presence of mental disorder and is equal in significance to more traditionally recognised forms of psychopathology (in this instance neurosis), the predominance of women in the statistics on mental disorder begins to disappear.

Another important source of material on self-reported psychological distress and on psychiatric symptoms in the UK is the Health and Lifestyle Survey, which is a longitudinal study of a nationwide sample, measuring changes in physical and mental health, attitudes and lifestyle (Blaxter 1990; Cox *et al.* 1993). The first survey (HALS1) took place in 1984/85 and the second (HALS2) 7 years later. Three measures of personality and a measure of mental health were used. The mental health measure was the number of psychiatric symptoms reported using the 30-item version of the General Health Questionnaire (GHQ) of Goldberg (1972). The GHQ is concerned with a person's current mental state, its questions dealing with psychiatric symptoms such as depression, anxiety, sleep disturbance, social functioning and general life satisfaction that have been present over the previous few weeks (Cox *et al.* 1993: 134). In common with other surveys, the GHQ was scored dichotomously, each symptom being rated as either present or absent, giving a maximum score of 30. In both surveys, women had higher scores than men. Based on earlier American research, the GHQ was also used as a screen for possible psychiatric disorder, taking a point between the scores of 4 and 5 as a threshold.

The results surprised even the authors of the survey report. They indicated that the proportion of survey participants with minor psychiatric illness was 25 per cent for men and 30 per cent for women (Cox *et al.* 1993: 135). Although this finding is not too far removed from the Stirling County Study, it is much higher than those of the OPCS surveys, and indeed the British authors suggest that it is an overestimate of the true prevalence of psychiatric disorder and results from a methodological error caused by the use of a threshold value validated in a general practice setting that may not be useful in a community setting. Data from this survey will be used in the discussion that follows, but the findings will be treated with a certain amount of caution.

Summary of contents

This text is divided into two parts, the first attempting a sociological analysis of current perceptions and professional practices in relation to mental disorder, the second providing a policy perspective on individual and social responses to the experience. In Part I (Chapters 2–5), the field of study is delineated in terms of the changing definitions of and perspectives on mental disorder, the gendered nature of the population seen to be at risk, the therapies (medical and non-medical) available to people who seek help with their mental health problems and, finally, academic debates on the interrelationship between concepts of normality, gender roles and psychiatric labels. Part II (Chapters 6–10) builds on the knowledge gained in the early chapters and focuses specifically on policy issues related to service development, legal changes and the special problems experienced by people who come into contact with both the criminal justice system and the health care system.

The discussion on the definitions of mental disorder contained in Chapter 2 begins with the official medical and legal definitions that form the basis for policy documents and research on mental disorder. Because these definitions are highly contested, these 'official' definitions are contrasted with alternative perspectives from mental health service users who reject psychiatric labels, and from researchers interested in the impact of culture on the concept of 'abnormal' behaviour and on professional classifications of this behaviour. Chapter 3 presents detailed research evidence on the population most at risk of suffering from mental health problems. Large-scale studies in the USA and Europe show complex relationships between psychiatric morbidity, ethnicity and gender. As we have already seen, gender patterns in psychiatric morbidity are changing as problems associated with men (substance dependence and personality disorders) are increasingly being recognised as mental disorders. In addition, research on inequalities in health has conclusively shown that generalisations about gender and vulnerability are not universally valid when ethnicity and socioeconomic circumstances are considered.

The use of the word 'treatment' in the title of Chapter 4 does not imply an acceptance of a medical model in dealing with problems that are often defined by service users as outside the health arena. Instead, it is assumed that these problems, which may be emotional or psychological in nature, often stem from social or economic disadvantage. The purpose of this chapter is to discuss the range of help available within the general framework of health care practice – the traditional hospital approach, the community care approach and the more recent user-initiated approach. In spite of the great wave of de-institutionalisation since the 1970s and the euphoria surrounding the introduction of community care programmes since the 1980s, there is evidence of a backlash in public opinion that may lead to a revival of the institutional approach to mental health care in the twenty-first century.

The title of Chapter 5 is also problematic as any discussion of normality must be contentious. Here, we consider some of the academic and literary debates spawned by psychiatry's efforts to conceptualise mental illness in terms that rely on stereotypical notions of behaviour for men and women. Because of the seeming overrepresentation of women in psychiatric statistics, feminist writers have constantly questioned the labels used to define 'abnormal' female behaviour and the structures in society that have placed unacceptable psychological burdens on women. The most recent public debate exposing different perspectives on women's mental health was that in relation to the inclusion of 'Premenstrual syndrome' in the American classification of psychiatric disorders (DSM-IV) (for a discussion, see Figert 1996). Similar problems with psychiatric discourse in relation to men are only now beginning to appear in the masculinity literature. The major debate during the 1970s and 80s was that surrounding the designation of homosexuality as a psychiatric illness and the controversy surrounding its removal from the American classification. The most current controversy is that surrounding the medicalisation (by psychiatric labelling) of diversities in sexual identity and role. As the discussion in this chapter shows, this is a new area of research that is developing rapidly as men's mental health becomes a focus for study.

In the second part of the book, the emphasis changes to incorporate a policy perspective into the exploration of gender and mental health and disorder. This may be quite a departure for some readers as, although there are a number of textbooks on health policy in general, there is relatively little public debate in the academic literature on mental health policy as such. Chapter 6 presents some of the most familiar approaches to the analysis of policy formation and implementation for those unfamiliar with this territory. This is rather a long chapter, but it provides the essential tools for analysing policy developments in the fields of both health and criminal justice. The perspective is then applied in some detail to recent developments in mental health services (Chapter 7) and mental health law (Chapter 8). Some of the service trends have already been introduced in Chapter 4, but here a much broader view is taken, and an attempt is made to answer the question, how do different countries deal with the problem of mental disorder? Both of these chapters touch briefly on policy assumptions underpinning legislation and service provision, with a view to providing the reader with some experience in the analysis of different approaches to mental health policy and law. It will be clear that the particular policy model adopted by a specific country will depend on factors that have little to do with mental health but are instead related to social attitudes, political will and financial commitment.

All of these influences are clearly evidenced in the data used as the basis for discussion in Chapter 9, on crime and mental disorder. Unlike other areas of mental health provision, where gender patterns are not always clear, the gendered landscape in relation to offenders with mental disorders is obvious. Although men predominate in facilities for this group of people (designated 'special hospitals' in the UK) as they do in the prison system, there is some evidence that, within the context of their small numbers in the prison system, women are overrepresented in special hospitals. Thus, any simplistic conclusions based on numbers alone will not be used as a basis for any conclusions drawn. As a general comment, it should be mentioned here that the rationale for the inclusion of crime in a text that is dominated by health issues is that it is in this area that the public perception of mental disorder is most obviously flawed.

The final chapter is simply a short discussion on some of the main themes that have emerged throughout the text, focusing on the importance of a 'gender-conscious' approach to research and policy-making, and implementation for a mental health service that is accessible and helpful to both women and men.

Part I

Mental Disorder

2

Defining Mental Disorder

A critical analysis of the experience of mental disorder and mental health service developments presupposes an awareness of hidden assumptions in research statistics, legislation and policy statements, as these assumptions influence the definitions used to measure the nature and extent of mental disorder. One of the main problems in measuring mental disorder and, by implication, defining the population at risk is the controversial nature of the concepts of mental health and mental disorder. Because there are no objective 'fitness' standards, there is an overreliance on 'illness' standards in the measurements used. Erik Stromgren, researcher for the WHO, suggests that the task of calculating the extent of mental disorder in the population should include studies not only of people in contact with psychiatric institutions, general practitioners and other community-based health professionals, but also of people who have never sought or received help with mental health problems (Sartorius *et al.* 1989: 70). In other words, any measurement of the extent of mental disorder should include but not be confined to mental health service users.

Sadly, in the past, there has been a tendency to do precisely this. This approach, although not adequate, has had some validity in the context of NHS services in the UK as the structure provided information on a national basis and with a fair degree of standardisation. However, this approach has been far from satisfactory in the USA and other countries in Europe where the range of service providers is much larger and more diverse. Of course, even if total coverage of health service use could be achieved, the problem of the meaning of the statistics would still remain. Research on service use may have a great deal to offer in relation to treatment and outcomes, but it tells little about the general state of mental health in the population at large or about the factors that impede or facilitate recovery. This was the kind of information sought in the surveys referred to in Chapter 1 – the ECA surveys in the USA,

15

the Psychiatric Morbidity Surveys and the HALSs in the UK, and the WHO surveys led by Sartorius (1986) and Jablensky (1986).

All of these surveys were based on definitions of mental disorder derived from two classification systems – the DSM of the American Psychiatric Association, and the ICD of the WHO. Although the purpose of any classification scheme is to minimise the bias in individual perspectives and to provide some kind of simple framework for conveying information between professionals, there are major difficulties in the use of both the DSM and the ICD. In this chapter, we will take a brief look at both classifications before broadening the debate to more critical perspectives on mental health and disorder. First, however, we will examine the definition used in mental health law.

Legal definitions

During the eighteenth and nineteenth centuries, it was generally accepted that medical and legal definitions of 'insanity' performed different functions. Abraham (1886: 13), in his major treatise on *Law and Practice of Lunacy in Ireland*, summarised the legal view of the period, a view that still has relevance today.

> The jurist views the condition of mind called lunacy or insanity with an exclusive eye to its effect upon the doings of the lunatic, whether in relation to the safety, the rights, and the accountabilities of that person himself, or to the safety and to the rights of the other members of the commonwealth, under the protection and dominion of the laws. Considered in his capacity of citizen, the person alleged to be of unsound mind may, through apparent absence or disorder of intellect, create the belief among his friends and neighbours that he ought to be placed under tutelage, for safety of person and property; and it is to the judicial ascertainment of the truth on this particular that the common inquisition of office is directed.

Judicial certification of 'lunacy', 'idiocy', 'insanity' or 'unsoundness of mind' was thus seen in terms of protection for the person from exploitation, or the protection of society from troublesome or dangerous citizens. One of the basic assumptions underlying nineteenth-century legislation was that the state should protect its citizens from loss of liberty or of property rights. The 'lunatic' continued to be a citizen, and decisions to remove the rights of citizenship had to remain in the public domain. Therefore, nineteenth-century law offered no definitions of what mental disorder was but instead considered the impact it had on the reasoning and behaviour of the individual.

The question for the current era is, should the law contain medical definitions? In the American legislative system, because of the civil libertarian movement of the twentieth century, definitions of what is meant by every legal description of mental disorder are considered to be an essential part of the law. However, the UK has no real medical definitions in the statutes. This has led to a certain amount of lobbying for clarification of the rather vague terms used in the law. One of the strongest lobbies is that for the removal of learning disability from the mental health legislation as, it is argued, the confusion between the two quite distinct forms of disability is stigmatising to both groups of people. The legal argument for the inclusion of both types of disability in the same piece of legislation has been that the impact is similar in terms of people's ability to manage their own financial affairs and to engage in legal contracts, even if the medical conditions are different.

The most controversial aspects of mental health legislation have nothing to do with property management or legal contracts but are aimed at setting parameters within which individuals can be treated, with or without their consent, in a public health system. The historical roots of this are to be found in the procedures for medical certification in nineteenth-century lunacy laws. With the introduction of a public asylum system throughout Europe and the USA, the law had to become more precise in defining those who had a right to treatment at public expense. Medical certification was used to confirm the presence of a mental disorder and thus establish the right of the individual to treatment. In addition, the person had to be acknowledged as poor in order to be eligible for care within the publicly funded system. In Britain, this was in the form of an application for admission to the asylum signed by the Poor Law Officer, who was the forerunner of the Approved Social Worker (ASW) in current legislation (Prior 1992).

The legacy of these early laws remains in current legislation – protection of the individual from unnecessary confinement and financial exploitation, and protection of the public from dangerous people, keeping in mind at all times the cost to the public purse. Recent legislation in Britain, the Mental Health Act 1983, although quite different from the nineteenth-century lunacy laws, outlines parameters for compulsory admission by excluding certain categories of people from the definition of mental disorder. The definition in the Act is very broad and relies on professional clinical judgements of who will be considered as eligible, within the broad categories of mental illness, mental impairment, severe mental impairment and psychopathic disorder. The exclusions are, nevertheless, very specific and are aimed at preventing any abuse of the legislation by families or communities who simply want to reject certain people because of their antisocial or deviant behaviour. Thus, nobody can be admitted (on a compulsory basis) for promiscuity, sexual deviance or immoral conduct, nor indeed for dependence on alcohol or drugs in the absence of a defined mental disorder. Although these exclusions were introduced to protect individuals from unnecessary hospitalisation, they have sometimes been used by psychiatry to abdicate responsibility for people with personality disorders, who may not be in need of compulsory treatment but who require recognition and care for their mental health problems. The impact of this piece of legislation in gender terms is also significant because of the higher incidence of men in the excluded categories. As shown in research by Barnes *et al.* (1990), over half of all compulsory admissions in 1986 concerned women, a pattern that prevailed in all age groups except the under-25s.

The law in other European countries reflects the state of service development as well as particular cultural perspectives on mental health problems. Since the late 1960s, most changes in legislation have been aimed at making voluntary admissions to mental hospitals easier, on the assumption that, as mental illness is similar to physical illness, people should have a right to a full range of health services including but not confined to hospital treatment. The first wave of these changes came in Britain in 1959, France in 1968 and Belgium in 1969. The most famous of 'new wave' legislation was Law 180, passed in Italy in 1978. This law led to a complete overhaul of the mental health system and made compulsory admission to psychiatric hospital treatment the exception rather than the rule. One of the most radical requirements was that no psychiatric unit should exceed 15 beds. The resulting changes in services, which included the closure of many large mental hospitals or their transformation into therapeutic work 'centres' or 'villages', has not been without its critics. However, the importance of this law cannot be overemphasised as it began the process throughout Europe of giving back rights to people who had no hope of regaining these rights without a change in law (see Louzoun 1993).

As we begin a new century, the value of rights without opportunities has also to be questioned. The debate on the 'right to treatment' has been strong in the USA for some time, and it is now beginning to appear on the agenda of user organisations in countries where hospitals have closed without being replaced by adequate community services. In Portugal, mental health law is still used to uphold a system of psychiatric institutionalisation. This is in keeping with a conscious philosophy that places mental illness within a medical framework dominated by hospital care (Freeman *et al.* 1985). Probably the only generalisation that can be made is that, in countries favouring hospital-based treatment, the definitions of mental disorder are broad and inclusive, concentrating on the need to protect the individual from exploitation and to establish a right to publicly funded care, whereas in countries where the non-institutional approach is dominant, the legal definition of mental illness is narrow and explicit to prevent unnecessary hospitalisation.

In the USA, although laws vary by state, it is clear that mental health legislation is quite different from that in most Western European countries, in terms of both its emphasis and its underlying assumptions. The civil rights movement of the 1970s, played out against a historical backdrop of commitment to the libertarian philosophy of John Stuart Mill, has ensured that the 'liberty of the subject' is seen to be of paramount importance. This was reflected in legal actions instigated by patients during the 1980s to secure the right to refuse treatment (Perlin 1992, 1993). These have been replaced in the past decade by legal action to secure satisfactory levels of care and treatment, which has in turn led to the development of 'therapeutic jurisprudence', a new area of legal expertise that seeks to protect individuals with mental disorders from the unintentional negative consequences of the law (La Fond 1994; Wexler 1990). Although some of the legal arguments about mental health issues may reflect the American propensity for litigation rather than any real commitment to social justice, it is likely that the outcomes of cases will eventually have a positive international impact on mental health laws (for a discussion, see Chapter 8).

Medical definitions

Surprisingly, the medical definitions of mental disorder are not much clearer than the legal definitions. This is in spite of an ongoing search for useful concepts that can be operationalised with the minimum of confusion, a search evident in the development work surrounding both the DSM and the ICD. The current ICD is based on a classification first formalised in 1893 as the Bertillon Classification or the *International List of Causes of Death*. In the sixth edition of the list, compiled in 1948, a special section on mental disorders was included – the first official attempt at classification. This early classification was rejected by many psychiatrists throughout the world, but since then it has been updated on a continuous basis by international committees working on behalf of the WHO and has gained international credibility.

The current version (ICD-10), which is very different from the first, relies primarily on research-based concepts and is widely accepted by psychiatrists. It now includes disabilities and factors influencing health status as well as factors that can cause death. The section on 'Mental and behavioural disorders', contains 1,000 categorical slots divided into nine groups (all conditions being coded with a letter of the alphabet, in this case F; Table 2.1).

Table 2.1   ICD-10: mental and behavioural disorders

F1:	Organic, including symptomatic, mental disorders
F2:	Mental and behavioural disorders due to psychoactive substance use
F3:	Mood (affective) disorders
F4:	Neurotic, stress-related and somatoform disorders
F5:	Behavioural syndromes associated with physiological disturbances and physical factors
F6:	Disorders of adult personality and behaviour
F7:	Mental retardation
F8:	Disorders of psychological development
F9:	Behavioural and emotional disorders with an onset usually occurring in childhood and adolescence

Source: Adapted from ICD-10 classification of mental and behavioural disorders, World Health Organization, Geneva, 1992

One of the most important recent developments in the ICD-10 is the idea of multiaxial presentation, which, it is hoped, will enhance the use of the classification on a worldwide basis. There are three axes: Axis 1 – Clinical diagnoses, to include mental and physical disorders; Axis 2 – Disablements, to assess the impact of an illness or health problem on social and physical functioning; and Axis 3 – Contextual factors, to identify any problems in the family or social context that might have a bearing on the health condition. This is a broadening of the notion of a mental health problem to one which includes the context necessary to achieve good mental health.

In parallel with the work on the main classification, the WHO has another that will be relevant to mental health services in the future. This is the *International Classification of Impairments, Disabilities and Handicaps* (ICIDH), first published in English on a trial basis in 1980 and now undergoing review. One of the important developments in this project is the endorsement of the concept of 'handicap' as follows. Handicap arises out of 'an interaction between (a) impairment and disability and (b) the environment where the individual lives, the resources available, and the social cultural setting' (Kaplan and Sadock 1995: 700). This is an attempt to incorporate current approaches to disability, which conceptualise it as being as much a function of a hostile (disabling) environment as of the individual's inherent physical or mental problem. Although the disability lobby has, in the past, often excluded non-physical problems from its definition of disability, there is increasing evidence of a growing recognition of mental disorder as a disabling condition with the same range of social and economic outcomes as physical conditions.

The other major classification, the American Psychiatric Association's DSM, has also undergone major revisions since its appearance in 1952. In the first version, the theoretical influence of Adolf Meyer was clear in the use of the concept of 'reaction' throughout. In Meyer's psychobiological view, mental disorders represented reactions of the personality to psychological, social and biological factors. Although the first revision, DSM-II, was quite different from the first version, as it omitted any reference to a theoretical viewpoint on non-organic disorders, it was the DSM-III that proved to be a radical departure from the two earlier versions. Debate continues among American psychiatrists on many aspects of the current version, DSM-IV, which came into use in May 1994. One of the aims of this latest revision was to co-ordinate it with the ICD-10. This made it more useful for psychiatrists interested in international research but more difficult for clinicians to use in daily practice.

While the general debates on each new revision of the classification will be forgotten, the more specific controversies over the 'declassification' (or exclusion) of homosexuality in the DSM-III (in 1980) and the classification (or inclusion) of 'Premenstrual dysphoric disorder' in DSM-IV (in 1994) will be held in folk memory for a long time. Each aroused passion and academic debate among clinicians and activists – in the first case, within the gay community, and in the second, within the women's movement. Each controversy was caused by a contradiction inherent in reconciling the negative and positive effects of placing a psychiatric label on people who are genuinely experiencing mental distress in relation to a condition regarded by a large section of the population as a normal healthy state (for a discussion of both issues, see Chapter 3 and Figert 1996). There is no doubt that, as with early classifications of mental disorder, historians working in the future will wonder about some of the current 'disorders', including 'premenstrual dysphoric disorder', 'attention deficit disorder' and 'gender identity disorder'. Only in the future will it be possible to judge their usefulness.

Meanwhile, we can expect each revision of the existing classifications to arouse both praise and criticism. Apart from actual controversies over the inclusion and exclusion of certain categories of disorder, the major criticism of the DSM has been in relation to the number of revisions it has been through in a short space of time. The main critics are those involved in training psychiatrists, but patients have also expressed discontent at changes in diagnostic labels, which they see as unnecessarily confusing. Notwithstanding these criticisms, there is no doubt that the latest version of the American classification – DSM-IV – has made progress in bringing the concepts used in the two major classifications closer together, a move towards a shared language in psychiatry throughout the world. The following extract will give the reader a flavour of the discourse surrounding the concepts of mental disorder in an earlier version of the American classification:

> Each of the mental disorders is conceptualized as a clinically significant behavioural or psychological syndrome or pattern that occurs in a person and that is associated with present distress (a painful symptom) or disability (impairment in one or more important areas of functioning) or with a significantly increased risk of suffering death, pain, disability, or an important loss of freedom. In addition, this syndrome or pattern must not be merely an expectable response to a particular event, e.g., the death of a loved one. Whatever its original cause, it must currently be considered a manifestation of a behavioural, psychological, or biological dysfunction in the person. Neither deviant behaviour, e.g., political, religious, or sexual, nor conflicts that are primarily between the individual and society are mental disorders unless the deviance or conflict is a symptom of a dysfunction in the person, as described above. (American Psychiatric Association 1987: xxii).

Those who oppose categorisation *per se*, on the grounds that labelling always has a negative effect, will see this description as a linguistic straitjacket, no less oppressive than the cloth straitjackets of the past. However, as the debate on the inclusion of premenstrual syndrome as a psychiatric category has demonstrated, a label can be liberating for some people because it represents public recognition of personal pain (Figert 1996).

But is it possible to measure personal pain, and is its absence a sign of good mental health? Some policy-makers make the assumption that the answer is 'yes' to both questions when they agree on indicators of mental health to be measured in the population. In keeping with the 1984/85 WHO target for the achievement of Health for All by the Year 2000, most countries have had to develop a strategy to improve all aspects of health, including mental health. In *The Health of the Nation: A Strategy for England* (Department of Health 1992), for example, there was no attempt to define mental disorder, but instead one outcome (death by suicide) was selected for action. The target is the reduction of the overall suicide rate by at least 15 per cent by the year 2000 from the 1990 levels of 11 per 100,000 of the population, and the reduction of the lifetime suicide rate of people with severe mental disorders by at least 33 per cent by the same year. Clearly, any reduction in suicide rates is desirable, but it may not necessarily mean a reduction in mental disorder. The other more general target in *The Health of the Nation* – 'to improve significantly the health and social functioning of mentally ill people' – will be very difficult to measure, although the newly revived debate on inequalities in health is pushing the agenda towards a focus on the areas and groups that seem to be in greatest health need. These policy targets are quite different from those of three decades ago, when the aims of mental health policy were articulated in terms of treatment provision rather than treatment outcome. In the USA in 1961, for example, the Joint Commission on Mental Illness and Health initiated a Community Mental Health Centre Programme in an effort to reduce the high rate of institutionalisation for people with mental illnesses (Robins and Regier 1991: 2). Similar targets were set in most countries in Europe during the following two decades, Italy being one of the first to introduce laws to prevent further hospitalisation in 1978 (Law 180), and Portugal being one of the last.

New targets are based on a definition of mental disorder different from that which prevailed in the era of mass institutionalisation. It is now generally accepted that disabilities linked to mental disorder can best be conquered in a community setting as isolation from society increases rather than decreases the disabling effects. It is also generally accepted that medical intervention alone cannot restore an individual to a mentally healthy life. However, in spite of this acceptance, there is evidence of an increasing use of medication in all psychiatric settings and a lack of financial backing for a substantial expansion of creative community-based, non-medical programmes.

Alternative perspectives

Because legal and medical definitions of mental disorder form only part of the picture in our enquiry into discourses on mental health and mental disorder, we will now look at some alternatives. As in other areas of health, it is clear that notions of mental health are gendered. Men and women think differently about their mental health and feelings of well-being, as is shown by studies of psychiatric morbidity in the community and of patterns of help-seeking behaviour (Anson *et al.* 1993; Barnett *et al.* 1987; Gomez 1993). Women more often define problems as 'illness' than do men, and health professionals are more likely to medicalise women's problems than men's (Jebali 1995; Shorter 1990; Showalter 1987). However, there are changes occurring in these perceptions.

Women have become stronger in looking for non-medical help for problems that might in the past have been revealed only to their general practitioner. Also, there are alternative services available for women who have experienced domestic violence or who have been sexually abused, problems that often went no farther than the office of the family doctor. Women are also more able to acknowledge that the cause of their distress may be socio-economic rather than psychological. These developments are a result of changes in the social climate in most Western societies, that allow women to think in different ways about their experiences of oppression or abuse and also allow for the expansion of avenues of help for women under stress. However, as these avenues are not equally accessed by all women, for example women from minority ethnic groups, it would not be prudent to over-generalise about changing patterns of help-seeking behaviour.

Men are also changing – in their perceptions of their health and in their willingness to admit that they have problems. However, this is not yet reflected in mental health statistics. Studies in Europe have found that men are less likely than women to report their problems at an early stage to their general practitioner and, because of this, are more likely to be referred directly to the psychiatric service (Verhaak 1993). Non-white men in Britain, in particular, are more likely to wait until there is a mental health crisis before coming forward for help, a factor that has only recently been acknowledged as one of the reasons for a higher proportion of compulsory admissions among Afro-Caribbean men (Bhui *et al.* 1995; Flannigan *et al.* 1994a). In the USA, young married men are the group in the population least likely to seek psychiatric help (Robins and Regier 1991).

For everyone, there are enormous barriers to be overcome before admitting to having a mental health problems. One of the main barriers is the fact that psychiatric labelling and treatment are often perceived as unhelpful and potentially damaging. The reality of the public services in many countries is that the majority of those who come into contact with the psychiatric system receive medication rather than psychotherapy or counselling, and few people are consulted about their psychiatric diagnosis. It would be foolish to assume that a continued use of the service implies agreement with psychiatric treatment – witness the vociferous lobbying from the ex-patients' movement against psychiatric labelling.

For people who are committed involuntarily, the situation is much clearer than for those who voluntarily seek psychiatric help. They have little faith in either the diagnoses or the treatment offered by psychiatry. Recent research in America shows that this lack of trust in the system affects treatment compliance and, consequently, treatment outcomes. Most forms of psychiatric treatment have been found to be ineffective in the long term when administered under conditions of compulsory hospitalisation (La Fond and Durham 1992). This has implications for countries that are considering the introduction of compulsory community treatment – will treatment also be ineffective in such circumstances? A small study in Britain of women in 'special hospitals' gives some insight into the views of involuntary patients on the psychiatric labels attached to them. These women, when asked about their perception of their own problems and the treatment meted out to them, were vociferous in their rejection of the psychiatric system. The 'special hospital' system in Britain is part of the prison system and houses offenders with mental disorders, some, but not all, of whom have been convicted of a crime. One woman dismissed her diagnosis of 'psychopathy' as 'just a title to call people', and another considered her diagnosis of 'schizophrenia' to be 'meaningless'. These and other women said that their diagnoses had never been explained to them, and, consequently, they had no idea what they meant (Eaton and Humphries 1996). What is interesting about this study, in relation to our discussion here, is the unspoken assumption (by the women) that the labels should benefit them. If so, they argue correctly that their usefulness might be enhanced if those labelled agreed with or even understood the labels. The question remains, however, of whether the label has to be meaningful for the patient. Is it just a therapeutic (or even neutral) tool of the medical trade (as claimed by doctors), or is it a powerful instrument of social control (as claimed by patients)?

Among those who see it as a powerful instrument of social control are two well known feminist writers who have experienced mental health problems and used psychiatric services – Sylvia Plath and Kate Millett. In *The Bell Jar* (1963: 142–3), Plath describes the inability of the fictional young woman, Esther, to communicate her obvious distress to the psychiatrist picked by her mother. Even her 'dull flat voice' did not 'impress' the doctor, who communicated his decision to give Esther 'shock treatment' (electroconvulsive therapy, or ECT) not to Esther but to her mother. The scene, which aptly describes the lack of power over decisions about treatment, is very familiar to many users of the psychiatric system. In Plath's story, there is little doubt that the young woman has mental health problems. However, what is of concern in this and other literary accounts is the lack of fit between the psychiatric system and the needs of individuals requiring care and treatment. As Plath's experience was based on services in the 1950s, one could dismiss it as a product of bygone times and therefore irrelevant in today's world. However, this would be the wrong conclusion to draw. Kate Millett's autobiographical novel *The Loony Bin Trip*, published in 1991, was written in the context of services in the 1980s in the USA and Ireland. It parallels Plath's experience of powerlessness – the loss of control over her mental state and personal liberty. Millett found herself being committed to hospital involuntarily on more than one occasion by people she regarded as being her best friends. She also had the terrifying experience of being sent to a large traditional mental hospital in Ireland during one of her literary tours. Millett does not question the fact that she had mental health problems at the time, but she rejects the label of manic-depression. She also views most of the medical treatment she received as at best unhelpful, and at worst physically and mentally damaging.

The story Millett tells is a familiar one to ex-psychiatric patients. After being involuntarily committed to hospital by her family in 1973, she at first accepted the judgement of her doctors and her friends that, in order to maintain mental stability, she needed to take lithium for the rest of her life. However, in 1980, when she was established as a successful author and a leading feminist academic, she decided to stop taking her medication. She explains her reasons:

> Then why quit taking lithium? Six years of diarrhea. Six years of hand tremor in public places, on podiums, at receptions, at the moment one is watched and observed. Six years of it in private while trying to draw... six years of a being on a drug that made one sluggish, the mind sedated, this suppressant. Rumors that it isn't good for you in the long run, the kidneys, the liver, maybe even the brain. Maybe the time had come to try living without it. (Millett 1991: 31)

Millett did stop taking her lithium and boasted about it to her terrified friends, who were not surprised when she began to talk too much, spend too much money and expect too much understanding. A second attempt to have her committed to hospital in the early 1980s did not succeed because, by then, she knew her rights under New York mental health law. Her description of the abortive attempt to 'capture' her is deeply moving. Situations like the one she describes usually end in the forcible removal and committal of the person to hospital or, more tragically, in the shooting by police of someone perceived as deranged and dangerous. Millett was 'saved' by the facts that she was an educated and articulate woman and that there was a policeman present who understood his duty to protect her rights not to be forced into an ambulance:

> And then it happens. The ambulance arrives. A siren. One ambulance inside the aura of that siren. Then another siren and another ambulance. And then a police car accompanying the ambulance. Its siren. Another siren and another police car. Two ambulances, three squad cars. The fear I have lived in for over an hour descends now like a plastic bag over my head. It is very hard to stand, not to tremble, not to weep, not to fall apart, become hysterical and scream – epithets, recriminations, everything. (Millett 1991: 164)

However, Millett was not so lucky later that year in Ireland, when she found herself locked up and isolated in an old-style psychiatric hospital near Shannon airport. There, the staff had never heard of the 'right to knowledge' about medication, nor indeed of 'the right to refuse treatment' – they were still working under legislation dating from 1945. They accepted medical authority without question. Millett eventually 'escaped' from the Irish mental health care system and returned to New York, where she admits to hitting 'rock bottom' before finally accessing help that included counselling and limited drug treatment. Her account of the depression she suffered during this time is poignant in its realness:

During depression the world disappears. Language. One has nothing to say. Nothing. No small talk, no anecdotes. Nothing can be risked on the board of talk. Because the inner voice is so urgent in its own discourse: How shall I live? How shall I manage in the future? Why should I go on? There is nothing ahead, my powers are failing, I am ageing. I do not want to continue into the future as I see it... One's real state of mind is a source of shame. So one is necessarily silent about it. (Millett 1991: 281)

The experiences of both Plath and Millett are echoed, if less eloquently, in the words of other survivors who struggle to articulate their feelings during a period of mental disintegration. Hatfield and Lefley (1993) collected a number of personal accounts from people who had experienced the trauma of psychosis and hospitalisation. It is clear from these accounts that, although individuals with mental health problems struggle to define themselves outside the psychiatric label, they are often submerged by their symptoms. For people with schizo-phrenia, for example, the loss of a sense of self is central to their perception of themselves:

It was just that sometimes I had a terrific sense of unreality. Suddenly, I found myself in the present and all the immediate cords to the present had been severed... everyone was so distant from me, there seemed to be a huge gap between me and the rest of the world, including my family. (Hatfield and Lefley 1993: 31, 115)

For those suffering from depression, the overwhelming emotion may be different, but it is equally frightening and disempowering. For George Fish, an American mental health advocate and freelance writer, 'being chronically depressed is like being trapped inside a bare, white room, a seamless monotony from which there is no escape' (Hatfield and Lefley 1993: 58). Knowing that hallucinations are not real and that depression will pass does not provide an instant path to re-entry into wider society. For most people who have used psychiatric services, the struggle to make sense of their own world is matched only by the struggle to cope with the negative attitudes of the outside world.

Some of these attitudes come from images of mental disorder derived from the media. Media images, of course, come from a number of sources and can seriously damage the cause of those trying to convey a more enlightened view of mental health problems to the public (Ramon 1996). Events such as a multiple murder or assault may be the basis for a television programme. Unfortunately, the media seize all opportunities to sensationalise these crimes further by labelling the perpetrator as 'crazy' or 'mad'. Sometimes, there is indeed a psychiatric history, but sometimes not, and it is difficult for the public to distinguish fact from fiction. The worrying part is that these images from television and newspapers may be the only sources of information for people with no personal experience of mental disorder.

The strength of these images is confirmed by the findings of a study carried out by the Glasgow University Media Group in 1993 (Philo 1996): even for people with personal experience of mental disorder among family or friends, media images eventually dominated their perception. For the most part, these are images of individuals (usually men) who are not in control of their impulses and are likely to harm or kill themselves or others. What is frightening about this is that, as long as the media continue to portray people with mental health problems as different and dangerous – as 'other' – the public remains ignorant of the fact that only a very small proportion of people using psychiatric services present a danger to others (for a full discussion, see Chapter 9).

Culture and mental disorder

The public perception of mental disorder is based in culturally constructed concepts of normality, abnormality, health and illness. There is a well-established debate within academia on the interrelationship between cultural constructs of mental disorder, personal experiences of mental disturbance and the medicalisation of these phenomena through the psychiatric system. The contribution of anthropology to this debate has been significant. Saris suggests that 'in their modern form, both anthropology and psychiatry derive in large measure from philosophical musings on the nature of rationality that developed out of the Enlightenment' (Saris 1994: 115). John Locke, the philosopher, preoccupied with defining the limits of reason, excluded certain groups of people from those who could reason. These included 'madmen' and 'savages', who then became objects for study and 'colonisation' by psychiatrists and anthropologists. Both disciplines contend that, although the context and expression of most forms of human behaviour differ, there are certain constants in human nature. In relation to mental health, those who are mentally healthy in any given society are those who manage to find personal fulfilment while being integrated socially and economically into that society at whatever level suits them. People who find themselves unduly stressed or isolated by the norms and expectations of their social situation have to find acceptable means of expressing their mental distress, otherwise they will become more

isolated or more stressed. For individuals living in a single cultural
setting, the discourses surrounding the expression of mental distress
and its recognition are usually clearly defined in terms accepted by the
public and health professionals (Shorter 1990). For those living in a
multicultural setting, the expression and recognition of distress is more
difficult as the discourses of the dominant culture (in which the psychiatric system is usually placed) may be different from those of the individual's ethnic group. Research has shown that problems are
particularly felt when mental distress arises from gender role conflicts
caused by clashes in cultural expectations in relation to the male and
female roles in society (Sargent and Brettell 1996: 17–19).

It is even more difficult for people who live in cultures that do not
recognise mental disorder as a socially acceptable condition. For
example, among Mexican American patients in California, all of whom
had a diagnosis of schizophrenia, relatives were reluctant to use
medical terminology ('mental illness') when talking about the patient,
showing a preference for local idiom (*nervios*) (Hopper 1991: 315).
The explanation given by Janis Jenkins, the researcher, was that acceptance of the person as crazy (*loco*) had repercussions for the family, for
the person and for the recovery process, repercussions that were viewed
as extremely threatening. The term 'mental illness' was seen in somewhat the same light. These people did not deny having a mental
problem, but instead they found that existing psychiatric labels and
concepts of health did not represent their experienced reality.

Similar differences in the words used to describe the problem and in
the perception of the experience are documented by Phan and Silove
(1997) in relation to Vietnamese refugees in Australia. They divide the
cultural factors that influence ways of describing mental disorders into
semantic factors, context-specific factors and concept-specific factors.
The semantic factors are fairly obvious – there are situations when the
term used in the English language has no equivalent in Vietnamese, or
when a similar but not identical term or phrase exists and is assumed to
be a direct translation. Phan and Silove discuss a number of phrases in
common use within psychiatric practice in Australia that have a
meaning completely different from that which was intended by the
translator. This is a problem that will always remain when the mental
health professional does not speak the same language as the patient, a
situation which is becoming increasingly common in Europe and the
USA. This difficulty could, to some extent, be overcome by having
comprehensive interpreting facilities available in all psychiatric units.

However, this kind of interpretative service across a range of languages is costly and therefore rare.

The other cultural factors discussed by Phan and Silove – context specific and concept specific – are not as easy to understand, but they are present in all cultures. These refer to both the physical and philosophical roots of the phrases used by a people to make sense of their lives. Words and phrases are not neutral and, even if directly translated, may have different meanings. An example of this is the meaning of the word 'suffering' to someone from the Buddhist tradition (as many Vietnamese refugees are). The authors suggest that the acknowledgement of suffering (the translation of *Duhkha*, one of the Four Noble Truths in Buddhist doctrine) will probably be interpreted negatively by the Western doctor rather than positively as the patient intends:

> Suffering can be transformed into an enlightenment experience through the appreciation of the impermanence of earthly things and a consequent focus on compassion for other beings. Acknowledging sorrow and sadness is one way in which Buddhists can gain insight into their *trishma*, which is the principle of redistributive justice in which past deeds in earlier incarnations affect a person's contemporary life. There is a risk that in the transcultural context the expression of *Duhkha* may be misconstrued as representing depressive symptoms, rather than an experience that is a virtue and indeed necessary in the quest for enlightenment. (Phan and Silove 1997: 88)

This is indeed a warning for mental health professionals working in multiethnic settings, a warning that is backed up by the message coming through from studies on the delivery of psychiatric services to different ethnic groups. The health system is permeated by institutionalised racism, characterised by a tendency to ignore certain individual characteristics of the patient and to expect stereotypical behaviour (Bhui *et al.* 1995; Compton *et al.* 1991; Halpern 1993; Nazroo 1997; Perkins and Moodley 1993; Sugarman and Craufurd 1994; Wade 1993). The research on ethnicity and mental health calls for a bottom-up approach to providing services in order to make it easier for people from minority ethnic groups to articulate their mental health difficulties in whatever way they wish.

Transcultural psychiatry

Some of the most interesting work on the interrelationship between culture and mental disorder comes from transcultural psychiatry, a research tradition attempting to quantify mental health problems throughout the world (see Corin and Bibeau 1988). The debate on the possibility of carrying out true cross-cultural comparisons rages in the two academic camps of psychiatry and anthropology. American psychiatric textbooks now quote anthropologists such as Melvin Konner, who suggests that two generalisations can be made about the cross-cultural incidence of mental disorders (Kaplan and Sadock 1995: 350). The first is that the major psychiatric symptoms and clusters of symptoms, which form part of what is regarded as a major mental disorder (including anxiety, mania, depression and suicidal ideation), are present in almost all societies. The labels used to define the problem and the approaches to treatment may vary greatly, but all are distinguished as being different from normal functioning. The second generalisation is that there are also some culturally specific conditions, which are not only culture-bound in terms of the discourse used to name and explain the conditions, but also that they might not exist outside the specific cultural framework. A current example in Western society is 'anorexia nervosa', which is found mostly among young middle-class women in cultures where body image and sexual confidence are important. A non-Western example is that of *amok:* 'a condition among traditional Malay men in which a period of brooding is followed by an outburst of frenzied, often homicidal violence ending in exhaustion and amnesia' (Konner, in Kaplan and Sadock 1995: 350).

The difficulties experienced by researchers attempting to reconcile classification systems within the Western world are described by Angst (1988) in relation to European studies on schizophrenia. Angst comes to the conclusion that the concepts of schizophrenia used in Europe and the USA are too diverse 'to allow for meaningful comparisons of course and outcome'. Research on schizophrenia by a WHO team sought to overcome this problem by concentrating on specific aspects of mental disorder for which the measurements could be validated across cultures – in this instance, the expression of psychosis (Katz *et al.* 1988). The work was part of the WHO collaborative study on the Determinants of Outcome of Severe Mental Disorders in a number of countries throughout the world (DOSMD 1976–85). An in-depth analysis of the WHO studies in Agra (India) and Ibadan (Nigeria) confirmed earlier findings – that the 'major formal elements of schizophrenia (disorders of thought, emotion and psychomotor behaviour)' appear common to the cultures in which the research took place, but that 'the content and quality of emotional expression and social behaviour differ across cultures' (Katz *et al.* 1988: 352). The Agra patients showed a 'more affective, more "self-centred" agitated quality', while the Ibadan patients presented 'a highly suspicious orientation, with bizarre fears and ideas' (p. 351). In each case, the content and expression of the disorder reflected either unresolved problems or dominant themes in the culture – a rejection or an exaggeration of cultural norms.

Some of the best known findings of the DOSMD studies occur in relation to the incidence and outcomes of schizophrenia. The researchers found very little difference between the 12 centres (in 10 countries) in incidence of schizophrenia but confirmed earlier research findings that outcome was consistently better for countries classified as 'developing' (as opposed to 'developed'). There was also a significant difference in the life course or pattern of the illness: 'Symptom free intervals were observed in nearly two thirds of the subjects in developing countries, compared with only 37 per cent in developed countries' (Hopper 1991: 304). Like other anthropologists, Kim Hopper is highly sceptical of this finding, which for her raises the basic question of the legitimacy of cross-cultural psychiatric research. She asks, 'does it make sense for Western clinicians to look elsewhere for entities so obviously their own making?' (p. 306). In an effort to standardise across cultures, the classification system used in the WHO research focuses only on core concepts. If a broader classification were used, it might yield different results. There are other criticisms of the WHO project, which also apply to other cross-national studies. They include the technical problems of translating questions into local idiom without losing the central concepts, and the difficulties inherent in comparing activities that may hold different meanings in different cultures. However, the research teams at the WHO continue to work towards the development of instruments that can be used to measure mental disorder across cultures as the need for accurate data on mental health needs is increasing all the time. As the findings of the ECA in the USA (Robins and Regier 1991) and of the National Community Survey of Ethnic Minorities in Britain (Nazroo 1997) have shown, differences in race and gender have a substantial impact on the incidence of mental health problems and on the help sought. Services that are either race or gender blind, or both, will not meet the mental health needs of today's world.

3

The Population at Risk

One of the problems in attempting to compare trends over time and space is that differences that appear in the data may not be real but may be caused by differences in measurement techniques and the interpretation of results. This is especially the case in relation to mental health. As we have seen in the last chapter, what is defined as mental disorder is changing, and these changes have had a significant gender impact on the size and shape of the population most at risk of mental disorder. For example, we now recognise that life is potentially as stressful for men as it is for women and that this fact has been masked until recently by different patterns of help-seeking behaviour and approaches to psychiatric diagnosis. Thus, a formerly hidden section of the 'at-risk' population should in the future become part of the visible landscape. For the moment, we have to rely on evidence from studies that have attempted to measure the size of the population suffering from mental disorder in terms accepted by psychiatry at the time of the study.

Gender and prevalence

Perhaps one of the most startling findings of the American ECA study was the following:

> The ECA results have overturned some erroneous views of the nature of psychiatric disorder in the community. Based on earlier studies, it was thought that women were particularly liable to psychiatric illness and that vulnerability increased with age. The stereotypic person with psychiatric disorder was a middle-aged anxious or depressed woman. The ECA has shown that disorders in men are as common as or slightly more common than in women and that most disorders begin in early adult life. (Robins and Regier 1991: 365)

As Robins and Regier point out later, the findings reflect the decision to include substance dependence and personality disorder in the calculation of mental disorder, although these two categories had often been excluded in earlier studies. With this in mind, we can look at the survey results. The main finding was that 32 per cent of American adults had experienced one or more psychiatric disorders at some time in their lives and that 20 per cent had an active disorder, defined as reporting symptoms in the previous year (Robins and Regier 1991: 327). When broken down in terms of gender, more men than women had a psychiatric disorder over their lifetime (36 per cent of men and 30 per cent of women), but men and women ranked the same in terms of their current (or active) experience of mental disorder, 20 per cent of both groups reporting symptoms during the previous year. The difference in lifetime prevalence is explained by the significant overrepresentation of men in two disorders – alcohol dependence and personality disorder. While women had much higher prevalence rates than men for somatisation disorder, obsessive compulsive disorder and major depressive episodes, the differential in overall prevalence rates was maintained because alcohol dependence was so common among men.

The ECA findings on the lifetime and annual prevalence of mental disorder pointed to a problem in the general population much greater than was expected from estimates drawn from service use. This is due to the fact that many people, although aware of mental distress, did not seek help from psychiatric services – only 19 per cent of people reported outpatient treatment in the previous 6 months or inpatient treatment in the previous year (Robins and Regier 1991: 341). There was also a gender difference in service use, women receiving more treatment than men (23 per cent of women versus 14 per cent of men). The group most likely to seek and receive treatment were single (never married) women who had completed high school (27 per cent), and the group least likely to do so were married men with low educational attainment (11 per cent). These findings are consistent with statistics on mental health service use, in which women usually dominate, and two of the most common risk factors associated with hospitalisation are non-marriage and low income – the latter highly co-related to low educational achievement. What is interesting is the suggestion that although marriage protects men from appearing in mental health treatment statistics, it does not necessarily protect them from the experience of mental disorder.

The other major source of information on the population experiencing mental disorder in the USA is the NCS (Kessler *et al.* 1994).

This study was carried out between 1990 and 1992, using a structured psychiatric interview based on DSM-III-R psychiatric disorders, with a national sample of 8,098 people aged 15–54 years (all living in private households). The lifetime prevalence rate for the presence of one disorder was very high, with only a small gender gap, the overall rate being 48 per cent (49 per cent of men and 47 per cent of women). The gender gap in annual prevalence (symptoms reported to have occurred in the year prior to the survey interview) was also small but in the opposite direction. The overall rate was 29 per cent – 31 per cent for women and 28 per cent for men. Consistent with other research, the authors found that most disorders showed declining rates with age and higher socio-economic status (see Kessler *et al.* 1994: 12).

The findings from the NCS on gender were also consistent with earlier studies, including the ECA, showing women to be more likely than men to have affective disorders (with the exception of mania, which showed no sex difference) and men more likely than women to have substance use disorders and personality disorders. The most common psychiatric disorders were found to be major depression and alcohol dependence, with social phobia and simple phobia featuring next. More than 17 per cent of the sample had a history of major depressive episode, 10 per cent of these reporting symptoms in the previous year. For alcohol dependence, the rate was just slightly lower – 14 per cent of the sample reporting a lifetime history of alcohol dependence and more than 7 per cent having been dependent during the previous year.

Perhaps one of the most important findings of this study was related to its original aim – to establish the level of co-morbidity between substance use disorders and non-substance psychiatric disorders. The vast majority of lifetime disorders were found to be concentrated in 14 per cent of the sample participants, all of whom had a history of three or more co-morbid disorders. Within this group of people, women had higher values than men for both lifetime and annual prevalence. This means that while mental disorder was not uncommon in the general population, the most severe burden was concentrated in one-sixth of those affected, women being at higher risk than men. Consistent with the finding that most people with mental health problems received no professional treatment, those with a history of three or more co-morbid disorders did not fare well, almost half reporting that they had never sought or received treatment from the mental health sector. The implications of this finding are that the population of mental health service users does not represent the population experiencing mental disorder either in terms of gender or seriousness of the condition. If this is to change, barriers that make services inaccessible to large sections of the community must be recognised and dismantled.

One example of these factors occurs in relation to people from ethnic minority groups (Fernando 1988; Hatfield *et al.* 1996b; Perkins and Moodley 1993; Phan and Silove 1997; Thomas *et al.* 1993). Nazroo (1997) echoes the feelings of a number of these researchers when he suggests that high rates of psychosis found among people of Caribbean origin in British hospital settings have more to do with the predominantly white medical profession than with the patients:

> How visible is mental illness to the agents of surveillance in our society – doctors, social workers, police and courts? How much of what to doctors is mental illness is perhaps a response to interactions between the potential patient and the doctor? (Nazroo 1997: vii)

The American research substantiates the argument that the relationship between health and ethnicity is highly complex. This is borne out by a recent study in London which found that there was quite a discrepancy between the diagnosis of depression in older African Caribbean people (in London), when tested using two instruments – the traditional Geriatric Depression Scale (GDS) and the new Caribbean Culture Specific Screen for emotional distress (CCSS) (Abas *et al.* 1998). The authors felt that the problem could be overcome by 'openness and genuine interest in symptoms, ethnicity and stressors' on the part of clinicians.

The situation is further complicated by the fact that the basic concepts of 'race' and 'ethnicity' are contested at both the theoretical and practical level. In mental health studies in the USA, 'race' is used as the distinguishing variable, whereas in the UK, 'ethnicity' has been more commonly used. Both the NCS and the ECA divided the population into four racial groups – black, white, Hispanic and 'other'. Within the context of this definition, the NCS found that black people had 'significantly lower prevalences of affective disorders, substance use disorders and lifetime co-morbidity' than white people (Kessler *et al.* 1994: 13). These findings are consistent with those of the ECA and are particularly interesting when one considers the stereotypical assumptions about the extent of substance dependence among young black people. It is also interesting when one considers that there are higher rates of hospitalisation and imprisonment in black young men than in their white counterparts for behaviour associated with substance dependence and personality disorders. The overrepresentation of black young men with these disorders in the institutionalised population indicates either an overzealousness on the part of the medical personnel in offering this form of treatment rather than others that are community based, or a failure of community services to support this section of the population.

European data on prevalence

In the UK, although the most recent research data on the extent of mental disorder are not directly comparable to those of the ECA or the NCS, the evidence points to similar trends in experiences of mental disorder. The most important recent study is the Psychiatric Morbidity Survey in Britain (England, Scotland and Wales), which had among its main aims the estimation of the prevalence of mental disorder, the identification of social disabilities associated with the experience, and the estimation of the extent of service use by those who identified themselves as having a mental disorder (Meltzer *et al.* 1995). Disorders were categorised as neurotic psychopathology, psychotic psychopathology and alcohol and drug dependence. The research found that 16 per cent of adults (aged 16–64 years) had a neurotic health problem, estimated as a score of 12 or more on the CIS-R in the week prior to the survey interview. The two most prevalent neurotic disorders were mixed anxiety and depressive disorder (8 per cent) and generalised anxiety disorder (3 per cent). Women had a higher overall prevalence than men, and the greatest risk factors were associated with marital status. Marriage, it appears, continues to offer protection from the experience of mental disorder to both men and women, the highest risks being associated with the break-up of a marriage rather than with the state of not being married:

> The groups with the highest CIS-R scores were divorced and separated women, and men who were separated from their wives – almost 30 per cent of these three groups had a CIS-R score of 12 or more. They were three times more likely than single, married and cohabiting men to exhibit significant neurotic symptoms. (Meltzer *et al.* 1995)

This last finding was a little different from that reported in research on the hospitalised psychiatric population. Married people have consistently occupied fewer psychiatric beds than any of the non-married categories of either men or women. There is growing evidence, however, that while being single (never married) presents the highest risk for men, being divorced, widowed or separated (previously married) presents the highest risk for women (for a discussion, see Hayes and Prior 1998a).

The other categories of disorder described in the Psychiatric Morbidity Survey included both the highest and the lowest users of mental health services – people with psychotic symptoms and with substance dependence. The annual prevalence rate for the functional psychoses (schizophrenia, manic-depressive psychosis and schizoaffective disorder) was similar for men and women, at 4 per 1,000 (or 0.4 per cent). The main gender difference was found for substance dependence. Here, the authors found an average prevalence of 5 per cent for alcohol dependence and 2 per cent for drug dependence. Men were three times more likely than women to be alcohol dependent and twice as likely to be drug dependent. As in the American research, the inclusion of substance dependence in measurements of mental disorder can either remove or reverse the predominance of women in psychiatric statistics because of the higher number of men in this category. The higher risk for men in relation to substance dependence was found to cross all the income bands. However, as one would expect, the highest risks for all types of mental disorder were found to be associated with unemployment. This represents a constant risk for both men and women, the highest rates of neurotic disorder, functional psychosis and substance dependence being seen among people in this position. One in four unemployed people reported symptoms such as fatigue, sleep problems, irritability and worry in the week prior to the survey. This is a group of people to whom services need to be targeted if equity of service provision is a goal.

Another major source of information in the UK is the HALS, a longitudinal study of a nationwide sample, measuring changes in physical and mental health, attitudes and lifestyle (Blaxter 1990; Cox *et al.* 1993). The survey was carried out in 1984/85 and repeated in 1991/92. In both surveys, women had higher GHQ scores than men. As with the American NCS, the results were much higher than expected, 25 per cent of men and 30 per cent of women scoring high enough (4–5) to be considered possible cases of minor psychiatric illness (Cox *et al.* 1993: 135). As the authors of the survey acknowledge, a different choice of threshold score would lead to different results and would perhaps be more appropriate for a community-based survey. However, this is a very important study because of the fact that the surveys were repeated over time, and it was therefore possible to study the impact of social and economic changes in participant's lives on their mental health.

One of the most interesting findings for the purpose of the discussion here was in relation to marital status. In line with the American studies, being married was associated with the best mental health for young men and young women (aged 18–39). Comparing the scores from both surveys, it was clear that becoming married was associated with an improvement in mental health, a more positive effect being seen for men than women. As one would expect, becoming widowed had the opposite effect. It was associated with a massive rise in the percentage of participants scoring over the threshold for minor psychiatric illness (5+) in both men and women, and was more striking in relation to men. For example, in the 40–60-year-old age group, there was a 30 per cent increase (from 26 per cent to 56 per cent) in the number of men with a score of over 5, while for women in the same age group, the increase was 12 per cent (from 25 per cent to 37 per cent).

More interestingly, in contrast to the American research, in which being divorced is usually associated with similar if not worse mental health outcomes than being married, this study found that becoming divorced in the time period between the two surveys had adverse effects on men but either led to a small improvement or to no change in women's mental health. For women, the stress of being in a bad marriage seems to be more harmful than the stress of going through a divorce. Another area that the HALS was able to examine was the impact of age on health – the Psychiatric Morbidity Survey had not included the over-60s. In line with previous research, the survey at both points in time found that elderly people who lived alone reported worse health – physical and mental. Both men and women aged over 65 and living alone had the highest GHQ scores, 40 per cent of men and 38 per cent of women having a score of over 5 (Cox *et al.* 1993: 137–8).

Research data from other parts of Europe, and indeed the world, are more difficult to incorporate into the discussion because of the diversity in cultural concepts of health and disorder, and also because of the diversity in the level of health service delivery. However, some of the comparative work carried out under the auspices of the WHO adds a broader perspective to the debate. The overall trends that are emerging from repeat studies are often contradictory. It is clear that social changes at both the national and international level have differential impacts by gender and race, and what is positive for one group may be negative for another. Sartorius *et al.* (1989; 176–8), who examined a number of studies, suggest that: (1) schizophrenia seems to be decreasing; (2)

depressive disorders are on the increase; (3) neurotic conditions seem to increase in reaction to socio-economic change; and (4) organic mental disorders in the elderly population will decrease in future.

Possible reasons for the decrease in the incidence of schizophrenia in the studies reviewed (carried out in Taiwan and the Danish island of Bornholm) were quite different, the latter being most interesting in terms of its gendered impact. The study in Bornholm, which was carried out in 1935 and repeated in 1983, found an increase in the prevalence of schizophrenia for men and a decrease for women. The interpretation offered was not that the incidence for women had decreased but that the difference resulted from the fact that women responded more positively to early treatment and therefore did not receive the diagnosis of schizophrenia in 1983. Sartorius *et al.* suggest that, although this is a possible explanation on that particular island, it may not be generalisable to all parts of the world, particularly the developing world. They suggest that the decrease is in keeping with the WHO worldwide study carried out in the 1970s, which found surprisingly low rates of schizophrenia, and 'could be explained by the theory that schizophrenia is a disease caused by a slow virus which is losing its virulence' (p. 176). Whether or not the virus theory holds, the fact that this very debilitating disorder is on the decline is to be welcomed.

The increase in depression documented in this review refers to a repeat study carried out in Lundby in Sweden in 1947, 1957 and 1972, which found a much greater increase during the second period than the first, being most remarkable for young men. According to Sartorius *et al.*, the increase has also been found in other studies of general practice throughout Europe, while in Africa, where depression was previously virtually unknown, it is now being frequently reported. It is not clear whether the increase is the result of a greater willingness among men in particular to seek help, to better survival chances for those vulnerable to depression, or to adverse socio-economic conditions, which impact on men more than on women.

The impact of adverse socio-economic conditions is clear in all research on mental health, with a consistent inverse relationship between wealth and mental disorder. The rate of socio-economic change has also been considered to be a factor in the mental health of a general population. Based on studies in a number of countries with different rates of change, Sartorius *et al.* put forward the hypothesis of a U-shaped relationship between problems facing the whole population and the frequency of neurotic conditions (Sartorius *et al.* 1989). They suggest that periods of economic stability and hope are related to low levels of neurosis, while periods of some instability or uncertainty bring an increase in the number of neurotic conditions reported. In periods of extreme political or economic instability, neurotic conditions decrease again and remain level until either stability has been restored or people have adapted to the situation, at which point they will again increase. However, it appears that this kind of hypothesis is much too simplistic as there are many more factors operating in the experience of mental disturbance. The complexity of the relationship between the larger sociopolitical context and levels of mental disorder in the community has been demonstrated in research in countries such as Northern Ireland, where political conflict has been part of life for the past half-century. Efforts to prove that high or low levels of mental disorder were related to particular time periods have been unsuccessful (for a discussion, see Prior 1993: 103–8).

The final trend to emerge in world research, a reduction in organic mental disorders among older people (over 65 years), is one that was also seen in the American ECA study. As most populations in the Western world move to a situation of coping with larger cohorts of older people, this finding is to be welcomed. The studies, which were carried out over time in Lundby, Sweden (1947, 1957, 1972) and in Samso, Denmark (1957–87), found similar patterns of lower rates of organic disorders among the old in each study period. The suggestion is that the combination of better living conditions and better health service structures has been instrumental in this trend. As with the other findings, this will have a gendered impact on psychiatric statistics as there are more women than men in the older age group. All of these trends point to the fact that, in the early part of the new century, the frequency map for mental disorder will be quite different from that which was taken for granted in the twentieth century. While women may continue to dominate in the older psychiatric population simply because there will be more of them in the population at large, men will replace women in the younger psychiatric population as their very real problems are recognised as being in need of care.

Mental disorders associated with women

Although sociological discussions on the nature and existence of mental illness (Goffman 1961; Scheff 1966; Szasz 1971) have not focused specifically on gender, there have been some debates in relation to the overrepresentation of women in psychiatric statistics. It is now clear that this is because of the exclusion from the statistics of conditions for which men have much higher prevalence rates – substance dependence and personality disorders. Explanations of female vulnerability included arguments about the intolerable constraints involved in traditional female roles, the acceptability of illness as a mode of protest and attention-seeking for women, and the inability of a male-dominated society to accept creative but different female behaviour (Allen 1987; Busfield 1989, 1996; Chesler 1972; Dennerstein 1993; Ripa 1990; Shorter 1990; Showalter 1987; Skultans 1979; Ussher 1991). Gove and Tudor, in their seminal article in 1973, documented the gender imbalance in community surveys – in first admissions to mental hospitals, in treatment by psychiatrists and in psychiatric treatment in general hospitals – explaining the higher number of women in all of these in terms of the position of women in society and the impact of a social role that is oppressive and problematic. Although Gove and Tudor had clearly defined what they meant by mental illness (including only neurotic disorders and functional psychoses), their definition was often forgotten in later work. Feminist writers expanded the debate by accusing psychiatrists of mysogyny, of stereotyping female behaviour so that many women found themselves in a 'Catch 22' situation of being easily defined as mentally ill for any deviation from the normal role or for close conformity to it (Busfield 1996; Ussher 1991). Edward Shorter offers a different explanation for the ease with which women entered the psychiatric system. Based on his research on hysteria in Austria at the turn of the century, he argues that not only was the discourse used by psychiatrists to describe hysteria more likely to be assigned to women, but also women used this specific diagnosis to express distress when other methods of protest or attention-seeking failed.

> The social historian of psychiatry must pursue three separate narratives: first, that of underlying biology; second, the story of the stresses and life experiences of individual patients; third, the story of changes in the models which the culture holds out for the communication of inner distress. (Shorter 1990: 3)

What is of most interest about Shorter's argument is not what it tells us specifically about women but instead what it reveals about the process of embarking on a 'patient career' (Goffman 1961). Individuals who become patients present themselves in specific ways, and if the mode of presentation is not acceptable, the distress will go unrecognised. The main diagnoses associated with women are depression and neurosis, which affect large sections of the population, and eating disorders (including anorexia nervosa and bulimia nervosa), which have a very low incidence rate except among adolescent girls in Western societies. The evidence for the proneness of women to all forms of depression is overwhelming. Although research continues into physical and psychological predisposing factors, it is now accepted by a growing number of psychiatrists that the explanations for it must be located in the social *milieu*:

> Women are twice as likely to become depressed as are men... The epidemiological difference does not appear confined to North America and Europe, but rather to occur with regularity cross-culturally... is not reducible to biological factors or methodological artefact but can be traced instead to extrinsic features of the social milieu and inequities with respect to cultural domains of power and interest. (Weissman *et al.* 1991, in Sargent and Brettell 1996: 279)

In the American NCS, women were found to have a 12-month prevalence of 14 per cent for any affective disorder (major depressive episode, manic episode and dysthymia), while for men it was 9 per cent. The greatest difference was for major depression, women being almost twice as likely as men to report at least one depressive episode in their lives – a lifetime prevalence of 21 per cent for women and 13 per cent for men (Kessler *et al.* 1994: 13).

Women are also to be found in great numbers in statistics on neurotic symptoms and disorders. In the Psychiatric Morbidity Survey in Britain, which distinguished between neurotic disorders (mixed anxiety and depressive disorder, generalised anxiety disorder, depressive episode, phobias, obsessive compulsive disorder and panic disorder) and non-neurotic disorders (functional psychoses, alcohol dependence and drug dependence), the gender patterns are clear, women showing higher rates for all the neurotic disorders, similar rates for the functional psychoses and much lower rates for alcohol and drug dependence. Within the neurotic disorders, the difference between men and women was greatest for the most common category – mixed anxiety and depressive disorder – for which 10 per cent of women and 5 per cent of men reported symptoms in the previous week. In the American NCS, the 2:1 differential for any anxiety disorder was confirmed, women having a 12-month prevalence of 23 per cent and men one of 12 per cent (Kessler *et al.* 1994: 12).

Some of the difficulties involved in making international comparisons were overcome by Regier and his colleagues, who attempted to put the American ECA findings into the context of material from other parts of the world (Regier *et al.* 1988). The available reliable data were for monthly prevalences, which makes the arguments even more confusing for readers who are already finding the statistics difficult to interpret. However, they are worth referring to in order to clarify the situation in relation to the gendering of mental health experiences. Regier *et al.* found that the overall monthly rate for affective disorders ranged from 5 per cent in Australia to over 7 per cent in European cities but was 19 per cent in Uganda. Figures for anxiety disorders ranged between 3 per cent and 4 per cent for Edinburgh, Australia, London and Uganda but reached a high of 8 per cent in Athens, Greece. The variation in rate perhaps serves to reminds us of the caution to be exercised in coming to conclusions on the basis of statistics with such wide variation. However, for the purpose of our discussion here, the gender imbalances provide an interesting focus:

> Affective disorders were found in women at about twice the rate as in men for London, Australia and Athens. Anxiety disorders were much more variable in their sex ratio, with rates four times higher for women than men in London and Athens, but a somewhat higher male rate in Australia. (Regier *et al.* 1988: 984)

Just as there is a growing interest among mental health practitioners and researchers in recognising the vulnerability of men to alcohol and drug dependence, there is a similar interest in the vulnerability of women to depression and anxiety (Bebbington *et al.* 1991; Jebali 1995; Leibenluft 1996; Paykel 1991; Pilowsky *et al.* 1991; Rogler and Cortes 1993; Roughan 1993; Walters 1993; Zerbe 1995; Zlotnick *et al.* 1996). For example, the research by Walters (1993) with Canadian women sought to clarify how women view their own health and illness. The 356 women studied reported very high levels of stress (60 per cent), anxiety (44 per cent) and depression (35 per cent). In the light of the studies already discussed, these are not surprising findings. What is new is the women's interpretation of the experience of these symptoms and their perception of the causes. The women spoke of multiple demands (from family and work), of overload (no time to rest) and of isolation (or lack of a confidante) in a way that dwelled not on personal culpability but instead on the inevitable impact of the social situation (work and family) in which they found themselves:

> Gendered caring roles, family structure, women's position in the labour market and their financial resources intertwined and threatened women's mental health. While private issues were not consistently discussed in public and political terms they were often located in this context. (Walters 1993: 401)

normal

These women did not medicalise their own condition as is sometimes suggested. Most of them defined their anxieties and stress as normal reactions to everyday life that they did not conceptualise as illness, although they did admit that they could be potential risk factors for physical illness. These modern Canadian women were describing the same process that Shorter (1990) found in his study of hysteria in nineteenth-century Austria, when women selected the medical route to help only when all other avenues of dealing with an overwhelming social burden were closed.

As we know, a higher proportion of women than men seek medical help for mental health problems. It has been suggested that this vulnerability to psychiatric diagnosis reflects a greater helplessness on the part of women. However, recent research on gender differences in reactions to negative life events has not upheld this view (see the discussion in Zlotnick *et al.* 1996). Given the same negative life events, men and women react in similar ways. The implication of this is that either women are exposed to more negative life events than men, or women experience life differently. A productive research focus has been on women's relationships – in particular the presence or absence of a confiding relationship. According to the gender-specific models of depression, if a woman's self-worth is grounded in her connections with others, a break in these connections (through death or separation) may lead to a loss of the sense of self, which predisposes to depression. In the context of changing social roles, it is possible that, in the future, 'self-worth' for women may be focused not as much on personal connections as on factors associated with the world of work – such as career and income. This, of course, may not necessarily lead to a reduction in depression or anxiety. Work by Zerbe (1995: 39) on anxiety disorders in women suggests that contemporary women, in all walks of life outside the family situation, 'tread new paths without the benefit of seasoned mentors or the same organizational supports as men, and without sustained affirmation from the family and larger social network'. She also suggests that anxiety can be viewed as indicating a positive survival advantage in women. It may be that women 'are more closely attuned to the environment than men so that they can protect themselves and their children'. If Zerbe is right, and if society develops in a less patriarchal way with plenty of well-trodden paths in all walks of life for women to follow, and if it presents less danger (in terms of socio-economic disadvantages) for women, women will perhaps not be presented with as many situations that promote both anxiety and depression. This will indeed be a new social order, in which not only will social structures be different, but also the category of 'woman' will be differently construed.

Mental disorders associated with men

Men have not featured in sociological writings on mental illness, mainly because they have not been visible in mental health statistics to the same extent as have women. However, the particular problems experienced by men are now being articulated in psychological and sociological literature on masculinity and are being confirmed in mainstream psychiatric research. In the past, the kinds of problem associated with men, such as alcohol and drug dependence or personality disorder, were often regarded as not being amenable to treatment and were often marginalised within mental health care systems (Barnett *et al.* 1987). There is also no doubt that, within a health care structure dominated by patriarchal values, it was easier to define the problems of women as illness and those of men as deviance and therefore unrelated to health issues. In this way, the macho image of the 'strong' man and the 'weak' woman was maintained.

Joseph Pleck, an American psychologist writing in the 1970s, was one of the first to suggest that the male role might be oppressive not only for women, but also for men (Pleck 1981) and that conformity to the male role might be psychologically damaging. However, his voice was not widely heard within psychiatry or psychology, and the link between this psychological damage and antisocial behaviour or substance dependence was not researched. Also, general patterns in psychiatric statistics were taken as evidence of a mentally healthy male population. Only in recent years have statistics on alcohol and drug dependence been taken seriously as indicators of mental disorder – a statistic in which men (particularly young men) feature prominently.

As we have already seen, the American ECA study was one of the first to acknowledge substance dependence and personality disorder as mental conditions in need of attention in the same way as depression or anxiety disorders. This inclusion led to results that overturned earlier views on patterns of mental health and illness. For the first time, men showed a higher prevalence for mental disorder than did women (a lifetime prevalence of 36 per cent for men and 30 per cent for women). The NCS found men to be twice as likely as women to have a substance dependence, with a lifetime prevalence of almost 36 per cent for men and 18 per cent for women, and a 12-month prevalence of 16 per cent for men and almost 7 per cent for women (Kessler *et al.* 1994: 12). In other words, over one-third of the male population have been dependent on alcohol or drugs at some stage of their lives. A further examination of the figures shows that alcohol dependence is a more widespread health problem than drug dependence, being second only to depression in the overall figures of mental disorder. One in five men reported having been dependent on alcohol at some time in their lives (a lifetime prevalence of 20 per cent), and more than one in 10 had been dependent in the previous year (a 12-month prevalence of 11 per cent). In contrast, one in every 12 women reported having been dependent on alcohol at some time in their lives (a prevalence of 8.2 per cent), while one in 27 (3.7 per cent) had been dependent in the previous year. The ECA reported similar trends, with a slightly higher lifetime prevalence for men (Robins and Regier 1991: Table 5-3). Both studies found that younger men had much higher rates of alcohol and drug dependence than did older men. For example, the NCS found that those in the 25–34-year age group were twice as likely as those in the 45–54-year age group to report substance dependency (Kessler *et al.* 1994: 15).

Similar patterns are found in Britain. In the Psychiatric Morbidity Study, men were three times more likely than women to be alcohol dependent and twice as likely to be drug dependent; within the male population, those aged 20–24 were found to be at particular risk, with a 12-month prevalence of 18 per cent for alcohol dependence and 11 per cent for drug dependence (Meltzer *et al.* 1995: 68). One interesting finding in the ECA was that, although alcoholism is still predominant among men and is increasing for all young people, there is evidence of a greater increase among young women aged 18–29 years (Robins and Regier 1991: 89). The patterns are different for drug dependence. Almost 8 per cent of men and almost 5 per cent of women said that they had been drug dependent at some time in their lives, 3 per cent of men and over 1 per cent of women reporting dependence during the previous year. The gender gap was reversed in the prison population. Almost half of the women in prison (45 per cent), against one-fifth of men (20 per cent), had been drug dependent in the year prior to the survey, and a staggering 70 per cent of women and 56 per cent of men in prison had been drug dependent at some time in their lives. The level of mental disorder in the prison population is a topic for discussion in a later chapter in this book, but for the moment it is worth considering that the probable level of health service provision to those in prison is almost certainly inadequate if drug and alcohol dependence are only now being recognised as genuine mental health problems.

Personality disorder, a mental health problem also associated with men, has until recently been regarded as untreatable by mental health professionals and has often been omitted from statistics on mental disorder. However, according to Robins and Regier (1991: 258), antisocial personality disorder, which 'is characterized by the violation of the rights of others and a general lack of conformity to social norms', meets all the criteria of a mental disorder in that 'its symptoms are highly inter-correlated, making it a coherent syndrome... it has a genetic component... and it occurs in and is recognized by every society no matter what its economic system'. It has been argued that to include this category is to medicalise badness and to ignore its significant association with deprivation and low income. However, it could be counterargued that the same could be said about depression and neurotic disorders, that it suits a patriarchal society not to label men's problems as illness because it indicates weakness, whereas the labelling of women's problems as illness never presented any such dilemma.

It is clear from current research that the great majority of both men and women cope with their mental health problems without any help from anyone, and that problems that have been defined as 'bad' rather than 'mad' have been excluded from the current health care system. People with these problems (including substance dependence and antisocial behaviour) have been further disadvantaged by being relegated to the prison system rather than the health care system. There is little chance that all inequalities of gender or of wealth will be removed from society, but there is a chance that highlighting the association between gender or poverty and mental disorder will result in a less punitive attitude to the individuals who have hitherto been regarded as 'bad' rather than 'mad'. It is from this perspective that the following data are offered to the reader. The authors of the ECA, aware of the criticism that the diagnosis of antisocial personality disorder simply medicalises criminal behaviour, tested for an association between a criminal history and the diagnosis of antisocial personality disorder. They were surprised to find that the correlation was not significantly high:

> In fact less than half (47 per cent) of those positive for the DSM-III diagnosis have a significant record of arrest (defined as two or more arrests other than for a moving traffic violation or any felony conviction). Rather than criminality, the adult symptoms that typify the antisocial personality are job troubles (found in 94 per cent), violence (found in 85 per cent), multiple moving traffic offences (found in 72 per cent), and severe marital difficulties (desertion, multiple separations or divorces, multiple infidelities, found in 67 per cent). (Robins and Regier 1991: 260)

In the total population, they found a lifetime prevalence of 2.6 per cent, but fewer than half of these people (1.2 per cent of the overall number) reported active symptoms in the previous year. As would be expected, men had a higher lifetime (4.5 per cent) and 12-month (2.1 per cent) prevalence than women (who had a lifetime prevalence of 0.8 per cent and a 12-month prevalence of 0.4 per cent). The NCS reported higher rates, but the gender trend was the same – the lifetime prevalence for men was 5.8 per cent and for women 1.2 per cent (Kessler *et al.* 1994: 12). As with crime statistics, young men were more prone to personality disorder than were older men, a finding that was consistent across ethnic boundaries. An interesting finding in relation to ethnicity was that no significant differences in the rate of antisocial personality were found between the three groups (white, black and Hispanic), although individuals from ethnic minorities are overrepresented in crime statistics in the USA. This would seem to confirm other research on crime and ethnicity that the probability of arrest for similar antisocial behaviour is lower for whites than for other ethnic groups.

Finding the population at risk

It is clear from existing knowledge based on reports of individual experiences of mental disturbances, and from that based on statistical data on the use of mental health services, that the size of the population depends on the definition of mental disorder. Mental disturbances are experienced by many more people than those who seek help from the psychiatric system. The result is that the services may be planned around false notions of the group most at risk of a mental disorder. The fact that women have sought psychiatric help in the past has had positive and negative effects for women, and the fact that men have not sought psychiatric help has had similar effects. While not arguing for the medicalisation of all mental problems, I suggest that an acceptance of substance dependence and personality disorder as real mental disorders in need of care and/or treatment must constitute progress in helping men to regain mental health and in rebalancing the view of mental disorder as a 'female malady'.

4

Approaches to Treatment

Different perspectives

Views on how to 'treat' people with mental disorders vary according to the position taken, by the proponents of these views, on what constitutes mental disorder. Those who view it as a medical problem will base their discussions on existing health care provision. Those who view it as a socio-economic problem will look for ways of changing social situations so that they provide more support and less stress for the individuals concerned. Others, of course, view the situation from a completely different perspective, one that is interested only in the negative effects on society caused by individuals who display antisocial conduct as a result of mental disturbance. For the latter group, the discussion will revolve around the issue of public safety and the need for surveillance and protective custody for people with mental disorders. Our discussion will incorporate these different perspectives, starting from the viewpoint of those who accept a health care perspective as an appropriate response to most forms of mental disorder.

From the context of health care in general, it is safe to say that most policy-makers and professionals strive to provide a mental health service that is responsive to the needs of both men and women. However, because of the traditional focus within psychiatry on certain disorders, such as depression and the neuroses (associated with women), and the neglect of others, such as substance dependence and personality disorders (associated with men), there has been an inherent gender bias in approaches to treatment. In other words, an already problematic situation in which men find it difficult to admit to emotional distress, or indeed to physical pain, has been exacerbated by unhelpful professional attitudes. The problem has been acknowledged in health literature:

Male social roles and cultural expectations may lead to denial of illness – a culturally approved behaviour for men,... Thus definition of, and access to, appropriate
treatment remain gender issues central to the creation of more equitable and
responsive health policy. (Sargent and Brettell 1996: 18)

However, even if gender equality were achieved, it would not solve
the larger question of how best to help people with mental health problems cope with them. For many people who experience mental disturbance, psychiatric services are a last resort rather than a first port of
call. Many object to taking long-term medication as a preventive
measure, even when they accept medical treatment in times of crisis.
This is due not only to the debilitating side-effects of most invasive
medical techniques, but also to the uncertainty surrounding the whole
issue of mental disorder. Thomas Szasz argues that mental illness is a
myth and that 'problems of living' can be sorted out through privately
contracted 'talking therapies' (Szasz 1961, 1970). Andrew Scull argues
that capitalism needs mental illness as a category of acceptable
'deviance' from the capitalist expectation that every individual should
contribute to economic growth. He sees asylums in the nineteenth
century and community-based services in the twentieth as equally effi-
cient ways of supporting capitalism – by providing an escape route and
repair service for the 'fall-out' from a system that, of its very nature,
supports the fittest (Cohen and Scull 1983; Scull 1991). Other labelling
theorists, such as Thomas Scheff (1966), agree with Cohen and Scull
that mental disorder is a convenient label for economic misfits who
eventually also become social misfits. An acceptance of this argument
assumes that mental disorders will disappear if we remove inequalities
in society. It also assumes that access to the market economy through
paid employment is one way of helping people to return to normality
and health. This perspective forms part of the background to current
developments in employment and housing projects for former psychiatric patients throughout Europe.

In non-Western societies, research on mental disorder points to the
reality of its existence as a phenomenon independent of culture. The
WHO International Pilot Study on Schizophrenia (IPSS), and other
research from newly established psychiatric institutes in Africa, contra-
dict early suggestions of a low level of depression there. One view on
low levels of disorder in poorer countries is that being mentally ill is a
luxury that some people cannot afford:

Relatively speaking, it is scarcity and the collaborative social world it makes
necessary in places where permanent 'sick roles' are an unaffordable luxury, that

heal. That is, a therapeutic virtue may spring from a subsistence necessity. Third World 'village' or 'peasant' communities permit the majority of those with mental disorders to find an appropriate level of functioning... to avoid disability and deterioration. (Hopper 1991: 305)

This is not a view with which I would agree. A lack of resources may prevent people seeking or using medical help, but there is no evidence in the Western world that poverty reduces mental disorder – in fact, quite the contrary is found to be the case. Also, the alleged therapeutic value of the traditional community can be overrated. Earlier studies in Africa had suggested that the extended traditional family cared for its disabled members, including them in their economic activity (usually farming), and thus protected them from unnecessary 'illness' labels. However, it is now clear that the situation is more complex than that, and generalisations from one tribe or ethnic group in a particular country to an entire continent are meaningless. It is also clear that, in countries where the average lifespan is less than 50 years and where only the fittest survive, it is more than likely that people who are mentally or physically disabled live very short lives indeed. Running alongside the somewhat romantic belief in the power of the traditional village community to offer emotional support is the belief that traditional medicine offers a physical cure. However, research on the use of traditional medicine (herbalists or medicine men as well as group rituals) in Africa is inconclusive (Edgerton 1980). The only clear pattern to emerge from the IPSS was that the recovery rate from schizophrenia appeared to be better for people from developing countries than for people from (economically) developed nations (Sartorius 1986). This generalisation has, however, been questioned by Hopper (1991) who suggests that there has been a lack of research on long-term patients with schizophrenia in Western countries and that the reasons for such a difference are therefore open to question. This finding could be attributed either to the efficacy of traditional healing approaches or to the different meaning that psychotic symptoms have for people in many African countries. If the symptoms are seen as temporary afflictions caused by external forces (either supernatural or unknown), the individual is not an outcast, does not deserve blame or punishment and needs to be maintained in the community (village or family) until the symptoms pass. In Western societies, we are less tolerant of psychotic symptoms, and we expect chronicity. The isolation experienced by former psychiatric patients who try to become integrated into the community at any level is evidence of our pessimistic attitudes.

Hospital care

> The blur of days in this place. I no longer know how many. Hours marked only by
> the tease of tablets, the cheat of watered tea, the fat rubberoid slices of bread. The
> turning on or off of lights, the troop from dormitory to dayroom, the barks of
> nurses that it is time to get up, make the bed for inspection. Time for the toilet or
> the pills, time for bed again. The television is on or off, the radio blares or is
> silent, the newspaper is a week old or yesterday's or today's... Was it October they
> caught me? When in October? (Millett 1991: 226)

Until relatively recently, most forms of treatment for mental disorder in
the Western world took place within institutional settings, usually
psychiatric facilities with roots in the public asylums and private
madhouses of the eighteenth and nineteenth centuries. In an era characterised by the expansion of state institutions to control all forms of
social deviance (Cohen and Scull 1983), the Western world prided
itself on the architectural splendour of the 'palaces' built for the poor –
the workhouses, prisons and asylums of the nineteenth century. One of
the most famous of these buildings was the Bethlem Royal Hospital,
founded in 1247 and rebuilt in 1674–76 (Stevenson 1996: 254). The
splendid design of Robert Hooke was criticised by Thomas Brown, a
satirical writer of that era, who felt that, this time, the governors had
gone too far in allowing such a sumptuous building to be commissioned for pauper lunatics:

> Bedlam... abounds with Amusements, the first of which is the building so stately
> a Fabrick for Persons wholly unsensible of the Beauty and Use of it: The Outside
> is a perfect Mockery to the Inside, and Admits of two Amusing Queries, Whether
> the Persons that ordered the Building of it, or those that inhabit it, were the
> maddest? (Thomas Brown 1700, quoted in Stevenson 1996)

However, in spite of the splendid appearance and the spacious
grounds that characterised many asylums and prisons, all were forms of
social control for the pauper classes, a fact that was proudly proclaimed
in annual reports of the Lunacy Inspectorate and reports of Royal
Commissions:

> All the witnesses who were examined in connexion with this subject, unani-
> mously admitted that pauper lunatics are largely drawn from the lowest and worst
> classes of the community, that is from the same classes which yield largely the
> inmates of prisons, thieves, prostitutes, drunkards, the idle and dissipated, persons
> leading turbulent lives and given to violence, persons unrestrained either by intel-
> ligence or morality. (Commission on Criminal Lunacy for England and Wales
> 1882: 11)

Early texts on the treatment of mental disorder show pictures of swinging chairs, of bloodletting and of (cold) baths as effective modes of treatment, but even these sometimes bizarre approaches were only available to a small minority of patients. The reality was that, for most people in institutions, there was very little attention from medical staff. For some asylum 'inmates', work and discipline were the main forms of therapy, while for others, it was harsh physical punishment and confinement in substandard conditions. As medical science developed in the early part of the twentieth century, infection was commonly associated with mental disorder, and a variety of physical treatments were pioneered, although some were quickly discarded. These included the following: shock treatment, at first through malarial and insulin therapy, and later on through ECT; surgery, for example the leucotomy popular in the 1930s and 40s; water therapy – the nineteenth-century plunge bath, which became twentieth-century hydrotherapy; and finally, the most generally used approach to therapy – manual work. For those who were rich enough to come into contact with therapists trained in psychology, psychoanalysis was an option in the first half of the twentieth century. However, for the majority of people in the public health care system, psychiatry had little to offer patients before what Kathleen Jones (1972) has called the 'drug revolution' of the 1950s. As we enter the twenty-first century, medication has replaced physical restraint, surgery and psychotherapy as the main method of treatment in hospital.

Of course, not all patients who were admitted to mental hospitals in the past remained there – some recovered and were discharged. Few, however, questioned the validity of an institutional method of treatment. It was a convenient way out for families who did not wish to disown or abandon the sufferer but were afraid of the stigma attached to insanity/mental disorder. Research on asylums in Ireland in the nineteenth century (Finnane 1981, Malcolm 1989) clearly shows that decisions to seek admission to or to oppose the discharge of a family member from either a public or a private asylum were more often based on financial considerations and potential social consequences than on the severity of the mental disorder. Since the 1950s, antipsychotic drugs (particularly the phenothiazines such as chlorpromazine) have transformed the lives of many people by making it possible for them to live in the community without the florid symptoms so frightening for both the individual sufferer and the onlooker. The numbers in psychiatric hospitals increased during the first half of the twentieth century and reached a peak in Britain in 1954, with 148,100 inpatients (Tooth and Brooke 1961), and in the USA in 1955, with 558,900 inpatients

(Scull 1984). This corresponded to approximately 350 per 100,000 population in Britain and 450 per 100,000 in the USA. By 1981, the trend had changed and the rates had dropped to approximately 155 per 100,000 in Britain in 1981 and 96 per 100,000 in the USA in 1983 (Hafner and An der Heiden 1989: 12). Recent research by Hayes and Prior (1998b), on psychiatric beds in Britain, has shown that women predominated in these beds throughout the century, a pattern that changed only in 1991 when, for the first time, men comprised over half of the psychiatric residential population.

As actual bed numbers have decreased in most Western countries, the composition of the hospital population has changed. As we approach the end of the twentieth century, the predominant group in public psychiatric care in the USA consists of young men who have been involuntarily committed to hospital because they are seen as being potentially dangerous either to themselves or to others (for a discussion, see Chapter 8). Within the young male population in both the UK and the USA, black males are more at risk of hospitalisation than white men, and are more likely to come to the hospital accompanied by the police than on referral from their primary care physician (Flannigan 1994a; Payne 1995, 1996: Robins and Regier 1991).

Private health care facilities cater for a different kind of population. These facilities include traditional psychiatric facilities, units for substance abuse, units for elder care and units for specific disorders such as eating disorders. As far as can be gleaned from reports from this sector, women still tend to dominate the ordinary psychiatric population whereas men dominate in substance abuse facilities (for a discussion, see Watkins and Callicutt 1997). This is a well developed sector, in contrast to the public mental health care system, which, according to many analysts of the American health care system, is rapidly deteriorating. As financial resources decrease, innovative staff are leaving, attracted by the inducements and opportunities offered by the private sector. This has a knock-on effect, as lower staff:patient ratios in the public sector can lead to a tendency to overuse compulsory treatment because of the shortage of time in which to 'persuade' patients of their need for treatment on a voluntary basis.

In the UK, where the emphasis is on the development of good community services, there is still a need for admission to hospital care. The service aims to keep the stay as short as possible because of the difficulties involved in reintegrating into the family and community after a long stay in hospital, and because of the possibility that what started as an acute admission might end up adding another person to the new long-stay hospital population. The recent national audit of new long-stay patients (the NLS) in Britain clearly showed that some patients are more at risk of staying in hospital than others. Among those included in the audit (905 people in all), schizophrenia was the most common diagnosis. All of the patients had 'severe social, as well as psychiatric, handicaps, three quarters had been unemployed prior to admission and only a small minority were married or had a partner' (Lelliot *et al*. 1994: 167). In addition to these characteristics, a high proportion of this new long-stay cohort were considered either to be at risk of self-injury or to pose a threat of violence to others. However, although there were certain common features in the mental disorders and lifestyle of the cohort, it would be a mistake to assume that it was homogenous:

> Young NLS patients (aged 18–34) were predominantly single males, often with a history of violence or criminality, and much more likely to be formally detained (35 per cent) than either the older NLS patients (16 per cent) or the proportion of all psychiatric patients admitted on a Section (about six per cent). The older NLS group (aged 55–67) included a larger proportion of women who were married at the time of the survey or had previously been married. These older patients had fewer positive symptoms but poorer physical health and were thought to have been at risk of self neglect if discharged. This age/gender distribution, with the younger NLS patients predominantly male and the older predominantly female, is a consistent finding. (Lelliot *et al.* 1994: 167)

This presents a picture consistent with recent figures emerging from census data on hospitalisation in Northern Ireland (Prior and Hayes 1998), where psychiatric inpatient populations of men and women are showing significant differences, older women and younger men being those most at risk of hospitalisation. In other words, these are two different populations requiring different types of care not only in a hospital setting, but also in the community. It is obvious that the mental health needs of these groups are not being met adequately in the community, otherwise they would not be showing up in hospital statistics to the extent evidenced in recent research.

Community care

The move towards a policy of 'care in the community' in the 1950s and 60s was precipitated by a new awareness of the growing costs of hospital care for long-stay patients, but it was made possible by the availability of new and effective therapeutic drugs. It was also supported, in most countries, by the liberalisation of the mental health laws, making it easier and more acceptable for people to seek psychiatric treatment earlier than had previously been usual. In the USA, there were a series of legal changes in mental health laws during the 1960s and 70s. The Mental Health Centers Act 1963, which was extremely innovative, introduced the idea of serving a small geographical population (200,000) from mental health centres staffed by a variety of health professionals. In the amended Act of 1975, the policy of community care was acknowledged as 'the most effective and humane form of care for a majority of mentally ill individuals'. In Britain, the Mental Health Act 1959 modernised all aspects of the legislation surrounding admissions to hospital, community-based service development and the monitoring of patients who were compulsorily detained. In continental Europe, legislative change was most radical in Italy, with Law 180 in 1978 rendering it almost impossible to admit anybody to a mental hospital. Similarly, in other countries, legal changes reflected the change in focus from hospital-based to community-based services (see Chapter 8 for a full discussion of the laws in Europe).

In most Western societies, the process of de-institutionalising long-stay patients and reducing the number of psychiatric beds is now virtually complete. Evaluations of the impact of the reduction in the number of beds have consistently found a lack of co-ordination and financial commitment to the development of alternative community-based services. There has been an increase in the number and proportion of people with mental health problems among the homeless and in prisons in a number of countries. The annual number of admissions to hospital has increased in the UK, and suicide rates have increased in Italy and Ireland (Kelleher 1998; Thornicroft and Bebbington 1989: 741–2). The link between statistics on homelessness, suicide and imprisonment is not straightforward, but existing evidence points to the increasing vulnerability of certain groups of former psychiatric patients who have lost touch with family and community.

While services in hospital have shrunk, there has not been a parallel increase in community services. In the USA, the responsibility for caring for people with severe mental disorder has shifted from the federal to the state level. This has resulted in a disproportionate burden of care on states with large areas of urban deprivation. The method of financing and organising health services in the USA, with the involvement of insurance companies and other commercial organisations in the sector, has also had a negative impact on publicly funded community services, many of the most experienced staff leaving the public sector. This has led to a situation in which the poorest often have to rely totally on an inadequately funded and poorly staffed public service. There are, of course, some pockets of excellence within the US system, where the non-profit sector provides a comprehensive mental health programme to the total community. One such service is the Monadnock Family Services Program, which runs a full range of mental health services in New Hampshire. Funded by payments for services to patients by private insurance companies and state health insurance schemes, the Monadnock Program has managed to survive recent health policy changes and provides a community service, which relies on very few hospital beds, to all members of the catchment area (for information on the programme, see Torrey 1997).

The situation is quite different in the UK, although it is changing in line with that in America. Mental health services are, for the most part, provided from within the NHS and local authority social services departments – publicly funded bodies. Legislation, enabling health authorities and local authorities to 'ring-fence' money from the former hospital budget and pool it with existing resources and new funding ('joint funding' initiatives), has not been as successful as envisaged. It has been more difficult than it first appeared to keep hospitals running at a low occupancy rate or to close them at no extra cost. In addition, plans to transfer resources from hospital to community have been limited by simultaneously timed financial policies aimed at reducing the cost of health care in all sectors.

Because of the increasing need for a financial justification for any new service development, there has been an ongoing debate on the cost of community care in the UK and continental Europe. Research has usually focused on specific groups of people who have been part of the de-institutionalisation process. For example, Salize and Rossler (1996), in their study of people with schizophrenia living in the community in Mannheim, Germany, found that the average cost of comprehensive community care was only 43 per cent of the cost of constant long-term care in a psychiatric hospital. In Britain, Martin Knapp and his economist colleagues at the Personal Social Services Research Unit (PSSRU) in Kent have been involved for a number of years in costing community care for different categories of vulnerable people. Although follow-up studies of discharged patients point to a lower level of cost for care in the community compared with hospital care (although not as low as predicted in the early years of the policy), there are different degrees of vulnerability and different levels of cost (Kavanagh 1997;

Kavanagh *et al.* 1995; Knapp *et al.* 1995). Some of the differences in cost are related to levels of vulnerability and some to other factors. For example, as part of the Friern/Claybury closure study, Knapp *et al.* (1995) attempted to predict community costs from a hospital baseline for 341 patients 1 year after discharge to care in the community. All of the patients were long stay (at least 1 year's continuous inpatient duration), so the information available on them was comprehensive.

One of the most interesting findings was that the actual diagnosis bore no relation to the cost of care in the community. However, all of the following characteristics increased costs: being male, being single (for both men and women), being widowed or separated (for men), having spent a large proportion of one's life in hospital, exhibiting negative psychiatric symptoms, non-specific neurotic syndrome or antisocial behaviour, and requiring daily nursing care. Similarly, some characteristics emerged as predictors of lower costs: being female, being old, having delusions and hallucinations, or having some social networks, none of these factors being related to each other. Contrary to expectations, they found that older people receive less costly community care programmes and that people with delusions and hallucinations, although they have a high level of need, do not regularly access services. They also found that the costs of community care for men are higher than for women, probably because men are assumed to be less able to care for themselves and are, therefore, directed towards more supportive (and more expensive) care packages.

Although there are many criticisms of community care policies, the overwhelming evidence is that they represent progress. Some of the positive outcomes of the policies are identified by Uffing *et al.* (1992) as being the prevention of admission to hospital in the first instance for an increasing number of people, a reduction in the number of readmissions, a shortening of the time spent in hospital, the expansion of 'protective environments' (such as sheltered housing and staffed hostels) and the integration of national and local services in many countries throughout Europe. The prevention of admission, of course, depends largely on the speed at which first indications of a problem are recognised and help is offered. In the UK and the Netherlands, general practitioners (primary care physicians) are the gatekeepers to specialist mental health services. Research in both countries reveals, however, that only a small proportion of these patients are referred on to psychiatric services. A study carried out in the Netherlands (Verhaak 1993) found that only 6 per cent of diagnoses of mental illness resulted in a psychiatric referral. They also found that there were certain groups of patients more likely to be referred than others. For example, even though younger men had the lowest level of identification of psychiatric morbidity, this group was most frequently referred. Verhaak's study also indicated that the training of general practitioners had a significant impact on the decision to refer or not, those who had an interest in and some knowledge of psychology being more likely to treat their patients themselves. In England, lower referral rates from general practice are found in practices with a psychiatric attachment (a psychiatrist undertaking one or more sessions at the practice site) and in areas where there is a multidisciplinary community-based mental health team, both developments resulting from community care policies (Uffing *et al.* 1992).

Therapies within mainstream psychiatry

For people who receive treatment in a psychiatric setting, either in hospital or in the community, advances in medical science have a significant impact on the types of treatment offered to them. According to Glen Gabbard, Professor of Psychoanalysis at the Menninger Clinic and of Psychiatry at the University of Kansas, the options available to psychiatrists practising today are myriad:

> Contemporary psychiatrists are blessed with an impressive array of treatments in their therapeutic armamentarium. Among these highly effective therapeutic tools are electroconvulsive therapy, highly specific pharmaco-therapeutic agents, sophisticated protocols for behavioral desensitization, hypnosis, family and marital psychotherapies, group psychotherapy, individual psychotherapy, and psychoanalysis. (Kaplan and Sadock 1995: 131)

Gabbard suggests that, as not all types of treatment suit all patients, decisions to use a particular form of treatment should be based not only on the particular disorder or problem, but also on a judgement of the patient's likelihood of adhering to whatever programme is drawn up. This is a highly optimistic view of psychiatric services. Even if all psychiatrists were versed in all of the therapies outlined by Gabbard, which they are not, it is unlikely that they would all be equally available to every person showing up with a mental health problem. It is true that, in the UK, in spite of changes in the model of health service provision, a range of therapies is available within most NHS facilities. Some geographical areas, such as cities with university teaching hospitals, may have more services than others, but there is always the possibility of being referred to a specialist service if it is seen as an essential part of treatment. In the USA, the situation is quite different as the kinds of treatment on offer are determined primarily by financial considerations – you get what you pay for.

The introduction of the American Health Security Bill (the Clinton Plan) in 1993 precipitated a major change in the delivery of health care in spite of the fact that it never passed into legislation. During the past few years, insurance companies and health maintenance organisations (HMOs), all commercial enterprises aiming at making profit, have expanded their managed care programmes to include all areas of health care, including psychiatry. This is already having a major impact on both the type and the length of treatment. Many HMOs allow referral to a psychiatrist only after an assessment and sometimes treatment by a general practitioner/primary care physician, a process that is usual in the UK but is not very popular with American psychiatrists as it may delay appropriate treatment and certainly limits referrals. Most managed mental health care (MMHC) plans limit the number of visits for psychotherapy or other behavioural therapy to an arbitrary figure of between five and 20 sessions per year, and they may also limit the number of hospital days to fewer than that suggested by the psychiatrist involved in the specific case (Kaplan and Sadock 1995: ix). People are also limited in their choice of psychiatrist (to one who is on the HMO's approved list), which is understandable from a commercial point of view but limits the treatment options available to the service user. The situation in the USA is regarded by mental health professionals as an extremely serious infringement of professional judgement. It could potentially damage people seeking help with mental health problems as their treatment might be limited or curtailed on the basis of a decision by an insurance company rather than on a professional mental health opinion. Although this particular debate is viewed as being particularly American (by those of us on this side of the Atlantic), it is worth a broader airing because similar systems of managed care may be duplicated in the future in the UK and other countries in Europe. At present, a number of governments are searching for alternative ways of financing an increasingly expensive health care system.

Within the context of different local limitations on service delivery, we will now look at some well-established models of treatment used within mainstream psychiatry today. These can be conceptualised fairly simply as the 'organic approach', the 'psychotherapeutic approach' and the 'behavioural approach'. The organic approach is based on assumptions about the link between the physical and the mental, the physical determining the mental. In other words, from the perspective of this model of causation, all mental disorders are secondary to physical disturbances or disorders. The psychotherapeutic approach represents a long tradition of psychoanalysis and psychotherapy in psychiatry on both sides of the Atlantic. Problems are conceptualised in terms of their historical roots in the conscious or unconscious reality of childhood. The behavioural approach, based on learning theories, focuses on ways of learning new ways to cope with old problems. Problems are conceptualised in terms of experiences and environments that have shaped learning along particular paths. These learning paths can be changed.

The organic approach

The focus on an organic basis for mental disorder is gaining increasing credibility, especially in American psychiatry, as the evidence of measurable physical disturbances or differences in people with specific mental disorders continues to grow. The main advances in recent research come from the neural sciences. As new ideas are tested, many of the old assumptions are being challenged and contested. The research is wide ranging, but certain aspects of it will have more impact on treatment than others. These include studies in neuroanatomy, with a special focus on functional systems of the brain, work on neurotransmitters and signal transduction, developments in measuring total brain functions, work on the central nervous system and, finally and perhaps most importantly, the major developments being made in genetics. In terms of the impact on treatment in the first half of the twentieth century, research on neurotransmitters has had the greatest effect, leading, for example, to the development of antidepressant and antipsychotic agents targeted on the monoamine neurotransmitter systems. Current research focuses on the development of more specific drugs with a greater therapeutic effect and, hopefully, without the adverse side-effects (such as tardive dyskinesia) now experienced by many long-term users of drugs for severe mental disorder. New developments in knowledge in relation to neurotransmitters have had an almost immediate effect on the treatments for schizophrenia and dementia currently in use (see Kaplan and Sadock 1995: chs. 1–3).

The application of research into ways of measuring total brain function is more controversial. New ways of assessing patient response to drug treatment, through the use of the technology of electro-encephalography (EEG), may make it possible for clinicians to predict which drugs will have the required effect before or early in treatment. However, the same techniques could potentially be used to diagnose people with abnormal brain functioning as a way of justifying compulsory treatment or institutionalisation. Horror stories from the USA concerning children who are labelled as potential murderers, resulting in punitive drug and behavioural treatment programmes, make us very wary of making direct links between brain functioning and mental health or ill-health.

However, there are a number of interesting subdivisions of research within this specialty, which are also of importance. Sleep research is gaining credibility in recent years as the importance of adequate sleep in the maintenance of good mental functioning is confirmed by research. Sleep problems are associated not only with specific sleep disorders, but also with depression, anxiety, stress and substance abuse. As the psychiatric population ages in line with demographic trends in the general population, this research will perhaps receive more attention as sleep problems affect a significant proportion of older people. After the age of 65, it is reported that one in three women and one in five men take over 30 minutes to fall asleep and that sleep time increases during the day and decreases during the night, although overall sleep time increases slightly (Kaplan and Sadock 1995: 83). It is not clear what the significance of this is, except that is its known that death rates are higher in those whose pattern of sleep is at either end of the continuum – too long or too short. Another interesting finding occurs in relation to depression. Sleep deprivation, either total or partial, has an antidepressant effect, but the positive effects wear off very quickly. Although this is not a satisfactory treatment for someone suffering from chronic depression, it is worth further research in an effort to develop non-pharmacological treatments for depression and other related disorders.

Another focus of increased research interest within psychiatry has been the central neural system. Advances in our understanding of the interaction between the neural system, the immune system and the endocrine system have been particularly visible in relation to acquired immune deficiency syndrome (AIDS). Success in establishing links in relation to AIDS has led, in turn, to research on the possibility of similar interactions in Alzheimer's disease and Parkinson's disease (Kaplan and Sadock 1995: 3). It is now accepted that a virus that affects the immune system may also, for example, cause depression or dementia. For the lay person, this kind of finding makes perfect sense, but what is less acceptable is the notion that behavioural and emotional difficulties are considered to be the effects of physical disturbances or disorders and amenable only to physical treatments.

One example of a controversial debate is in relation to the menstrual cycle. Nobody disputes the impact of certain hormonal changes on the subjective experience of well-being. However, in the past, the female menstrual cycle has been used to label a variety of deviant or distressing behaviours as mental illness. The most well-known example of this is hysteria, the condition usually associated with women, which means 'wandering womb' and derives its name from the original Greek word for womb – *hustera*. Elaine Showalter, the feminist historian, documented the ways in which the reproductive cycle, a constant reminder of female sexuality, was assumed to be the root cause of almost all of women's ills. Some Victorian doctors made great efforts to regulate the menstrual cycle and delay sexual development for as long as possible:

> Dr Edward Tilt argued that menstruation was so disruptive to the female brain, that it should not be hastened but rather be retarded as long as possible, and he advised mothers to prevent menarche by ensuring that their teenage daughters remained in the nursery, took cold shower baths, avoided feather beds and novels, eliminated meat from their diets, and wore drawers. (Showalter 1987: 75)

The menstrual cycle has also been used in the justice system to excuse women from culpability for all kinds of crimes, ranging from stealing to acts of aggression (Allen 1987; Heidensohn 1996; Smith 1981). The debate continues to rage over whether or not premenstrual tension and menopausal disorders are caused simply by hormonal changes or by other factors completely independent of the physical factors but related to the particular stage of life. The strength of feeling involved in the debate was evident in the controversy surrounding the inclusion of the classification for premenstrual syndrome in the DSM-III-R and DSM-IV (Figert 1996). The lobby that favoured the medicalisation of the syndrome as 'Premenstrual dysphoric disorder' won. The question is not resolved, however, and research on the inter-action between the hormonal system and experiences of emotional and behavioural disturbances continues to be a valid and controversial focus for study.

Genetics research is perhaps the area in which the most creative leaps will be made in the very near future. The Human Genome Project (in the USA) aims to explore the whole human genome (all human chromosomes) in the next two decades. Kaplan and Sadock (1995: 155) suggest that 'this historical mission promises to unveil the approximately 50,000 human genes, the DNA sequences that regulate their expression, and, presumably, many unknown characteristics of the human genome'. The new information, and there are bound to be new discoveries, will have a major impact on all aspects of medicine, including psychiatry. The degree of influence of genetic characteristics on the emergence and pattern of different mental disorders is highly debated, although there is general acceptance that there is probably a genetic predisposition in disorders such as schizophrenia, manic-depression and perhaps also alcohol-related disorders. Evidence on genetic links in specific mental disorders is gathered from the relatives of known sufferers from that disorder and contrasted with a control group from the normal population. In schizophrenia, for example, the morbidity risk among first-degree relatives ranges from 3 to 7 per cent, in contrast with the risk of approximately from 0.2–0.5 per cent in the relatives of the control group.

Other studies, in a effort to distinguish the relative influence of heredity and environment, focus on twins (both monozygotic and dizygotic) who have been adopted or reared separately. The evidence points to a strong genetic link in manic-depressive disorders, with concordance rates of 80 per cent in monozygotic twins, and also in schizophrenia, with a concordance rate of over 50 per cent, the concordance rates in both cases being much lower in dizygotic twins. However, because in all of the studies a significant proportion of the monozygotic twins did not develop the disorders, the research also points to the need to identify other factors in the environment that have an impact on their occurrence. As the Human Genome Project progresses, there is no doubt that it will have a major effect on our understanding of the major mental disorders. However, a word of warning comes from mainstream psychiatry itself:

> For psychiatry to avoid the twin pitfalls of becoming either mindless or brainless, clinicians must acknowledge the complex relations between neurophysiological and psychosocial factors in the cause and the pathogenesis of psychiatric disorders. To say that a chemical imbalance, for example, is the cause of a disorder is reductionistic. Neurophysiological or biochemical, processes in the brain are mediating mechanisms, rather than causal agents. The subjective meaning of the information perceived from the environment sets the biological processes in motion. (Kaplan and Sadock 1995: 473)

The psychotherapeutic approach – DRUGS.

Taking prescribed drugs may be easy for some people, but they are potentially of little use in the resolution of some disorders such as anxiety disorders (the neuroses in the American Psychiatric Association classifications up to DSM-III), where there is little research evidence of genetic predisposition and a general acceptance of a causal link with unresolved conscious and unconscious conflicts. Drugs are of little value in resolving the problems on a long-term basis without some form of 'talking' therapy, whether this be in group, family, marital or individual sessions. Psychotherapy is offered in the hope of helping the person experiencing mental disorders to understand the mechanisms that have precipitated the current crisis or are inhibiting recovery. For example, classic psychoanalytical theories of depression explain it in terms of anger turned against the self as a result of unresolved negative feelings against one's parents or an inability to live up to the real or imagined expectations of a loved one. The aim of therapy is to help individuals to redirect their anger outwards or to realign their expectations of themselves in line with what they really can achieve, thus removing some of the self-hatred and, hopefully, reducing the depression.

Most current ways of working are based on the work of Sigmund Freud, whose theories of the mind are almost 100 years old. His lasting contribution is the analysis of the influence of the unconscious on conscious behaviour and of early childhood on adult life. Because of the particularly paternalistic and sometimes mysogynistic thrust of his sexual development theories, many women reject Freudian psychotherapy and turn to therapies informed by other schools of thought. Feminist psychologists working during the 1970s attempted to integrate feminist ideology into their therapeutic approaches. Juliet Mitchell, in her influential work *Psychoanalysis and Feminism* (Mitchell 1975), argued for a revised understanding of Freud to one which sees Freudian theory not as a prescription for a patriarchal society but instead as an analysis of one that existed in his time. However, critics of Mitchell regard her arguments as a rather weak rationale for the continuing use of a theory that is obviously suffused with theoretical underpinnings unflattering and unhelpful to women.

More acceptable to many women are the therapies deriving from the 'object relations' work of Melanie Klein (who worked in England from the mid-1920s) and the psychodynamic theories of the American therapists Eric Fromm and Karen Horney. Horney, in particular, was one of the first psychotherapists to validate womens' experiences of the destructive impact of oppressive marital relationships. Jane Ussher, a psychologist currently working in England, echoes other psychosocial therapists (both men and women) when she suggests that the only form of psychotherapy helpful to women is feminist psychotherapy, offering a context within which they can come to some understanding of both the aspects of their individual psychological development that have led to current patterns of emotional reaction, and the negative or oppressive factors in their current life that have precipitated a mental health crisis. Ussher criticises traditional psychiatric approaches to women's mental health problems and suggests that feminist psychotherapy is the only productive way forward:

> The labels applied to women, labels which so cleverly place the problem within her as a person, distracting from the social reality of her life, serve to mystify the reality of her oppression, a process buttressed by the gender bias in psychiatric nosology, the labelling process itself. (Ussher 1991: 168)

It would be wrong to assume that there is general agreement on the value of either traditional psychotherapy or feminist psychotherapy in alleviating mental health problems caused primarily by social or economic circumstances. Joan Busfield, for example, while acknowledging the contribution that feminist psychological theories have made in mainstream psychiatric settings, is critical of them on two counts:

> There is a tendency to generalise too freely about human psychological development, which when applied to gender differences, leads to forms of psychic essentialism. There is also a tendency to attribute too much to the inner world (albeit often held to be socially generated) and too little to external situational pressures and events, as in the classic psychodynamic focus on phantasy rather than reality (with the attendant danger of denying the reality of external events). (Busfield 1996: 186)

Busfield makes an important point that must be considered in relation to all forms of therapy. If problems arise primarily from internal emotional conflicts, it makes sense to use psychotherapy as the treatment of choice to help solve the problem. If, on the other hand, the problems derive mainly from economic or social circumstances, it makes little sense to concentrate on psychological explanations. Research has consistently found a strong correlation between poverty and mental disorder (Belle 1990; Regier *et al.* 1993; Viinamaki *et al.* 1995), but it also does not preclude the existence of mental disorder within situations of socio-economic advantage. Therefore, the possibility of primary causation being rooted in internal emotional conflicts has to remain on the agenda.

The behavioural approach

The importance of therapies based on learning theories has increased enormously in recent years. Drugs may help to alleviate distressing symptoms, psychotherapy may help the individual to understand the roots of the problem, but behavioural approaches have been found to be the most effective in changing behaviour in the short term. Different learning theories form the basis for this approach:

> The basic concept of learning is that the organism acquires new behaviors as a result of experience. Much of the disordered behavior that characterizes the syndromes of interest in psychiatry is learned and maintained within a social context, particularly within the family. (Kaplan and Sadock 1995: 300)

Therapy involves unlearning old patterns of behaviour and relearning new ones, with a view to decreasing situations of internal and external conflict. The approach is best described in relation to a particular area of human behaviour – aggression. Aggressive behaviour results from a combination of learned patterns of response to specific situations perceived as threatening. The individual learns aggressive modes of acting, reacts to particular stimuli and receives reinforcement from the social context. Programmes to change aggressive behaviour have to be aimed at all stages of the sequence if possible.

As men are more prone than women to labels of personality disorder (which always includes violent behavioural outbursts), this is an important area for research because of the gendered impact on service development. While behaviour therapy is used fairly widely to help people living in the community who are violent within the family (to spouses or children), there is little or no commitment to it in prisons, where some of society's most violent people find themselves. Because other less intractable behaviour problems are more amenable to change, they usually receive more attention in the psychiatric system. All kinds of phobia, and certain types of anxiety and addiction, respond well to learning programmes involving desensitisation and the relearning of new patterns of response. While work continues to develop these programmes further, it is to be hoped that more resources will be devoted also to those whose antisocial behaviour is linked to mental disorder.

Behavioural programmes were not popular when first introduced within psychiatry and social work as they appeared to use techniques associated with brainwashing and were used in isolation from other approaches. Now, in an era in which people feel free to make choices that may involve rejecting old ways of being and developing new ones, it is more acceptable to participate in a behavioural programme. It is also more usual to see behavioural programmes being used in conjunction with other forms of therapy. For example, in the case of anorexia nervosa, it is common practice to use a behavioural programme to try to bring about an immediate change in eating patterns and psychotherapy to help the individual understand the origins of the problem and find other more healthy ways of dealing with it. One of the disadvantages of psychotherapy, regardless of what the specific theoretical basis happens to be, is the length of time it takes for the individual to resolve the conflict in such a way as to reduce stress and cause a change in attitude or behaviour. In the case of anorexia, the patient, usually a young woman, may die from starvation before she understands why she has to engage in this self-destructive behaviour. In the case of more dangerous antisocial behaviour linked to mental disorders, such as long-standing patterns of sexual abuse or violent physical assault on others, the person may offend again if some attempts are not made to change behaviour.

Although the behavioural approach has been shown to be successful in specific situations, it is open to criticism, mainly because of the overtly manipulative nature of the programmes and the short-term nature of the 'cure'. However, because of the overwhelming evidence from psychiatric and prison statistics that antisocial behaviour in young men (in particular) is often linked to some form of mental distress or disturbance, more resources in terms of personnel and research must be devoted to this area of treatment, which seems to work when others fail. The alternative is the long-term incarceration of men in a prison system offering no hope of recovery.

Non-medical approaches

As recent research on psychiatric morbidity in the USA has shown, the majority of people with active mental disorders do not gain access to professional medical help of any kind (Robins and Regier 1991: Table 13-5). In the ECA study, only 19 per cent of the household residents with an active disorder had received either inpatient treatment in the previous year (2.4 per cent) or outpatient treatment in the previous 6 months (16.4 per cent). When looking for variables that had an impact on the likelihood of receiving treatment, the researchers found a relationship between gender, marital status and education. Women (with an active disorder) received more treatment than men – 23 per cent as against 14 per cent; unmarried men and women received more treatment than those who were married – 20 per cent compared with 17 per cent ; and men and women who had completed high school were slightly more likely to have received treatment than those who had not. The group most likely to have received treatment were unmarried women who had completed high school, and the group least likely to have done so were married men without high school education – 27 per cent versus 11 per cent. What is clear about these findings is that, even for the group who were the highest users of services, almost four out of five people did not receive any treatment.

If these are the people who might perhaps seek alternative sources of help, it is worth looking at the ECA findings more closely to see who are the least likely to receive treatment within conventional medical settings. Conscious of the fact that not all of those who sought help through their general practitioner received it, the researchers asked participants if they had ever brought their symptoms to their doctor's attention (Robins and Regier 1991: 361–2). Although there was great variation across disorders, some patterns emerged. The disorders most likely to have been discussed were panic, schizophrenia, depression, mania and somatisation disorders. This confirms research carried out in psychiatric settings that points to depression and anxiety being the disorders most commonly seen by mental health professionals. The disorders least likely to be reported were phobia, alcoholism, drug dependence, personality disorder and cognitive deficit. As we saw in the discussion on prevalence, the ECA study found the most common disorders in the community to be alcoholism and phobia. This is in contrast to research carried out in populations receiving medical treatment, which describes very different patterns of mental disorder. The result is highly gendered. The disorders found to predominate in hospital – anxiety/panic disorders and depression – are more often associated with women, while those which predominate in community studies – drug and alcohol dependence and personality disorder – are more often associated with men. The need is clear: to expand the services available to men and to develop new flexible approaches to the care and treatment of substance dependence and personality disorders.

However, there are perhaps other avenues of help open to people who do not use medical services. Do they use alternative treatments? Interestingly, this question is rarely included in research on mental disorders in Western countries. However, because of the importance of traditional healing in India and Africa, it was included in the WHO's DOSMD study. In this, traditional and religious healers were regarded as important sources of information on all kinds of mental disorder: they were the source of referral to the study of 30 per cent of the patients in Agra, India, and of 28 per cent in Ibadan, Nigeria (Katz *et al.* 1988: 334). It would be extremely interesting to include faith healers and providers of alternative therapies in studies of service use in Europe or the USA. That kind of information is not currently available, but it may become so in the future – some research on ethnicity and health is beginning to incorporate questions on traditional healing.

Self-help organisations

We have seen a great expansion in recent years in the number of self-help organisations, including groups initiated by existing or former users of psychiatric services, their relatives and professionals, some of these organisations being linked to mental health services. In the USA, the President's Commission on Mental Health (1978) estimated that there were over 500,000 self-help groups in existence at the time (Kiesler 1980). Some of these organisations are aimed at helping the individual sufferer to find a solution to and to move on from the mental disorder; one of the best known examples of this is the worldwide organisation Alcoholics Anonymous (AA). Others aim to give support to people who accept that their condition is chronic – for example, the National Schizophrenia Fellowship (NSF) in the UK and the National Alliance for the Mentally Ill (NAMI) in the USA. Although organisations based on AA, such as Narcotics Anonymous and Gamblers Anonymous, are exposed to criticism from many quarters, they have been found to be helpful to many thousands of people to whom the traditional psychiatric services can offer no cure.

The secret of success seems to lie in the link to a new social group, which supports the individual through times of 'failure' but which has as its aim the changing of the problem behaviour for all of its members. The message is simple and unambiguous, and blame is not assigned. The major criticisms of AA are that it is based on a Christian ideology and is thus only meaningful in Western Christian cultures, and that it is based on the assumption that alcoholism (or any other addiction) is a disease. Both criticisms are valid and might have led to the demise of AA in the face of an increase in secularism and of an acceptance of the multicausal origins of addiction. However, this has not been the case, and the AA format continues to thrive in groups that neither acknowledge the Christian way of life nor are totally committed to the disease model of addiction.

Other user organisations (including those initiated by relatives of people with mental disorders) have increased in number and in strength, as psychiatric services decrease in Europe and North America. The rise has coincided with a greater awareness of citizenship rights by people who had previously taken for granted their exclusion from many social and economic opportunities. User organisations have been strong in the USA and Canada for many years and are becoming more visible in many European countries as lobbyists for the rights of people with mental health problems. For example, at a European meeting in 1991, representatives from nine countries debated the issues of rights and government responsibility in relation to mental health. People spoke of the 'tyranny' of having to cope with chronic mental disorder, of the 'abandonment' by the state of responsibility for certain groups of sufferers such as young adults whose mental disorders derived from drug abuse, and of the need for some kind of 'normality' for families and users of services (Louzoun 1993). The range of user groups is wide. Older user organisations, such as the Finnish Mental Health Association, founded in 1897, usually provide services to support existing psychiatric services – day centres, housing projects, leisure projects and rehabilitation and education. Newer organisations are much more influenced by the civil rights movement and are involved in promoting the individual and group questioning of services and policies through advocacy schemes and lobbying tactics (see Sundram 1995). Research by Barnes and Shardlow with three user groups in England demonstrated the increasing strength and confidence of people who would not, in the past, have 'taken on' the system:

> The groups that we have studied demonstrate that people who have used mental health services can be active agents, not only in controlling their own lives, but also in providing services to each other, and as participants within decision-making networks... They also have a role to play in revitalising the relationship between users and service provided within the welfare state. (Barnes and Shardlow 1997: 298)

However, although they are expanding in number, many user organisations are disappointed by the lack of progress that the movements
have made in terms of making an impact on changes in policy directions. In the UK, for example, user organisations are increasingly being
asked to sit on committees of service users to give feedback to the NHS
trusts responsible for mental health services. However, there is very
little power attached to such committees, and any changes made are
usually fairly minor. Perhaps in future we will see more direct political
lobbying for change from these organisations.

Housing and employment programmes

Many people with serious mental health problems have great difficulty
in maintaining their link to the world of employment and therefore to
an adequate income. The social and economic isolation that follows
from this precipitates stresses that inhibit recovery. Increasingly,
projects with either housing and employment components, or both, are
being seen as the backbone of long-term rehabilitation. The more traditional highly staffed rehabilitation hostels, usually located near a
psychiatric hospital, are seen as short-term measures only, suitable as
half-way houses for people who have been institutionalised for a long
time. Other hostels or group homes, based on the model of a therapeutic community, suit people who have behavioural problems but who
would have difficulty living alone. More innovative are the housing
projects that include one or two group homes and some independent
apartments nearby, with flexible staffing arrangements allowing for as
much or as little independence as the residents can cope with. These
projects provide a social network for people who find it difficult to
form their own networks and professional support when necessary.

However, the main problem with all of these housing initiatives is
that they are rarely welcome in residential locations. Over a decade
ago in the USA, Dear and Wolch (1987) documented various attempts
by local residents to prevent any housing developments that would
cater for former psychiatric patients, particularly if they were men. The
problem has now escalated, as the run-down hotels in some seaside
towns fill up with the former patients from nearby hospitals that have
been closed. This has resulted in the growth of what has been called
the 'psychiatric ghetto' as localities fill up with former patients and
other people gradually move out. Fortunately, this is not yet a European phenomenon.

However good housing projects may be, there are a number of issues that could be debated concerning them. Apart from the fact that they can cater for only a small minority of people already known to mental health services, there are questions surrounding what kind of home life, if any, can be provided and to what extent this kind of project can encourage true independence, leading eventually to the resident moving away from the therapeutic group. Sociological research by Lindsay Prior on patients living in 'independent' situations in the community in Northern Ireland clearly demonstrated how difficult it is for former or current psychiatric patients to link into alternative worlds: for many, their world outside the hospital continues to be made up of people from the world inside the hospital – mental health professionals, day centre staff, therapeutic leisure group members and colleagues from sheltered work situations (Prior 1993). In other words, there is little difference between the social world of the patient in a hospital and that of the same patient in a community-based residential facility, integration with the broader community continues to be almost impossible for a psychiatric patient, regardless of location. However, the ultimate goal must be to have a less exclusive society that tolerates some differences, including disabilities, in its midst. Unfortunately, as life becomes more privatised and larger sections of the community find themselves increasingly excluded, housing projects offer short-term, high-quality solutions to people who would otherwise find themselves totally isolated.

All of the arguments in relation to housing can also be made in relation to employment projects. Work as a form of therapy has been highly valued since the early nineteenth century, primarily because of the influence of the Tuke family, who pioneered 'moral management' within the first Retreat in York, England. Before the demise of the large mental hospitals in the middle of the twentieth century, most of them had a farm, a laundry, a shoe shop and a tailor's shop attached to them. Patients who were well enough worked in all of these departments, the work being strictly divided on gender lines. Women did not work in the shoe shop nor men in the laundry. Sometimes, the work extended outside the asylum, either for the good of the society at large, for example in times of labour shortage, or for the good of the patient, for example to maintain his or her existing links with the working community (Hopper 1991; Prior 1995). Current work projects in Europe are supported financially from the antipoverty programme of the European Union (EU) and include a range of activities, from sheltered workshops producing components or goods for industry, to individually negotiated work placements with independent employers. People involved in these projects are those who value work for its own sake and do not object to the low level of wages offered. For them, it is a lifeline to the 'normal' world of work. For others, it is akin to slave labour, which serves to reinforce the existing divisions in society, divisions that place those with a mental disorder at the bottom of the heap. The philosophical debate is succinctly summarised by Kim Hopper:

> Isn't it a bit awkward, to suggest on the one hand that when work is a socially valued and supported activity, its effects are therapeutic, while maintaining on the other that even when it is soulless and ill-paid, similar benefits may be reaped? As Marx never tired of noting, social utility does not necessarily translate into individual benefit. (Hopper 1991: 317)

Hopper's discussion on work is in relation to the value of work in different cultures and in different economic situations. It raises the basic question of the value and meaning of any approach to helping people cope with or recover from mental disorders. The reality is, of course, that for the majority of people with mental disorder, no intervention takes place. They get on with their lives alone, trying to live in a society that is becoming increasingly intolerant of those who cannot compete in the market place. The most neglected groups, we know, are those who are known to be substance abusers or who engage in antisocial acts. These people are the least likely to succeed in accessing help in either the medical or non-medical sector. As these are mostly young men, it perhaps points to the need for more research into the particular problems experienced by young men in today's society. One starting point for this debate forms the basis for the next chapter – how society defines and controls 'normality' in ways which leave very little room for manoeuvre in male or female gender roles.

5

Gender and Normality

All descriptions of mental disorder assume some criteria for defining what is normal – what is acceptable and tolerable for the individual and for society. These definitions of normality are almost always tied to gendered notions of behaviour and ways of thinking. Because people have different levels of tolerance not only for emotional stress, but also for behaviour that is outside the norm, differences of opinion arise among individuals and their families over whether or not professional therapeutic help is required. Often, what is experienced by the individual as a small personal difficulty, which will pass without any outside intervention, is seen by friends or relatives as mental disorder in need of treatment. Both views (that of the individual and that of the relatives) are valid positions, representing the two opposing camps in the debate on the role of medicine in helping people with mental health problems. According to the well-known 'antipsychiatry' psychiatrist Thomas Szasz (1961, 1970), the very existence of a publicly funded mental health system is an unnecessary medicalisation of 'problems of living' that could be solved privately. He argues that this system enhances the powerful position of a medical élite and does little to help the individual experiencing mental distress. For Marxist theorist Andrew Scull, the same system not only medicalises problems of living, but also selects some of these for particularly controlling interventions because it suits the particular developmental phase of capitalism (Cohen and Scull 1983).

Whether or not one accepts the 'power élite' type analysis of Szasz or the economic analysis of Scull, one has to accept the fact that public mental health services have, for the most part, been perceived by consumers of these services as meeting some need other than that of helping them to live a more mentally healthy life that will integrate them into society. This has been primarily due to the fact that, for the past two centuries, the majority of the population using publicly funded mental health services (until recently, mainly hospital inpatient treatment) have come from disadvantaged socio-economic groups in the population (Davies *et al.* 1996; Finnane 1981; Flannigan *et al.* 1994a, 1994b; Robins and Regier 1991; Viinamaki *et al.* 1995).

This is particularly the case where hospitalisation is concerned. In the past, when psychiatric beds were plentiful, poor men and women had an equal chance of being admitted. However, evidence is emerging that, as psychiatric beds become scarcer, the risk of hospitalisation increases for men (Payne 1995, 1996; Prior and Hayes 1998; Sanguineti *et al.* 1996; Sommers and Baskin 1992; Sugarman and Craufurd 1994). This has been attributed to the fact that there has been a change in the conceptualisation of mental disorder to one which has given more prominence to the individual's potential for dangerous behaviour – the perceived risk to the public. This has led to subtle changes in admission practices, which place men at greater risk of hospitalisation than women.

However, these new patterns of professional practice have not made a great difference in terms of overall psychiatric treatment. It still remains a fact that the mental health problems of women receive more attention than those of men. Recently, both the overrepresentation of women and the underrepresentation of men in mental health programmes have led to a severe criticism of psychiatry by feminists and, to a lesser extent, by the newer theorists of masculinity.

Feminism

Because of the known gender differences in the diagnosis and treatment of mental disorder during the past two centuries, this area has provided fertile ground for feminist research. Two different perspectives have been evident in this research. One is a social constructionist perspective, which focuses on how diagnoses are constructed, and the other is a social causation perspective, which focuses on the stress caused by traditional female roles (for a discussion, see Pugliesi 1992: 44). Reasons given for the overrepresentation of women in psychiatric statistics have included arguments about the intolerable constraints involved in traditional female roles, the acceptability of illness as a mode of protest and attention-seeking for women, and the inability of a male-dominated society to accept creative but different female behaviour (Allen 1987; Barnes and Maple 1992; Busfield 1986, 1996; Ripa 1990; Shorter 1990; Showalter 1987; Skultans 1979; Ussher 1991).

Feminist writers accuse psychiatrists of being mysogynist, of stereotyping female behaviour so that women are caught in a 'Catch 22' situation of being easily defined as ill for any deviation from the normal
role or, on the contrary, for close conformity to it (Busfield 1996: 101;
Chesler 1972: 56; Showalter 1987):

> women who *conform* to the female model, as well as those who *reject* it, are likely
> to be labelled psychiatrically ill... The description of a *healthy* adult, either male
> or female, conformed to the masculine stereotype, while the feminine stereotype,
> of passivity, conformity, less aggression, lower achievement motivation etc., was
> seen as psychologically *unhealthy*. (Ussher 1991: 168)

The image of the feminine as synonymous with 'madness' provided
the basis for *Female Malady* by Elaine Showalter (1987). She argues
that the link between femaleness and insanity goes far beyond statistical evidence of an overrepresentation in psychiatric reports. Within
literature and art, women stand on the side of irrationality, while men
stand firmly on the side of rationality:

> While the name of the symbolic female disorder may change from one historical
> period to the next, the gender asymmetry of the representational tradition remains
> constant. Thus madness, even when experienced by men, is metaphorically and
> symbolically represented as feminine: a female malady. (Showalter 1997: 4)

It is certainly true that representations of certain types of madness in
the world of literature and art have often been female, but this is not
true of all types of madness. The images of a crazy woman locked in an
attic or a wandering Ophelia-like character are part of this tradition, but
there have also been images of 'madmen' – in chains because of their
uncontrollable violence.

The images of female madness provided the justification for the
imposition of treatments sometimes for the woman's benefit, always
for the benefit of her immediate family and sometimes for the benefit
of the therapist. Showalter is scathing in her criticism of one the leaders
of the antipsychiatry movement of the 1960s – David Cooper. Like
selected therapists of the era, Cooper approved of sex with clients as a
way of establishing a bond:

> He is confident that he can detect the 'non-orgasmic personality' (predictably
> female) by 'minute ocular deflections and by sentences spoken to one that fail to
> connect because they are never properly ended'. Cooper seems blind to the
> ethical issues involved when he picks up a beautiful twenty year old schizo-

phrenic woman... a mute whom he takes home and 'makes love with'. (Showalter
1987: 247)

As Showalter points out, there is very little difference between the use
of male power in this situation and that exercised by asylum staff who
raped women in their care.

Of course, most women are not exposed to this kind of abuse but to a
more subtle form of oppression, which is based on assumptions about
both mental health and the female role. Feminists have pointed out that
this oppression crosses social class boundaries. Some articulate,
middle-class, educated women find themselves as consumers of
psychiatric services; for example, two of the most famous feminist
writers of the 1970s had personal experience of mental disorder. Sylvia
Plath was diagnosed as having schizophrenia and Kate Millett as being
manic-depressive. Plath wrote about her experience in the form of
fiction, while Millett told her story in the form of an autobiographical
novel. The two accounts are quite different, but both confirm the awful-
ness of the experience. Sylvia Plath was terrified of ECT; the doctors
knew she was terrified, her mother knew she was terrified, but this did
not stop her having to endure it. She tells us how her fictional character,
Esther, felt. Through half open eyes, Esther saw the bed, the ECT
machine beside the bed and a number of 'masked people' on both sides
of the bed. She was reassured by the nurse that she would not 'feel a
thing' and that she would be 'perfectly all right'. Her last recollection
of receiving the treatment was of being enveloped by darkness and of
being wiped out 'like chalk on a blackboard' (Plath 1963: 226).

The debate on the right to refuse treatment had not yet begun when
Plath was writing, but, in her account, she rejects the social system that
virtually primed her for mental illness, and the private medical care
system that controlled her benevolently without helping her to deal
with the social pressures causing her distress.

Writing over 20 years later, Kate Millett tells us about another type
of treatment, which, although not physically invasive, was also terrifying. To her surprise, she found herself in 'seclusion' in a psychiatric
hospital in Ireland – locked in solitary confinement as a method of
controlling aggressive behaviour. (Seclusion is now rarely used except
in the prison system.)

And then the door slams. Forever. So the wheel, prayer, was all that was left, the
last resort. And I amused myself with it all night long, entertained myself with my
own mind, with pictures, covering the walls with pictures, the wave pattern, the
light of a swimming pool. When you discover that this room has not only no

natural light but no natural air either, you begin to grow particularly anxious: blackouts, power failures. You are kept alive by air-conditioning only. And it there were a power failure would the fools in charge realize you have no air in these cells? (Millett 1991: 91)

Millett had only to endure one night of seclusion, but even this was extremely distressing. She uses this and other stories about the occasional loss of control of her life, when committed involuntarily for treatment, to articulate the cause of men and women who have experienced similar intrusions on their civil rights. As with other feminist writers, Millett acknowledges that the problem for women is not their femaleness but rather their lack of power, a theme that is reiterated in the recent work of the British sociologist, Joan Busfield:

> Women's relative lack of power in many situations in comparison with men, and the perceptions surrounding their lack of power, means they are doubly disadvantaged. On the one hand, their lack of power makes it more likely that their behaviours may be viewed as indicative of mental disorder. And, on the other hand, it makes certain experiences more traumatic or distressing. (Busfield 1996: 236)

The impact of this lack of power and opportunity has led to valuable research into the effects on mental health of marriage and childbearing (Bebbington *et al.* 1991; Paykel 1991; Pilowsky *et al.* 1991), of gender role expectations (Chesler 1972; Dohrenwend 1975; Gove and Tudor 1973) and of the lack of employment opportunities (Dennerstein 1995). All of this research has shown conclusively that there are specific risk factors in women's lives that are highly related to social expectations and a lack of economic opportunities.

Perhaps even more important than this is the general psychiatric research that is now beginning to take gender and race into account. The ECA and the NCS surveys have confirmed the most basic feminist argument – that women have been overrepresented in psychiatric statistics simply because the definitions of mental disorder have included only the symptoms and conditions most often associated with women (Kessler *et al.* 1994; Regier *et al.* 1988, 1993; Robins and Regier 1991). The social construction of mental disorder, as reflected in measures of psychiatric morbidity and diagnostic categories, tended, in the past, to make women highly visible and men almost invisible. If the disorders included in the calculations of mental disorder are confined to anxiety, depression and the myriad of conditions classified under the neuroses, women will predominate. If,

however, substance dependence, personality disorders and schizophrenia are included, the picture changes to one in which men are
clearly as vulnerable (if not more so) to mental health problems as
are women.

The male perspective

Men have not been the focus of sociological analysis of the diagnoses
and treatment of mental disorder in the same way as women have,
mainly because an absence from the psychiatric statistics was (and can
still be) taken as evidence of good mental health. An exception to this is
the work of Mark Finnane on Ireland, who found (not surprisingly in
the aftermath of a great famine) that single, young, landless men dominated asylum statistics during the second half of the nineteenth century
(Finnane 1981). This was in contrast to most other historical research,
which found that women predominated in the asylum system (Ripa
1990; Showalter 1987).

   The main reasons usually given for the underrepresentation of men
in psychiatric statistics are as follows: men are not good at help-seeking
behaviour; men are more likely to externalise problems (in crime rather
than illness); men are discouraged from acknowledging distress; male
doctors are unlikely to see male distress as illness; and, finally, men
have fewer real-life problems than women (for a discussion, see
Barnett *et al.* 1987; Busfield 1996: 106–7). Evidence is now coming
through from a number of sources that some, if not all, of these statements are no longer true. There has been an increase in the number of
men (especially the young and unemployed) entering the psychiatric
system for substance dependence and personality disorder (Robins and
Regier 1991). There has also been an increase in suicide rate among
young men (Bille-Brahe 1993; Kelleher 1998; Lesage *et al.* 1994). If
we accept the 'social causation' explanation of gender difference in
mental disorder, this means that men are experiencing more stress in
life. If, on the other hand, we accept the 'social construction' explanation, it means that the conceptualisation of mental disorder has changed
so that men are now more likely to be diagnosed as having psychiatric
problems. In other words, men are more likely to conform to models of
mental disorder and illness than in the past. On the negative side, this
could be taken as a tendency to medicalise new areas of life. On the
positive side, it could mean that the discourses and models of disorder
today are more sensitive than previous ones to male distress signals.

According to the sociologists Connell (1995) and Edley and Wetherell (1995), the current psychiatric system is not 'man friendly', in other words not flexible enough to be helpful to men experiencing difficulties in relation to the male role or identity, or to men having personal problems that might make them appear weak. They argue that this was not always the case as early attempts to construct a theory of masculinity were firmly based in the work of Sigmund Freud: 'Freud understood that adult sexuality and gender were not fixed by nature, but were constructed through a long and conflict ridden process' (Connell 1995: 9). Freud questioned traditional assumptions on the nature of gender identity and on sexual orientation. He argued that humans are constitutionally bisexual and that masculine and feminine characteristics co-exist in everyone, with the result that adult masculinity (and indeed femininity) is a 'precarious, construction'. Psychoanalysis moved to the right between 1930 and 1960, and leading psychoanalysts such as Erikson (1950) and Reik (1967) no longer stressed the contradictions involved in developing a gender identity or the difficulties of balancing social order with individual desires. 'Rather their message identified mental health with gender orthodoxy, especially conventional heterosexuality and marriage' (Connell 1995: 11). Because homosexuality was pathologised, psychoanalysis and other forms of psychiatric treatment were used by patients and therapists alike to help individuals to become more normal by 'adjusting' to heterosexual behaviour (see Bancroft 1983).

This approach was enhanced by a new emphasis on the 'sex role' (rather than any difference in mental functioning) as being the differentiating feature between men and women. If masculinity and femininity are defined as internalised sex roles, conformity is essential for social stability. It was this perspective which aroused most hostility from academic women interested in the issue of mental health. While women were (and still are) more vulnerable to medical labels of dysfunction, particularly in situations where the definers of mental illness (doctors) are mainly male and the defined (patients) are mainly female, men are also negatively affected (Gove and Tudor 1973):

> The socially prescribed male role, however, requires men to be non-communicative, competitive and non-giving... and to evaluate life success in terms of external achievements rather than personal and interpersonal fulfilment. (Kimmel and Messner 1995: 247)

There is a price to pay for this kind of success. Joseph Pleck, the American psychologist writing in the 1970s, was one of the first to suggest that the male role might be oppressive not only for women, but also for men (Pleck 1981), and that conformity to the male role might be psychologically damaging. David and Brannon (1976) described the stereotyped male role in terms of four dimensions. They summarised them as follows. The first, *No Sissy Stuff,* is the need to be different from women. The second dimenison, *The Big Wheel,* is the need to be superior to others. The third, *The Sturdy Oak,* is the need to be independent and self-reliant, and the fourth, *Give 'Em Hell,* is the need to be more powerful than others, through violence if necessary. It is now recognised that the way in which men lead their lives contributes to their higher rates of mortality and consequent shorter life expectancy than women (Kimmel and Messner 1995). However, there is very little work on the impact of the male role on mental health. Masculinity theorists such as Connell have focused on mental health problems associated with sexual orientation and gender identity rather than on the broader issues.

The situation is changing, however, as it is clear that substance dependence statistics and suicide rates among men cannot be ignored. A number of studies have attempted to assess the level of psychiatric morbidity among young men who have been successful in their suicide attempts. These studies have been carried out because the suicide rate among young men has been increasing in most Western countries over the past two decades and because there are higher suicide rates among people with mental disorder. Research in Denmark suggests that men have always had higher suicide rates than women and that, prior to the 1970s, the risk increased with age, older men being more at risk than younger ones. However, this changed during the late 1970s, when the rate for young men increased by more than 600 per cent in 4 years (Bille-Brahe 1993: 26). Since then, there has been an overall increase in attempted suicide by men and an increase in completed suicide for men in their thirties and forties.

In Quebec, in an effort to reconstruct a profile of young men who had committed suicide, Lesage *et al.* (1994) studied the cases of 75 men aged 18–35 whose deaths had been classified as suicide and matched them to a random sample of young men in the same geographical area. This study confirmed the findings of other research in the 1990s that mental disorder is an important factor in suicide, the random control group in the community showing much lower levels of psychiatric morbidity than the group who had committed suicide. This was determined by diagnoses received from mental health professionals by all the participants in the 6 months prior to the suicide or to the study. In the suicide and comparison subjects respectively, 64 per cent and 16 per cent had had a diagnosis of at least one of three disorders (major depression, alcohol or drug dependence and borderline personality disorder) in the previous 6 months (Lesage *et al.* 1994: 1066). The authors discuss the limitations of their study and call for further research to broaden the debate on why this group of young men are particularly vulnerable. In Ireland, there are similar research programmes that seek to explain the rise in suicide among young men over the recent decades – some suggestions of causation link the increase to the broader social situation of changing norms in relation to religion, marriage and gender identity.

In Britain, Sarah Payne has studied admission rates to hospital over the past two decades (Payne 1995, 1996). She suggests that redundancy, not only from employment but also from a meaningful male role in the family, has had an impact on how society views young men. They are increasingly seen as disconnected from the normal channels of social control – the economy and the family – and therefore as in need of more public control. Payne relates changes in both psychiatric and penal discourse on men and women to changes in patterns of employment and of family life. The young men most at risk of hospitalisation and of imprisonment are most likely to be unemployed and single:

> Thus as young men have become more detached from the world of paid work, and from family and paternal responsibilities, they have become more visible in their discontent, and at the same time the need for control of this group has increased and become more visible. In the psychiatric system, the discursive rendering of men shows them to be vulnerable to suicide and violent in reaction to this loss of employment. (Payne 1996: 174)

More recent research, using British census data on residents in psychiatric beds between 1921 and 1991, has found evidence of similar processes at work (Hayes and Prior 1998b). In 1991, men outnumbered women in psychiatric beds in Britain for the first time this century. The change had been occurring since the 1950s in that, as overall bed numbers decreased, the fall in the number of female residents was more rapid than that in males. If the trend continues, men will become the majority population in psychiatric institutions, as they already are in prisons.

It is obvious, therefore, that there is a great need for the theorists of masculinity to apply their analyses to the emerging patterns of institutionalisation of men (particularly young men) in psychiatric hospitals and prisons. Whether this is due, as Payne suggests, to an increase in state surveillance of this group as a perceived threat to public order, or to an increase in mental distress among men, is a question that needs urgent research.

Sexuality

> Homosexuality was invented by a straight world dealing with its own bisexuality. But finding this difficult, and preferring not to admit it, it invented a pariah state, a leper colony for the incorrigible whose very existence, when tolerated openly, was admonition to all. We queers keep everyone straight as whores keep matrons virtuous. (Millett 1991: 97)

This is 'fighting talk' indeed by Kate Millett. It was not merely a criticism of the medical profession but of society as a whole, which ostracised people who were different, especially those who rejected the constraints of traditional sexual behaviour. This criticism is echoed in the work of masculinity theorists such as Bob Connell, who has specifically criticised psychiatry for the way in which it handles problems associated with sexual orientation (specifically homosexuality) and gender identity. We will now take a look at how these are perceived and 'treated' within psychiatry as a professional discipline. In Hill *et al.* (1986), the chapter on sexual disorders is one of the shortest in the textbook. The authors express satisfaction with the progress made in terms of conceptual developments and approaches to treatment:

> The liberalization of values over the last 25 years has led to a lifting of the legal and cultural sanctions which define deviation and has induced people to question the ethic by which people with a deviation so defined were persuaded towards treatment. (Kellett and Bebbington, in Hill *et al.* 1986: 261)

The authors (British) argue that patients who wish to change their sexual orientation should not be deprived of the opportunity to try to do so but point out that therapies to change orientation or behaviour have differing success rates. In the USA, any such treatment would be unethical. One of the most controversial diagnoses within psychiatry was that of homosexuality, which only disappeared recently from classifications of mental disorder. In one of the most comprehensive current American textbooks for trainee psychiatrists, homosexuality is discussed (under the heading of sexual dysfunction) in language carefully constructed in order neither to identify a cause nor to make a moral judgement:

> Homosexuality is best conceptualised as a final common pathway/sexual activity that represents many different sources, some conflict based, some not conflict based and many about which only speculation is yet possible. (Kaplan and Sadock 1995: 1321)

This is quite a change from psychiatric literature of the not too distant past. In the first edition of the DSM-I (1952), homosexuality was defined under the heading of 'Sociopathic personality disturbances' as a sexual deviation involving pathological behaviour. In the later DSM-II (1968), the term 'sociopathic personality' was omitted, but homosexuality remained as sexual deviation. Under pressure from the gay liberation movement, the American Psychiatric Association finally 'declassified' homosexuality as a mental illness in 1973, and the DSM-III (published in 1980) omitted it as a diagnostic category. However, as critics of the continuing medicalisation of problems encountered by gay men and lesbian women point out, it was 'merely reclassified, first as "sexual orientation disturbance" and still later as "egodystonic homosexuality"' (De Cecco and Parker 1995: 25). Ego dystonic sexual orientation also appeared in the ICD-10 (World Health Organization, 1992). Treatment regimes are still an area of contention throughout the Western world. Any attempt to change a person's sexual orientation is deemed unethical in the USA and highly questionable in Europe.

Estimates of homosexuality in the population are difficult to verify, and almost any estimate is controversial. According to Kaplan and Sadock (1995: 1349): 'Predominant or exclusive homosexuality is estimated at four per cent for men and 1.5 to two per cent for women.' Other estimates are higher. In research in the USA, between 4 and 10 per cent of people identified themselves as homosexual (Hellman 1996). Adding to this statistic the fact that it is also estimated that, each year, five million Americans suffer from severe mental illness this means that 'an estimated 200,000 to half a million gay men and lesbian women may have severe psychiatric disorders' (Hellman 1996: 1093).

Recent academic literature reflects a new interest in the mental health problems of gay men and lesbian women who, although they do not wish to have their sexual orientation medicalised, do not want the difficulties they experience because of it trivialised or forgotten. This is to argue not for an approach based on individual pathology but for one based on the model of a disabling society. Kathleen Erwin (1993: 437) proposes 'that the significantly higher rates of depression, substance dependence and attempted suicide among lesbians and gay men than among heterosexuals in the USA... [are] due to social isolation and the internalization of negative stereotypes'. Research on suicide and substance abuse conducted since the early 1970s in the USA have highlighted the particular vulnerability of lesbians and gay men, particularly in the younger age group. In a study of over 5,000 lesbian women and gay men in the USA and Canada in 1977, Jay and Young (quoted in Erwin 1993: 438) found that 40 per cent of gay men and 39 per cent of lesbian women had attempted or seriously considered suicide, over half of the men and one-third of the women saying that their homosexuality was a factor. These findings were confirmed in 1978 by Bell and Weinherg, who surveyed 575 white gay men, 111 black gay men, 229 white lesbians and 64 black lesbians. The significantly higher rate of attempted suicide by gays over heterosexuals was consistent across race and gender. More than half of them had made the attempt at age 20 years or younger. Also, in 1989, a study by Gibson on the causes of death among gay and lesbian young people found suicide to be the main reason, accounting for at least 30 per cent of all adolescent suicides. Based on these and other research findings, it has been estimated that the risk of suicide among gay and lesbian youth is three to six times that among heterosexual youth (Erwin 1993: 439).

Just as the significantly high number of women in depression statistics makes it unlikely that the problem is caused primarily by individual pathology, so Erwin argues that any theories of inherent psychopathology in the homosexual population must be discounted. Instead, it is much more likely that the heterosexism (institutionalised exclusion as well as individual homophobia) of the larger society is internalised by lesbian women and gay men. This leads to psychological conflict, especially for those who are just beginning to define themselves in terms of their sexual orientation. The difficulties are intensified for ethnic minority lesbian women and gay men, who are often not supported by their own cultural group. The work of Beverly Greene (1994: 244) on ethnicity and sexual orientation clearly shows that 'sexuality and its meaning are contextual. Therefore, what it means to be a gay man or lesbian will be related to the meaning assigned to sexuality in the culture.' She suggests, for example, that, although in Latin

American cultures, same-gender sexual behaviour is not uncommon, the overt acknowledgement of a gay or lesbian identity will undoubtedly meet with disapproval more intense than the homophobia in the dominant Anglo culture. This is also true in African American communities, with particularly negative effects on lesbians, who 'find themselves at the bottom of the racial and gender hierarchical heap'.

Gender bending

Some of the same exclusionary processes are at work towards people who want to change or expand their sexual identity or role – transvestites (cross-dressers) and transsexuals. The available data on prevalence are questionable, but research (from the UK, Sweden and Australia) suggest a prevalence rate for transsexualism of about one case per 50,000 adults. The number of transvestites (usually men) is unknown as only a minority join cross-dressing organisations and very few look for psychiatric help. According to Hill *et al.* (1986), it is not an uncommon phenomenon, and they estimate the number at 30,000 in the UK.

Kaplan and Sadock (1995: 1334), in their psychiatric textbook, trace the changes in medical discourse. In the DSM-I (1952), transvestism and transsexualism were seen as sexual deviations and placed within the category of 'Sociopathic personality disorder'. In the DSM-II (1968), sexual deviations were still seen as characteristic of a personality disorder, although the word 'sociopathic' had disappeared. In the DSM-III (1980), paraphilia (a subcategory of which was transvestism) was included under the heading of 'Psychosexual disorders', which also included gender identity disorders, psychosexual dysfunction and ego dystonic homosexuality. The DSM-IV (1994) no longer includes a category for transsexualism but has one for gender identity disorder. The behaviours in themselves have been demedicalised, and current psychiatric thinking is along the lines that only if the individual has problems with his or her sexual orientation or identity should it come to psychiatric attention. This approach is still problematic as it implies that the difficulties are the result of individual psychopathology rather than general social intolerance of 'gender-bending' behaviours. Cross-dressing is an acceptable and interesting leisure activity in some subcultures and is gaining credibility in popular culture. However, it would be foolish to think that it is acceptable to everyone, and one of the reasons for cross-dressing men coming to the attention of mental health professionals is the discovery of the behaviour by a partner (Brown *et al.* 1996). Literature pointing to psychological dysfunction among cross-dressing men has usually been based on research with men who have presented at clinics. An example of this is the work of Stoller in the 1960s (Stoller 1984), which suggested that 'transvestic fetishism' was an erotic form of hatred. Other studies have found high levels of neuroticism and introversion. Recent research has not found any evidence of these negative attributes. A study with 188 men who are members of cross-dressing organisations in the USA found that most of the participants 'have personality and sexual functioning profiles that are similar to normative populations of men' (Brown *et al.* 1996: 271). The main difference was that the cross-dressing men showed higher levels of openness to experience and excitement-seeking. The researchers admit that the participants in their study could not be taken as representing all cross-dressing men but only those who were confident enough about their sexuality and identity to 'come out', but it does confirm the positive impact that social tolerance has on the individual experience of living outside the norm.

Changing one's gender identity is also becoming more acceptable as new surgical techniques make it physically possible. In contrast to people who cross-dress, those who wish to change gender almost always seek help in adapting to a new identity. For a British view on this topic, we turn to the psychiatric textbook by Hill *et al.* (1986: 273). Transsexualism, which is defined as 'a deviation of gender role characterised by the strongly held conviction that, by a cruel stroke of fate, gender identity is misrepresented by anatomy', is said to be rare – one per 34,000 males and one per 108,000 females in the UK. Sex reassignment surgery can be accessed through the NHS and is usually the most satisfying outcome for people who are convinced that they have been born into the wrong sex.

The most comprehensive research on transsexualism comes from the Netherlands, where there is a special clinic (in Amsterdam) that 97 per cent of all hormonally treated transsexuals use. The Netherlands is one of the only countries in which there is a reasonable degree of acceptance of crossing the gender divide, in which the government reimburses the cost of sex reassignment surgery and in which people can assume a new legal sex status after completing the change of identity (Bakker *et al.* 1993). Researchers at the Amsterdam clinic suggest a higher prevalence of transsexualism that that generally accepted in other countries – at one in 11,900 men and one in 30,400 women. The only other country that has higher recorded rates is Singapore, where rates are reported as being four times higher than this. Both Singapore and the Netherlands report a ratio of three men to one woman, which seems to be the pattern in the USA and other Western European countries. This is in contrast to central and eastern Europe, where the sex ratio is in the opposite direction (Bakker *et al.* 1993: 238). Research on the possible reasons for this difference in gender patterns has yet to be carried out.

As medical technology has made it possible for individuals to change their physical appearance and live as members of the opposite sex, countries are being forced to change their laws to allow them to take on a new legal identity and to marry if they wish to do so. Sweden was the first to reform its law in 1972, followed by Italy in 1982 and the Netherlands in 1984. Other countries are in dispute with the European Court of Human Rights on the issue of respect for private life. The Court ruled in 1992 that a discrepancy between the sex declared and that on the birth certificate 'placed individuals in a situation incompatible with respect for their private life' (Gromb *et al.* 1997: 29). This ruling came as a result of a case brought by a French transsexual and led to changes in French law. It is probably only a matter of time before other countries are forced to move in the same direction, although some will be slower than others. In Portugal, it is illegal to perform sex reassignment surgery (Costa-Santos and Madeira 1996), and in Ireland it is not even discussed.

Psychiatry and the gender debates

Some sociologists have defined psychiatrists as the arch social control agents of our society – more frightening than the forces of official law and order because of the covert nature of the control that they exercise, shackling their patients with what the historian Roy Porter calls 'mind-forged manacles'. Psychiatrists are also accused of being misogynist (Allen 1986; Busfield 1996; Showalter 1987; Ussher 1991), being members of the power élite (Laing 1960; Scull, 1984; Szasz 1961, 1970) and stereotyping masculinity (Clatterbaugh 1990; Connell 1995; Edley and Wetherell 1995: ch. 2; Gomez 1993), and encouraging those who come into contact with them to conform to traditional gender roles rather than question their social situation (Prior 1996). In the psychiatric literature, sociological and anthropological research is often ignored, although some psychiatrists have recently incorporated the questioning of assumptions and models of disease into their thinking and research (Clare 1976; Hill *et al.* 1986; Pilowsky *et al.* 1991).

During the past 30 years, there have been significant changes in both the sociological debate on gender and the psychiatric debate on mental health and disorder. Psychiatry has gone through major revisions of the internationally recognised classifications of mental disorder – the DSM has had four revisions and the ICD 10. Sociology has been influenced by feminism and by newer writings on theories of masculinity, and both disciplines have also been influenced (especially in the USA) by the gay liberation movement. However, there is mixed evidence on any real change in attitudes to gender and sexual orientation in the psychiatric literature.

The language used in the American psychiatric textbooks is a model of gender neutrality, largely because of the influence of the feminist and gay liberation movements. This is a significant shift as earlier literature on mental disorder was clearly gendered in both language and underlying assumptions. As an example, Thorley (Hill *et al.* 1986) reminds us of the characteristic traits given by Chodoff and Lyons (1958) for an hysterical personality; these included egotism, vanity and self-indulgence; irrational, unbridled and capricious emotionality; and lasciviousness, sexualization and coquetry, as well as sexual frigidity and a fear of mature sexuality. He agrees with Foulds (1965) that all that was lacking was a 'Thurber drawing of a predatory female bearing down on a timorous male psychiatrist' and suggests that the description of this personality type 'is a distorted caricature of femininity' (Hill *et al.* 1986: 242). This kind of language is indeed now disappearing, but it will take some time before we can assume that changes in discourse reflect a true change in the underlying assumptions about the natures of womanhood and manhood.

Not only is overall descriptive language changing in American psychiatric literature, but diagnostic categories are changing too, as are research approaches – social characteristics (including gender) are now being more rigorously analysed in current psychiatric literature. In Kaplan and Sadock (1995), for example, gender is considered in relation to every psychiatric condition. In the discussions on 'mood disorders', the distribution of cases by age and sex, race, lifetime prevalence, incidence and setting are discussed and causes are identified as including demographic factors (sex, age and race), socioeconomic status and marital status, as well as family history, early childhood experience and personality attributes, together with social stress and social support. As this is a good example of the language

used, the paragraph on sex (as a causal demographic factor) is quoted
in full:

> Almost all community based epidemiological surveys of mood disorders find that
> women are twice as likely as men to be experiencing an episode of major depres-
> sive disorder. Few investigators discount the finding as an artefact of prejudice in
> the diagnostic criteria for major depressive disorder or of increased help-seeking
> behaviour among women, yet female sex has not been demonstrated to be a risk
> factor per se. The social environment of women and a higher threshold for
> reporting depressive symptoms in men may account for the increased association.
> (Kaplan and Sadock 1995: 1084)

It seems that the issues raised by Showalter (1987), Ussher (1991)
and Shorter (1990), on the ease with which diagnostic categories were
constructed to fit female rather than male presentations, has been taken
into account, albeit not resolved. In looking at the DSM-IV the fact that
women are more likely to feature in statistics for major depressive
disorders is also included but not explained:

> Major Depressive Disorder (Single or Recurrent) is twice as common in adoles-
> cent and adult females as in adolescent and adult males. In prepubertal children,
> boys and girls are equally affected. (American Psychiatric Association 1994: 341)

An examination of the criteria used in the diagnosis of a major depressive episode does not show any obvious gender bias in the symptoms,
although it could be argued that all the symptoms used to define the
illness are inherently sexist. For example, 'feelings of worthlessness or
excessive or inappropriate guilt nearly every day' (American Psychiatric Association 1994: 327) may be a reflection of the position of
many women in their own household or social setting, a position that
induces feelings of worthlessness and guilt.

The British textbooks, Gelder *et al.* (1989), Hill *et al.* (1986),
Kendall and Zealey (1988) and Sims and Owens (1993), are not as
comprehensive as Kaplan and Sadock (1995) and do not include gender
as a risk factor in the same way. Male and female prevalences are
given, and case histories, when included, usually refer to the gender
most likely to present for the disorder under discussion. For example,
in Gelder *et al.* (1989), there is a male representation for personality
disorders – a man with an antisocial personality may be provoked into
anger when he feels rejected by women' (p. 149) – and for schizophrenia – 'a 20 year old male student [who] had been behaving in an
increasingly odd way' (p. 270) and a 'middle aged man who... is
usually dishevelled and unshaven and cares for himself only when

encouraged to do so by others' (p. 272). The representations for anorexia nervosa are female – 'it generally begins with ordinary efforts at dieting in a girl who is somewhat overweight at the time' (p. 437) – as are those for agoraphobia – the 'house-bound housewife syndrome' (p. 187). It could be argued that there is no way out of this dilemma, as case illustrations have to generalise to some extent from the most common cases to prevent the identification of specific people. However, perhaps the way forward is either to include male and female case presentations or to exclude both.

Theory and practice

At first glance, psychiatric literature seems exemplary, striving to avoid gender-bound diagnoses and carrying out research on mental disorder consciously searching for a gender component. However, those who criticise psychiatry for taking precisely the opposite approach are those who have experienced the psychiatric system personally as consumers (Millett 1991; Plath 1963), have worked as mental health professionals (Laing 1960; Prior 1996; Ussher 1991) or have carried out research with former patients whom feel they have been labelled rather than helped (Busfield 1996; Chesler 1972; Connell 1995). The dissonance between the two accounts (the theory and the practice) of what is actually happening may be caused by the fact that current psychiatric practice is almost two decades behind the academic research of the discipline. Individuals who found themselves as patients during the 1980s did indeed experience a 'psy' system (Castel *et al.* 1982) swayed more by discourses of an earlier era, because mental health professionals are inevitably more influenced by their own socialisation and more prone to uphold traditional values than are those in academic psychiatry (Prior 1996).

Thus, deeply embedded stereotypical notions of normal male and female behaviour provide the baseline against which constructs of mental disorder are measured. Feminist researchers have argued that, in the past, the particular construct of mental disorder that prevailed was almost synonymous with stereotypes of female characteristics. Thus, women were more easily identified as having mental disorders than men. However, just as social attitudes change, so can constructs of mental disorder, and there is some evidence that the new conceptualisation includes notions of dangerousness and risk to the public. If this is so, stereotypical male behaviour will draw the attention of psychiatry, and thus mental disorders associated with men (substance dependence and personality disorder) are likely, in the future, to become more visible in the psychiatric statistics on diagnosis and treatment. Of course, as was the case (and continues to be the case) with women, only certain sections of the male community will be at risk of being exposed to the most oppressive forms of treatment (such as long-term hospitalisation); these are likely to be those who are already marginalised by society by virtue of race, poverty or other socio-economic characteristics regarded as a threat to the *status quo*.

Part II

Mental Health Policy

6

Defining Mental Health Policy

Mental health policies throughout the Western world can, at the present time, be summarised as policies geared towards the provision of a community-based range of therapeutic services for people with mental disorders, supported by the least possible number of publicly funded psychiatric beds and therefore costing as little as possible to the tax-payer. Throughout Europe, and especially in the UK, this has led to a reduction in the number of publicly funded psychiatric beds and the expansion of independent sector providers of community services. It has also led to the phenomenon referred to as 'trans-institutionalisation', in which many former psychiatric patients find themselves in other institutions, such as prisons or shelters for home-less people (for a discussion, see Heller *et al.* 1996; Ramon 1996; Rogers and Pilgrim 1996; Torrey 1997). The change in focus, from a hospital-based service to a community-based one, has been supported by changes in the law – both on mental disorder itself and on the general delivery of health services. On the one hand, the law has allowed for a more flexible approach to treatment, but on the other hand, it has become more prescriptive in defining the people who need to be treated not only for their own safety and well-being, but also for the safety of the public. Thus, current policies reflect the ambivalent attitude of the public to mental disorder – one which purports to be more tolerant of people needing care and treatment, and, at the same time, requires assurances that people who are dangerous will be locked away. It is often difficult to see the total picture, especially if one is either a professional working in the mental health care system or a user of this service. The purpose of the discussion in this chapter is to look at this broader picture, with a view to understanding some of the factors at work in the process of policy-making and policy implementation.

The specific aim is to position the reader within the perspective taken by the author by referring to some of the literature that informs the questions being asked and the particular issues being dealt with.

A conceptual framework

There is no ready-made framework available for the student or policy-maker as theorising on mental health policy is relatively uncharted territory. The perspective taken throughout the text therefore derives from a combination of two distinct academic traditions – British literature on social policy and American literature on the analysis of public policy. It calls for an analysis of issues in relation to mental health policy within the broader national and international framework of political and public policy decisions, keeping in mind the impact that these have on the individual (with a mental disorder) as a citizen and as a consumer of health services.

Ideas on the role of the state in meeting individual need, as well as debates on concepts such as equality, equity and citizenship, derive from the social policy perspective. Ideas on decision-making and implementation come from the literature on public policy analysis, which provides the conceptual tools both for the exploration of processes of government and models of political decision-making and for the analysis of the formation and implementation of specific policies. Together, the two disciplines form a rich theoretical framework for the evaluation of mental health policy. This evaluation includes questions on how and why policy decisions are made, what impact these decisions have on service users and on the general public, how these policies compare with those in other countries, and what the ideological and gender assumptions built into these policies are.

We look first at American public policy literature on policy-making and implementation (see Anderson 1994). Although there is no direct reference in this literature to mental health policy as such, it is included in health policy, which is one element of public policy. Definitions of what should be included under the heading of 'a policy' are myriad. Christopher Ham, a leading health policy analyst in the UK, and Michael Hill, a social policy theoretician, outline a number of theoretical definitions, ranging from that of Friend *et al.* (1974: 40, in Ham and Hill 1988), for whom 'policy is essentially a stance which, once articulated, contributes to the context within which a succession of future decisions will be made', to that of Jenkins (1978: 15, in Ham and Hill

1988), who sees policy as 'a set of interrelated decisions taken by a political actor or group of actors concerning the selection of goals and the means of achieving them within a specified situation'. Both are valid positions and can refer to the same thing from different points of view.

Modelling the policy system

When carrying out research on mental health policy in Northern Ireland, I found a systems model, derived originally from the work of Easton (1965), to be the most useful in unravelling the processes at work in a country that belongs geographically to one nation and politically to another (Prior 1993). The model used is easily applicable to a variety of countries and political systems. For Easton, a policy consists of a 'web of decisions and actions that allocate values' within the context of a political system. His theory of political systems and processes is not a normative theory but rather an analytical tool to examine formal decisions (for an elaboration, see Hill 1997a, 1997b). It is a useful approach, not only because of its logic, but also because it lends itself to the study of policies over time, the interrelationships between policies, and the study of non-decisions.

For Easton, all political activity in a given country can be viewed as a system akin to a biological system, consisting of a number of interacting subsystems (for a diagrammatic elaboration, see Jenkins, in Hill 1997b: 33–35). Like biological systems, political systems exist within a constantly changing environment. Within this perspective, the relationships between the political system and its environment are conceptualised as *inputs* and *outputs*. The most significant inputs, seen in terms of their relevance in producing or reducing political stress, are described as *demands* and *supports*. A *demand* is an expression of opinion that something ought to be done (resources allocated or the law changed) in relation to a particular issue. Of course, not all *wants* or *interests*, as expressed by individuals or groups, are converted into demands, nor are all demands channelled equally through the political system. Therefore, in order to come to some conclusions on what led to the final outcome, the factors at work in the *initiation* and in the *regulation* of each demand have to be examined. In other words, the question is, why do some demands get through the system and command action while others do not?

Another major *input*, according to the systems model, is that of *support*. There are two kinds of support – support for the specific change in law or services under consideration, and general support for the government in power and for their approach to that aspect of policy, in this instance mental health policy. It is easy to forget the importance of 'diffuse support', which enables governments to act in specific instances in ways that are damaging to some individuals or groups. Diffuse support is, in fact, the 'stock' or the 'credit' of a government and 'locates the prevailing boundary of tolerable discontent' (Hall *et al.* 1975: 483). At any given time, the progress of a demand through the political system is influenced by the general level of support for the government and by the estimated effect of any change in policy. This support is constantly changing, and governments sometimes overestimate what the public will tolerate, so inevitably suffer the consequences at election time. For example, the reluctant acceptance by the public of the retraction of the NHS in the UK during the 1980s reflected a level of support for the Conservative government. The defeat of the same government in 1997 showed that the boundary of tolerable discontent had been reached. Among the policies questioned by the public were (and still are) the continuing drive towards a reduction in the number of psychiatric beds and the lack of financial commitment to expanding community-based services.

Analysing policy processes

But how exactly do individuals or groups make an impact on policy? How are demands for changes in policy initiated in the first place? What is the process whereby some of these demands are translated into issues worthy of attention while others make no impact on the political system? On what basis are decisions to act or not to act made by policy-makers? The answers point to the factors that are most significant in determining the progress of a demand from the point of initiation to the point at which there is a change in policy as a result of this demand. For example, within the health care arena, we need to know whether the particular demand was initiated from an interest group of consumers (for example, MIND or the National Schizophrenia Fellowship) or professionals (for example, the Royal College of Psychiatrists or the British Association of Social Workers). We also need to know whether it was backed by the political and/or professional *gatekeepers* (for example, the Chief Medical Advisor to government) or whether it simultaneously conflicted with other demands on the health agenda. Alternatively, the demand might have initiated from outside the country's own political system. This is happening more frequently in Europe at present as the policies of individual countries are constantly under pressure to change if they fall behind general developments in laws or services in other parts of the EU.

As well as knowing how demands are initiated, we need to know exactly how they are regulated. Clearly, all demands that enter the political arena cannot be met. Resources such as manpower, finance and political support are limited, and demands have to compete with each other. Furthermore, at each stage of the process of policy-making and implementation, there are individuals and groups with gatekeeping functions. Demands that are not rejected in the first instance can be regulated by being combined with other demands or reformulated by these gatekeepers, both leading to a diminution or dilution of the original demand. Some of these patterns can be clearly seen in the progress of different mental health policy initiatives. For example, demands for the removal of judicial procedures in compulsory admissions to psychiatric hospital treatment were successfully initiated by the medical profession in England during the 1950s. Their lobby was highly influential and led to many of the changes in mental health legislation in 1959 (Mental Health Act). By the time the legislation was being changed again in 1983, the power of psychiatry had begun to diminish, and there was a partial return to the more judicial language and ideology of earlier laws. Now, as we enter a new century, public opinion is more concerned with issues of public order than with those of unnecessary incarceration, and while these issues dominate the policy-making agenda, the chances are that the influence of the medical profession on any demand going through the system will be subordinate to that of the legal profession.

At each stage of the process of policy formation, decisions are made on what goes forward. Even with agreement in principle that a change needs to be made in some aspect of policy, choices have to be made about the timing and extent of the change. The criteria for measuring the level of priority and the extent of the resources to be devoted to a particular policy change are too numerous to describe here, but the most important in relation to decisions on mental health policy is perhaps that of legitimacy. Legitimacy, which is the basis for government intervention into the lives of individual citizens, is determined by the answer to the question, 'Is this an issue with which government considers it should be concerned?' (Hall *et al.* 1975: 475). This question will be answered differently across time and place as it depends largely on the values that are held in highest esteem in a country at any given time. There are certain areas, such as public order and public health, which are rarely disputed as legitimate targets for state intervention. Disputes, however, often arise at the boundaries of these areas. Where do public health and order end and personal health and security begin? As social values change over time, so do attitudes to state intervention. Policies with high legitimacy will receive priority over those with low or questionable legitimacy. Public order issues usually have priority over health and welfare issues. The problem for mental health policies is that they are sometimes law and order issues and sometimes health and welfare issues. The question of legitimacy is particularly important in times of constraint on public expenditure as decisions on the use of public funding have to be constantly justified. When mental health services have high legitimacy, as they have had in most Western countries for almost two centuries, public money is allocated for costly institutional-based services, with very little dispute on the principle of the expenditure. If, however, they lose legitimacy, either because they are no longer regarded as useful for social cohesion, or because the public funding approach is no longer seen as necessary to ensure their continuance, the only services to merit funding and expansion may be those for people seen as a threat to the public – in other words, this is a public order issue rather than a health issue.

Understanding decision-making

In order to understand how policy change occurs, we need to know more about the ways in which decisions are made at each stage of the process. Two very important debates in relation to decision-making within public policy contribute significantly to our understanding. These are on the relationship between decision-making and power, and on the relationship between decision-making and rationality. The debate on the link between power and decision-making is often confined to issues related to the influence of different interest groups on the initiation or regulation of a demand as it moves through the system. There are, however, two other situations that merit attention. These are occasions when power differentials prevent issues being either expressed or transformed into a legitimate demand. This happens, for example, when dissatisfaction or conflict is ignored or suppressed so that the issue never becomes part of the political arena (for a discussion, see Ham and Hill 1988; Hill 1997a, 1997b). It also happens when people do not make demands because they simply do not experience conflicts of interest with those of the dominant class or group. In the words of Lukes (1974: 24): 'People accept their role in the existing order of things, either because they see it as natural and unchangeable, or because they value it as divinely ordained and beneficial.' In these kinds of situation, where less powerful sections of society make no attempt to change the existing order even if it creates problems for them, more powerful sections seek to influence policies that maintain the balance of power in their favour. There is abundant evidence that lunacy policies in the nineteenth century and mental health policies in the twentieth have consistently reinforced the hierarchical divisions between rich and poor (Belle 1990: Finnane 1981: Viinamaki *et al.* 1995; Wilkinson 1996), between men and women (Busfield 1989, 1996; Showalter 1987; Ussher 1991) and between majority and minority racial groups (Bhui *et al.* 1995; Chung *et al.* 1995; Sugarman and Craufurd 1994).

The debate on the relationship between rationality and decision-making alerts us to a different range of possible interpretations of mental health policy developments. It focuses on the actual process of decision-making by policy-makers (civil servants and politicians) in terms of the information on which these decisions are made and the outcomes envisaged. It is easy to assume a rational approach to the planning and implementation of policies, but early policy analysts, such as Braybrooke and Lindblom, see the process as much more haphazard. They suggest that most policy-making and implementation are the result of 'muddling through' rather than of a series of rational choices between alternatives. Although there are examples of a rational planning model of decision-making in some aspects of mental health policy, most bear more resemblance to what Braybrooke and Lindblom (1963: 73) describe as 'disjointed incrementalism', in which 'a policy is directed at a problem; it is tried, altered, tried in its altered form, altered again, and so forth'.

More recent debates have dismissed the rational planning model as a useless tool and have turned to other models of decision-making that lack any rational basis (see Hill 1997a, 1997b). March and Olsen (1989) developed what they called the 'garbage can model of organizational choice', which fits some organisations (such as universities) better than others (for example, government departments) but is still worth examining. The organisation in their model is not a coherent structure but a 'loose collection of ideas' in which the members do not always understand the actual organisational structures very well and often drift in and out of decision-making. The members know their own jobs well and the organisation can survive, but the processes of decision-making are anything but rational. Whenever a decision has to be made, a number of participants become involved, all with their own agenda and solution to the problem in hand. This is the 'garbage can' into which 'various kinds of problems and solutions are dumped by the participants as they are generated'. The final decision (or outcome) will depend on the mix of 'garbage', which now includes the participants' personal and financial resources as well as the original problems and solutions. It also depends on the way in which the 'garbage' is processed, that is, the length of time available for the decision-making process, not to mention the staying power of the participants. For example, this model of decision-making explains the sometimes unexpected twists and turns in the progress of a piece of legislation through national and European parliaments. Different actors are involved at different stages of the process, and the final solution often looks more like a new configuration of available solutions rather than any coherently planned change.

The important point about these different models of decision-making is that they should alert the reader to some notion of the kinds of process at work every time a policy change takes place. The outcomes, in terms of the kind of formulation in both law and government documentation (which becomes the blueprint for health and social services organisations), are subject to so many influences that it is impossible to predict how an issue will be resolved. However, as users of mental health services or as professionals working in those services, some knowledge of how a 'private problem' becomes a 'public issue' (to use the words of C. Wright Mills) is absolutely essential for those who wish to make change happen.

The impact of ideologies

In order to round off our view of the process of policy-making, we need to draw on another body of literature – that of the British social policy tradition, which offers ways of understanding the ideologies that guide policy direction and targets. Since the introduction of a welfare state in Britain after the Second World War, it has been taken for granted that the state has not only the right, but also the responsibility to use collective resources (gathered through taxation and national insurance contributions) to redistribute wealth and to protect the vulnerable in society. However, although there is consensus in general about a central role for the state in ensuring some form of social justice, there is little agreement on what exactly this role should be or indeed on what is social justice. Early social policy analysts, such as Brian Abel Smith, Richard Titmuss, Peter Townsend and David Donnison, all of whom were associated at some time with the London School of Economics (LSE), may not have been in total agreement on whether the goal of social policies should be equality or equity, but all saw the overall aim as being one of striving for a more just society. Policies were evaluated in terms of their success in achieving this aim. Current debates in British social policy continue largely in the same ideological vein but focus more specifically on issues of citizenship for all groups in society; on the need to retain a strong direct state presence in areas such as health and social care services which are increasingly being privatised; on the need to promote policies that will not disadvantage future generations; and on the need to evaluate policy outcomes in terms of their differential impact by gender, ethnic origin and ability (Lister 1996; Marshall 1981; Oliver 1990; Williams 1989).

One exciting research initiative is the welfare state programme at the LSE headed by Julian Le Grand and John Hills. The programme is involved in a continual evaluation of different areas of social policy in terms of their redistributive effect and has led to extensive debates on the meaning of equality as a goal of social policy. Le Grand (1982) suggests five distinct ways of defining equality, any or all of which can be used as measuring tools in evaluating the redistributive effect of social policies. The two definitions most useful in relation to mental health services are what Le Grand (1982) calls 'equality of final income' and 'equality of cost'. In relation to the first, if the aim of a particular policy is equality of final income, public expenditure should be directed to those who have most initial need so that the income of a family is not adversely affected by the use of the service. This was part of the ideological basis for the introduction of the welfare state in Britain, influenced by the philosophy of Tawney (writing in the 1930s), whose view of a good life for all included the universal availability of health and education services in such a way so as not to depend on or reduce the income of the family.

The second definition of equality, which provides a useful way of looking at mental health services is 'equality of cost', more often described as equality of access or equal opportunity. According to Le Grand (1982), the cost to the individual of using the service (per unit) should be equal, and if two individuals wishing to do so incur different costs, access to the service has not been equal; this includes opportunity costs and actual costs. As mental health statistics show, although people from low-income backgrounds are high users of mental health services, there are obviously barriers to the use of services for a number of individuals and groups. If the findings of the American ECA study are generalisable, only one in five people with mental disorder receives help from the psychiatric system (Robins and Regier 1991: 341). People with substance dependence problems or personality disorder, for example, do not perceive psychiatric services as offering them any hope of recovery. This means that, even within the NHS structure, which has high credibility as an accessible service, there are barriers impeding access to some services for sections of the community.

This exploration of the concept of equality gives the reader some idea of the kind of debate in the British social policy literature. This and others, such as that on citizenship, form the basis for any critique of current mental health policy outcomes. Citizenship in the context of changing national boundaries throughout Europe and Asia has become a 'hot' topic in the academic literature of politics and social policy, particularly when viewed from the perspective of gender or ethnicity (Yuval-Davis and Anthias 1989). Being a citizen of a country no longer simply means having the right to participate in political life through voting. As T.H. Marshall (1981) argues, having achieved political and legal rights, citizens can expect also to enjoy a reasonable standard of living, which includes access to certain publicly defined life chance outcomes. Social or physical characteristics, including gender, race and disability (such as mental disorder), should not limit access to these life chances. However, people with mental disorders, particularly those who have been hospitalised for treatment, often find themselves excluded from many social and economic opportunities (Dear and Wolch 1987; Dennerstein 1995; Ezzy 1993; Hopton and Hunt 1995; Perlin 1992; Viinamaki *et al.* 1995; Wade 1993).

Claude Louzoun, a French psychotherapist who leads an organisation dedicated to raising issues in relation to citizenship rights and mental health, has gained increasing support during the past decade from mental health professionals as well as from user groups throughout Europe. The work of the Comité Européen: Droit, Ethique et Psychiatrie (CEDEP), of which Louzoun is president, centres around the tension between the individual's right to freedom and full participation in social and civic life, and the need to protect the public from harm. CEDEP argues that these rights to freedom and participation do not disappear when a person develops a mental disorder. Undoubtedly, however, some of the most basic rights and duties associated with citizenship are often problematic for people with psychiatric symptoms. Raymond Hickman states the case very eloquently:

> How can duties to contribute financially be fulfilled by those largely absent from, or excluded from the labour market?... Why should rights to legal protection through contract or otherwise be afforded to the dangerous? How is the right to free speech to be guaranteed to the deluded and the unintelligible? (Hickman 1995: 11)

One of the difficulties in discussing mental disorder (as opposed to race or physical disability) as a factor in the exclusion of individuals from mainstream society is that the external manifestation (physical or behavioural) regarded as abnormal, irrational, dangerous or simply unwelcome is not permanently present. This means that rights which might be removed legitimately in one given period of the individual's life must be restored at others. One of the means used by countries to ensure the protection and restoration of rights of people with mental disorders is through the appointment of guardians and advocates (see Fennell 1992; Sundram 1995). Under current legislation throughout the UK, guardianship is mainly used for people with learning disabilities rather than those with mental illnesses. The practice is also authorised in a different form in the 1968 French law for *Les Incapables Majeurs*. The law of 1968 made a clear distinction between the need to protect the patient's civil rights and the need for treatment by introducing regulations for *la tutelle* (translated into English as supervision or protection) and *la curatelle* (legal guardianship). In France, the system is already over-stretched, while in the UK, the underuse of guardianship is not publicised by mental health professionals because of the resource implications its extension would involve. There is a further practical problem in the separation of advocacy from treatment. However, guardianship is only a partial solution, and the debate on how best to protect the rights of individuals with mental disorders in order to enable their full participation in social life has to continue at all levels of society.

Gender and ideology

Before leaving the discussion on ideologies that underpin welfare state provision, a final point needs to be made that is relevant to all areas of social policy in the Western world. This occurs in relation to the deeply rooted cultural notions of both womanhood and manhood that underpin most social policies, particularly those in relation to health and the family. For example, stereotypical notions of the male as breadwinner and the female as wife and carer have a significant impact on community care policies. The research on carers shows conclusively that the burden of caring for the people with mental disorders (particularly men) often falls on the female members of the family, as it does in other situations of long-term care (Benson 1994; Biegal *et al.* 1995; Hatfield *et al.* 1996a; Kuipers 1993; Salize and Rossler 1996; Subotsky 1991; Young 1996). The fact remains that the role of women in caring for sick or disabled members of their families has largely been ignored in the past. However, the situation is constantly changing as the population of carers becomes more visible and more demanding of recognition and of payment for carrying out this very onerous task. Hopefully, in the future, payment for different kinds of work carried out in the home (usually by women) will be universally recognised so that people with chronic mental disorders will be able to avail of family members as carers without loss of income or of dignity.

Changing trends in health policy

To conclude our discussion on the parameters within which we need to view mental health policy, we will look at the broader trends in social policy in general, and health policy in particular, in Europe and the USA. One of the most striking features in many European countries during the past two decades has been the strong political lobby for a lessening of the involvement of the state in areas of social service delivery that had, up to then, been regarded as essential welfare provision. This trend is related to the growing realisation among policymakers of the ever-increasing cost of publicly funded health services, caused by technological advances in medicine and the demographic reality of an increasing proportion of older people in populations of the future.

Countries such as Ireland, Greece and Italy, which have what Munday and Ely (1996) describe as the 'Latin welfare model' of social provision, have always been characterised by a 'mixed economy of care' approach to health and social care. The role of the state in these countries has been to support the non-statutory, non-profit sector (family and charitable organisations) in meeting health needs. Interestingly, even in these countries, the state has traditionally played a much more central role in the provision of mental health services than in any other branch of health care. Ireland, for example, was one of the first countries to establish a network of public 'district lunatic asylums' in the nineteenth century (Prior 1993). General hospitals, which were developed in a much more *ad hoc* manner, included voluntary hospitals for those who could pay and publicly funded workhouse infirmaries for those who could not.

The reason for the difference in provision was the relationship between mental disorder and vagrancy – in other words, the need to prevent social disorder. As Cohen and Scull (1985) have argued, with regard to similar developments in Britain and other Western European countries during the nineteenth century, social control was the main aim of the system, care and treatment being a secondary concern. In Britain, the development of asylums and workhouses supported a society that was rapidly becoming industrialised and urbanised. In Ireland, industrialisation was much slower, so Scull's theory does not adequately explain the expansion of the asylums in a country economically devastated by famine in the middle of the nineteenth century. A more probable explanation was the need to ensure social order in a population permanently on the brink of revolt against its coloniser. In terms of the conceptual framework outlined in the beginning of this chapter, public expenditure on a centrally organised system of incarceration for people with mental disorders was acceptable because of the high level of legitimacy this public service had, in common with prisons, the police force and other social control mechanisms.

What is more interesting about Ireland is the continuance of public funding for mental health services in the twentieth century in the context of a new political system committed to quite different ideologies. In all areas of social policy, particularly in health care, the new Irish government supported the 'principle of subsidiarity', which is of interest as it is making an appearance in debates on the role of the state in welfare provision in other countries where the Latin welfare model is evident (Munday and Ely 1996). According to this principle, responsibility for meeting individual social need should rest at the lowest level of social organisation, and a higher level should intervene only when this has not materialised. The only exceptions to this are services that aim to protect individuals or groups from threatening or violent behaviour from other members of the public. Asylums in the nineteenth century obviously met this criterion. However, with developments in knowledge about mental disorder and with the introduction in the 1950s of antipsychotic drugs, the risks associated with mental disorder decreased significantly over the past three decades. This has meant a reduction in the legitimacy of a high degree of state intervention in the provision of these services – thus providing the ideological justification for any reduction in public funding to this sector

The same argument holds for countries that have characteristics of a residual or liberal welfare state – countries such as post-1979 Britain, and the USA, which are now showing similar trends even though they have quite different approaches to the financing and provision of health services. In the USA, the state has not been the main provider of mental health services for over two decades. The de-institutionalisation movement, which started earlier there than in Europe, coincided with the withdrawal of public funding from this sector to bring it into line with other health services. Currently, in a system that is financed equally by the public and private sector and provided mostly by the private sector, mental health services are experiencing problems similar to those seen in other areas of health care. The stranglehold of commercial health insurance companies is reflected in the successful operation of 'managed care' (strict budgetary guidelines for all treatment programmes) in spite of professional and consumer objections (Carson 1993; Kavanagh 1997; Watkins and Callicutt 1997). Citizens who are adequately covered by insurance policies, and who have a satisfactory service provider (HMO or preferred provider organisation – PPO) can access the full range of mental health services, although there is a time limit on funded treatment. However, for those on Medicaid (the poor), the situation is much more dismal. Mental health services are difficult to access, and, as was clear from the ECA study, the majority of people with psychiatric symptoms do not seek specialist help. Current debates on health funding and provision in the USA indicate that Medicaid, which was established as the safety net for all those not covered by other health insurance schemes, is decreasing in terms of its coverage of the population, leaving approximately 40 million people without health cover of any kind and twice that number with no insurance at some time during any given year. Without health insurance, those on low incomes, who have been shown in numerous studies to be the most vulnerable to mental disorder, have little hope of receiving treatment unless, of course, they break the law.

In the UK, the situation is different, but health policy is increasingly being influenced by ideas similar to those characteristic of the USA health care system (Shepherd *et al.* 1996; Thornicroft and Bebbington 1989). Mental health services have been an integral part of the NHS since 1948, when the welfare state was established to provide a comprehensive range of publicly funded health services free at the point of access. Although part of a larger budget, the mental health budget was safe from use in other parts of the health care system as long as it was allocated to hospital provision. The current state of affairs is much more precarious as a result of two quite different trends – the first within mental health services themselves and the second within the wider health care system. De-institutionalisation and the shift of services to the community has meant that some of the mental health budget has been 'poached' for other more expensive medical services; this is in spite of government attempts to impose 'ring-fencing' on funds saved as a result of hospital closures. At the same time, what have become known as 'the NHS reforms', initiated in the early 1980s by the Thatcher Conservative regime and followed through, to a large extent, by the Labour government, have irrevocably changed the NHS structures. On the advice of American economist Alain Enthovin, an internal market was created within the health services, new providers (non-profit and commercial organisations) have been encouraged to enter the arena, new funders (insurance companies) are being sought by service providers, and the principle of a free service for all has been eroded (for a discussion, see Ham 1992; Jenkins 1994). The changes have very quickly impacted on all levels of health service provision, with a 'two-tier system' (of those who pay and those who do not) appearing for the first time since the 1940s. Within this 'mixed economy of care' approach, it is already evident that certain health services are more profitable than others and therefore more attractive to non-statutory providers. For example, commercial companies invest in hospitals providing specialist cardiology and surgical services (including cosmetic surgery) and also in long-term care of the elderly, all of which are lucrative. The non-profit sector has taken over the role of the public sector in other less profitable areas – long term care and special supported housing and employment schemes for people with disabilities, both physical and mental. With the exception of elderly care, chronic conditions and those which are linked to social problems are neither lucrative nor attractive. Mental disorders fall into both of these categories. The future of mental health services in the UK is therefore very precarious, and it is difficult not to be pessimistic.

In contrast to the UK and other liberal welfare states, there are two other groups of countries in Europe using a model of welfare state provision that is not residual. These are countries which can be described as having either a social democratic welfare model of provision or an institutional or corporatist model. The former is used to describe Scandinavian countries, where the statutory sector is the main provider of universal services, and the latter to describe Germany,

Austria and Central European countries (Munday and Ely 1996). The traditional Scandinavian approach to health and welfare provision, which was envied by citizens from other countries, has begun to be somewhat diluted. Because of the acceptance among the public of the need for a high level of personal taxation, and the expectation that this would provide an adequate and equal level of service provision for all sections of the community, there has been no need for service provision from the independent sector (commercial or non-profit-making). In Denmark, for example, where the basic income tax rate was 50 per cent in the late 1980s, a comprehensive range of social provision is publicly funded and provided with very little need for non-state provision. The services have traditionally been guided by notions of citizenship that are now just beginning to appear in many other countries. Users of services (people with disabilities and illnesses, and older people) are seen to have the same rights to participate equally in social and polit-ical life as their less vulnerable fellow citizens. This has resulted in the integration of all specialist services into mainstream services – for example, services for people with learning disabilities falling within the main educational system – and an acceptance of the rights of users to participate in service delivery (Philpot 1989). This has led to strong support in Denmark and other Scandinavian countries for the inclusion of users of mental health services in committees that plan, implement and monitor policies that affect them. In current experiences of mental health provision in Europe, the Scandinavian countries are ahead of the game in terms of government commitment to the provision of a comprehensive health care system. However, there are signs that changes are on the way as new incentives are put in place to encourage the independent sector (including groups of citizens) to become providers of care (Munday and Ely 1996: 36).

The other model of health and welfare provision that is found, for example in Germany and Austria, is based on assumptions about the economy and employment. Often referred to as the Bismarkian model of welfare, the focus is on labour market solutions to problems of indi-vidual social need (MIRE 1995). Insurance contributions by employees and employers, and agreements about service provision between employers and government, ensure the delivery of a comprehensive range of social protection services (including health care). People who are not employed are catered for outside this system by voluntary organisations (usually church linked), which are highly subsidised by the state. As in Italy and Ireland, where there is a much heavier reliance on the voluntary sector, the principle of subsidiarity is the guiding principle in government support for the sector. While the level of employment was high in countries such as Germany, the system worked well, the majority of the population being comprehensively covered for a full range of good-quality health services. However, the system came under intense strain when unemployment rose during the 1980s, and, for the first time, alternative ways of funding and providing health care are being discussed. What is particularly worrying about these changes is the increased vulnerability of people with mental disorders in a society where unemployment is rising. Whether or not unemployment is a cause or an effect of mental illness, the result is the same – many people with mental health problems remain outside the labour market, and, as economic opportunities decrease, the likelihood of remaining in work also decreases. The non-profit (voluntary) sector is also affected by an increase in the proportion of the unemployed population – a sector that catered well for a small population may find it impossible to finance or provide services for a larger one, while, starting from different baselines, there is a certain convergence in health policies.

The overall picture emerging throughout the UK and continental Europe in relation to social policies that include health is one of dualisation – governments being increasingly willing to allow those in employment to subsidise a comprehensive service structure provided by either employers, commercial insurers or both, and to offer financial incentives to any non-governmental organisation (either commercial or non-profit making) to provide a minimum range of services for those who are not employed. In many countries, this is a break with the traditions of the past, where there was a commitment to a publicly funded universal provision based on need rather than on participation in the labour force or ability to pay. There is also evidence of a second trend – this time in the USA as well as in Europe – towards a localisation of responsibility for the poor. While still contributing central funds to local services, the central state is slowly moving to a position of having very little control over the extent or quality of local service provision. The kind of ideological rhetoric associated with this trend can include debates on the principle of subsidiarity (in Europe) and on the rights of local communities or states to manage their own affairs (in the USA). All have the same effect – those who are economically disadvantaged are increasingly disempowered as local communities make decisions that, more often than not, fail to meet national or international standards of care or protection.

7

Mental Health Services

The more hopeless you were, the further away they hid you (Plath 1963: 169).

The picture painted by Sylvia Plath for her fictional character Esther, who had mental health problems, is one of a lifetime of increasingly inadequate and exclusionary care. It had a resonance for many of her contemporaries in the same position because of the danger of being comitted to a large state hospital when the family could no longer afford private care. The situation now is different – we pride ourselves on having moved away from institutional care. But is the experience of using mental health services any less bleak? Studies carried out in the 1980s on families' perception of services consistently found dissatisfaction with what was on offer (Benson 1994; Biegal *et al.* 1995; Hatfield *et al.* 1996a; Kuipers 1993; Mueser *et al.* 1996). This contrasted sharply with the perceptions of professionals and policymakers, who saw the changes in systems of mental health care as an improvement on the earlier era (Hafner and An der Heiden 1989; Rogers and Pilgrim 1996; Watkins and Callicutt 1997). Feedback from studies carried out during the 1990s has been mixed. Families surveyed by NAMI in the USA in 1993 were positive in their overall responses (Hatfield *et al.* 1996a). Nevertheless, they had not used the full range of services in the proportions suggested by official and professional reports:

> Of all services used, medication was reported by the largest proportion, followed by individual therapy, hospitalization, and case management. Only about a third of the consumers had used crisis care, day care, residential services, and rehabilitation. Use of group therapy was reported by nearly half, and family therapy by about a fourth. (Hatfield *et al.* 1996a: 826)

Families were asked to rate the services as having 'no', 'some' or 'considerable' value. The findings are interesting in the light of discus-

116

sions on mental health and disorder that favour a demedicalisation of approaches to care. The highest value was placed on medication (97 per cent), followed by hospitalisation (90 per cent). The medical treatments, including medication and hospitalisation, were used by the greatest number of consumers (over 90 per cent in the case of medication and almost 60 per cent in the case of hospitalisation) and were rated by more respondents as being of considerable value. In contrast, the psychosocial treatments, which included residential care, crisis services, case management, day care services, consumer groups and rehabilitation, were used by only one-third of the consumers and were rated by more families to be only of some value. However, having a place to live was seen as one of the essential components of any community-based programme of care, and for the families (16 per cent) whose relatives were in residential care, the ratings of the service were high.

The authors of the study offer some possible explanations for the uncomfortable finding that people continue to find hospital-based services easier to access and more satisfactory when they do access them, in spite of efforts to move mental health services outside hospitals and into the community. The most controversial explanation is almost certainly the most important – that 'more resources and attention have probably gone into tailoring pharmacological treatments for individuals than into tailoring psychosocial treatments' (Hatfield *et al.* 1996a: 831). The pharmaceutical industry obviously has more money to pour into the development of their products than does any government into the development of other approaches that are not commercially attractive to outside providers. Another explanation offered is that psychosocial treatments, especially crisis care and case management, are only recent developments, needing more time to consolidate staff training and the expansion of services. This is a depressing argument for those involved in mental health service delivery in Europe and elsewhere. The USA programme of de-institutionalisation started at least 20 years earlier than elsewhere in the world. If community-based programmes are not being accessed easily there, the situation is bleak for other countries such as Ireland and Greece that have only just begun this process.

Other studies on the carers and relatives of people with mental disorder point to the continuing burden on families of being responsible for someone with a chronic disorder in the community. For example, Mueser *et al.* (1996), in their study of the relatives of people with schizophrenia and bipolar disorder, found that professionals often underestimated the burden of specific symptoms. This confirmed earlier evidence on the experiences of caring in similar families, which showed that, even when professionals were aware of the burden of caring for people with schizophrenia, this did not have the effect of increasing services for them (Kuipers 1993). In other words, although the rhetoric of supporting carers has entered policy documents, this has not led to a great expansion in services to support people with chronic mental disorders and their carers in the community. Against the background of these sobering reminders from consumers and their families that official reports on progress do not always reflect the experience on the ground, we will now look at patterns of service delivery that have been developing in the second half of this century.

Recent trends

When examining recent trends in mental health services in any country, we have also to include trends in the law relating to the provision of these services, changes in the methods of funding services and any changes in the public perception of mental disorder that affect the kinds of service that people are willing to use. All of these changes emanate from different sources and interests. Some are guided by public policy, some by commercial interest and some by developments in knowledge. Because some or all of these factors present themselves in different forms and configurations in specific countries, it is sometimes foolhardy to make generalisations. This is particularly true in Europe, where nations are at different stages of economic and social development, and have undergone quite different political experiences in the past 30 years. Notwithstanding these limitations, however, I feel that there are some general trends worth discussing.

Perhaps the most dramatic development in terms of its impact on people with mental disorders has occurred in the sphere of law. This sphere includes laws to protect the individual's rights in situations where liberty is removed and also laws that provide the basis for the establishment of services funded from the public purse. In the first half of the twentieth century, the link between the two sets of laws was much stronger than it is now because of the origins of mental health policy in the vagrancy and lunacy laws of the nineteenth century. Laws to protect individuals from unlawful confinement were passed concurrently with those to allocate money to establish and run public asylums.

This was seen as an essential protection measure for the already disempowered poor, who found themselves being confined in a rapidly growing network of lunatic asylums. A more detailed analysis of the role of the law is included in the next chapter so, for the purposes of our discussion here, suffice it to say that current laws are no longer linked in the same way. As the proportion of people receiving hospital treatment on an involuntary basis (known as 'detained' patients in Britain) has decreased throughout the Western world, the emphasis has also changed to the protection of the individual's rights to appropriate treatment regardless of the legal status of the treatment (voluntary or involuntary).

The increase in the willingness of people to receive treatment on a voluntary basis was related, in most countries, to the integration of mental hospitals into general medical care. During the early part of the twentieth century, the medical profession offered an alternative explanation and treatment for behaviour that had, until then, been viewed as beyond medical treatment. The positioning of mental health services within mainstream health care provision has also had implications for the funding of services – in terms of both the maintenance of existing services and the development of new ones. The nineteenth-century link between social disturbance and mental disorder, although negative from almost every angle, did guarantee a certain level of both central and local funding for service provision, that is, for the building and running of public asylums. As services have moved out of institutional settings, mental health professionals have fought to keep the same level of funding for community-based services. In spite of the fact that some policies have been aimed specifically at a transfer of funds from hospital to community – for example, in the joint funding initiatives in Britain in the 1970s and 80s, and in the Italian anti-institutional policies of the same period – community services are the most vulnerable to cost-cutting exercises. As Thornicroft and Bebbington (1989: 741) point out in relation to the NHS in Britain, only 5 per cent of joint funds (between local authorities and health authorities) have been used for mental health services, and the constraints on new spending have been in line with general health spending:

> The funding of psychiatric services generally has reflected wider trends in public sector spending within the last decade: resource control through cash and manpower limits, cost containment through efficiency savings and self-funding, and the centralisation of decision making. (Thornicroft and Bebbington 1989: 741)

The trends in most Western countries towards a mixed economy of health care, with an increasing proportion of commercial interests involved in all sectors, will certainly have a major impact on the pattern of mental health service provision of the future, but it remains to be seen which aspects will expand and which will disappear. What *is* clear is that governments have a less direct say in guiding policy when the majority of services are run by non-statutory organisations. In the Netherlands, for example, where health services are provided by insurance companies and large non-profit charitable foundations, the government has had difficulties in implementing policies of de-institutionalisation. This is in spite of the fact that a substantial proportion of the funding for these provider organisations comes from the government (Munday and Ely 1996: 54; Ramon 1996: 29). In other words, central policies and strategies are becoming more difficult to implement as service provision becomes increasingly diversified.

Current services in Europe

One of the targets of the 1972 WHO's strategy on mental health was the 'development of general hospital units as the mainstay of inpatient psychiatric care' (Freeman *et al.* 1985). This target was set within the context of a general agreement that mental hospitals should be cut back, if not replaced altogether by the new units, and that these units would be a resource for expanded community based services. Sweden, for example, aimed to provide a general hospital psychiatric unit in each county while reducing the number of mental hospital beds to 10,000 (from a peak of 27,000) by 1990 (Freeman *et al.* 1985: 84). It has not reached either target yet, but it is much more advanced than most countries in its efforts to move away from specialist mental hospitals. The UK, together with Norway and France, began the process of moving in this direction around the 1940s, but it was not until the 'pharmacological revolution' of the mid-1950s that the reduction in the number of mental hospital beds began to take effect. France was one of the first countries to establish multidisciplinary teams on a national level to provide an alternative service for those who were being discharged from psychiatric hospital – there were 800 set up in 1960, with 24-hour back-up from hospital services (Uffing *et al.* 1992: 275).

In Britain, as we have already seen in an earlier chapter, the number of patients in mental hospitals peaked at 155,000 in 1955 and has been falling ever since, reaching 50,000 in 1993 (Shepherd *et al.* 1996). One of the main problems with this process is that, while all of the 'old' long-stay patients have been relocated to other housing projects and residential units, a 'new' long-stay population is taking its place. Many of the general hospital psychiatric units do not wish to keep long-stay inpatients. They prefer to transfer them to the remaining mental hospitals, which have reduced in size and expanded in terms of personnel and the range of available treatments, or to residential facilities provided by both statutory social services departments and independent organisations. Decisions on the transfer of patients often depend not only on the availability of residential places in either the health or social service sectors, but also on the relationships between the psychiatric unit and all the other providers in the locality. For example, some of the problems for these acute units are clear in the report on an audit of mental health admissions to two inner London health districts during the early 1990s. In the absence of a comprehensive range of community residential facilities, including some for crisis care, clinicians found the new level of acute care grossly inadequate. The level of provision, based on norms on bed complement set out in *Better Services for the Mentally Ill* (Department of Health and Social Security 1975), was found to underestimate the need in areas of high psychiatric morbidity, for example central London. According to these clinicians, 'it has become increasingly difficult to admit patients even in acute crisis' (Flannigan *et al.* 1994a: 756). This study supports claims being made by mental health professionals all over the UK that a reduction in the number of hospital beds must be accompanied by an expansion in community services.

The specific recommendations of the Inner London audit may not apply equally to other areas that have cut back the number of hospital beds, but they can be seen as an 'ideal type' – a combination of services needed to provide a comprehensive mental health service. These are presented here in a summarised form:

1. special facilities for the assessment of mentally ill people who may require admission to hospital – accident and emergency rooms are not appropriate;
2. experiments in hostel-wards for acute care (like those which exist in some areas for medium-length stay);
3. respite houses (such as shelters for the homeless) with professional back-up from the psychiatric services to prevent some admissions;

4. a register of all patients assessed as being in danger of a relapse, supported by a simple way for those listed to contact a mental health professional in an emergency.

The authors of the audit suggested that, if all of these recommendations were put in place, the number of acute admissions would be reduced and the number of available beds or places for longer-term care and treatment increased (Flannigan *et al.* 1994a: 757).

However, it is very unlikely, in the current climate, that a great expansion in services will take place. In spite of the change in government in the UK to a Labour government that has promised to abolish the 'internal market' within the health services, the legacy of the NHS reforms remain in place. In particular, the 1990 National Health Service and Community Care Act has adversely affected services for people with mental disorder. Lead responsibility for this sector was given to local authority social services departments without sufficient funding – they were given approximately 15 per cent of the available resources for the development of community services, while health authorities received the remainder to meet medical and psychiatric needs (Shepherd *et al.* 1996). In addition, the split between the 'purchasers' and 'providers' of services and the introduction (for a brief period) of general practitioner fundholding has led to great diversity in service delivery and a tendency to move away from investment in community-based care. Instead of cementing co-operation between the health and social services departments, the reforms led to great competition between service providers, competition that may have brought benefits to acute medical care but not to community services. According to some mental health professionals, the reforms have unfortunately 'managed to create a complex system from a relatively simple one' (Shepherd *et al.* 1996: 1355). Although there are plans for the development of multidisciplinary 'primary care groups' to redress the imbalances of the past decade, it is unlikely that there will be a major shift in the funding available for community-based services in the near future.

In Spain, Ireland, Romania, the Czech Republic and Greece, services are at an earlier stage of development and are still dominated by the large mental hospitals, although a number of psychiatric units in general hospitals (often attached to university departments) have been developed. In Greece in 1985, for example, there was only one unit in a general hospital. Following the exposure of the scandalous conditions that prevailed among psychiatric patients on the island of Leros, a grant of 8 million ECU was given to Greece by the EU for the development of new mental health services. As a result, 33 psychiatric units have since been opened in general hospitals, and 10 community health centres have been established (Ramon 1996: 21). Rumania reported to the WHO in the early 1980s that it had developed 15 psychiatric units in general hospitals. However, it is clear from the description of the units that these were mental hospitals that were integrated in name only into general medical care. Six of the units had more than 500 beds each, and nine had over 200 beds – all of them designated as mental health beds (Freeman *et al.* 1985).

Italy was probably the most radical in its approach to changing the face of mental health services with the passing of Law 180 (in 1978). Under this law, only wards or other residential facilities with 15 or fewer beds could be designated as psychiatric units. As a result of this legislation, the number of mental hospital beds per 10,000 of the population had fallen to 7.6 in 1983, and there was also a decline in the number of private psychiatric beds (Thornicroft and Bebbington 1989: 742). This level has continued to decline, and although provision must be inadequate for at least some areas, it has forced Italians into creating alternative living arrangements and approaches to mental health services. There are as many critics as there are supporters of the Italian model of provision, but perhaps the main lesson is that the service in any area is only as good as the resources (in terms of both personnel and finance) available to them. What is most interesting about the experiments is that they have shown that it is possible to change a large institution from within by involving patients in making their own decisions about how to run their lives rather than their waiting to move successfully to a community that had abandoned them in the first place. This, as Ramon (1996: 31) suggests, is perhaps the only way forward for hospitals such as the Kashenko Hospital in Moscow, which has 5,000 patients and 5,000 staff. Within the current economic climate in Russia, it is unlikely that resources will be devoted to the rehabilitation of these people. Their only hope of survival is transformation from within the institution.

Non-residential mental health services

There are major difficulties in compiling and comparing data from different countries on non-residential (or ambulatory) services, which include outpatient clinics, specialist day care (including employment projects), domiciliary care by specialist staff, and primary care services. What is counted as a psychiatric outpatient attendance in one country may not be in another. For example, a large number of people who might attend an outpatient clinic in the UK are seen by private medical practitioners in Germany. Also, some psychiatric clinics in general hospitals and domiciliary visits by non-medical mental health professionals (nurses, psychologists and social workers) are often not recorded in the psychiatric statistics. Comparisons are, therefore, virtually impossible with the current state of data, not only because of the lack of statistics from many countries, but also because of the difficulties in interpreting what is available. However, what is available gives a basis for discussion.

In the WHO report of the mid-1980s on outpatient and day care, the picture was grave: 'The available statistical data indicate very little progress indeed, and the report texts also suggest relatively slow progress' (Freeman *et al.* 1985: 85). France, the UK, Norway and Sweden seem the most advanced in terms of providing extensive outpatient facilities to all sections of the population. In Finland, Italy and Poland, facilities have increased considerably during the 1980s, while in Greece and Spain, the WHO pilot study areas have benefited from the extra resources devoted to them, although progress is slow elsewhere. In Eastern European countries, where the emphasis is on delivering a comprehensive primary health care system, psychiatric outpatient clinics are integrated into the network of polyclinics. In Bulgaria, for example, these polyclinics cater for a population of between 100,000 and 500,000 people. In the Netherlands, the government has made finance available to local bodies for the development of outpatient facilities, but, as with other countries where they are seen as a threat to private practice, they have been slow to develop.

Day care is equally difficult to compare as it includes a wide range of projects with a variety of functions – therapeutic, rehabilitative, occupational and social – each type of service catering for different groups of people. According to the Audit Commission in Britain in 1986, there were only 9,000 day centre places available (32 per cent of the target number set out in *Better Service for the Mentally Ill*) and 17,000 day hospital places (17 per cent of the target number) (Department of Health and Social Security 1975; Thornicroft and Bebbington 1989: 749). The traditional day hospital provides the transition between inpatient living and living in the community, while the traditional day centre, run by either social services departments or independent organisations, serves as a form of daily respite for carers and a social club for the person with a mental disorder. Neither of these facilities is particularly attractive to young adults who want to be more integrated into the larger community of work and leisure. For this group, work-related day care is more useful. There is anecdotal evidence that community-based services have expanded since 1990, but, because of the diversity in providers that has followed on from the 1990 NHS and Community Care Act, it is very difficult to get accurate, up-to-date information on these services in the UK (Heller *et al.* 1996; Rogers and Pilgrim 1996).

During the past 20 years, as a result of the infusion of money from the antipoverty programme of the European Social Fund, a number of employment projects were initiated throughout the region, encompassing a broad range of different approaches:

> The range includes sheltered workshops with traditional assembling jobs, employment training workshops where a variety of skills are taught (such as the use of computers, office skills, printing, picture framing, catering), supported work experiences, on the job training, social firms, work co-operatives, the use of high street employment placement agencies, and employment as a support worker. (Ramon 1996: 154)

Most of the projects do not operate as viable commercial organisations and rely for their continuance on some funding from either the national government or the European Social Fund. Since the purpose of these projects is to prepare people to work in a less sheltered environment – the real market place – they are significantly affected by the state of the economy and in particular the availability of employment opportunities. Over the past two decades, when Western European economies suffered from higher levels of unemployment than those experienced since before the Second World War, the opportunities for people with disabilities (whether mental or physical) have been severely limited. In this context, specialist employment projects take on a different function – one of providing long-term employment for people with mental disorder. In times of high employment, this function disappears. The largest, and one of the most famous, co-operatives is in Italy, *la Nuova Cooperativa* in Turin, where 95 per cent of its 200 members are users of psychiatric services. The main difference between it and other businesses is the fact that workers are not dismissed for missing work but are encouraged to return when they feel able to do so. Another version of this kind of employment project exists in Trieste and Pordenone, also in Italy. In order to overcome the problems of a sometimes absent workforce, they incorporate a number of businesses in a consortium that has some workers who have a mental disorder and some who have not. For example, the Pordenone consortium provides cleaning services to offices, collects money from public telephones and provides home care services for disabled people. In Trieste, the consortium includes a hotel, a restaurant and a building firm (Polak and Warner 1996). Both of these examples are large organisations, but there are also a number of smaller and successful co-operatives in Ireland, England and Germany.

Before leaving the discussion on Europe, it is also important to raise the issue of the kind of staff necessary for a changing mental health service. The WHO report was pessimistic about staff qualification and training. While most countries have sufficient (if not too many) psychiatrists, who are the most expensive personnel in the mental health system, many also employ large numbers of untrained staff (Freeman *et al*. 1985: 89). In addition, even in countries such as Spain, where there are enough trained psychiatrists, there are great regional differences in their availability, rural areas being poorly served. In the UK and France, the problems are different in that, although they have a sufficient number of qualified staff, many of them find it difficult to adapt to the newer modes of working. In particular, nurses who have undergone training focused on hospital care are not well prepared for multidisciplinary, community-based teamwork. Training programmes inevitably lag behind service development, and the difficulties are compounded by the increase in the diversity of settings within which most mental health professionals are now asked to work.

Current services in the USA

In common with the UK and other Western European countries, the number of psychiatric beds in public hospitals increased during the first half of the twentieth century, reaching a peak of 558,900 in 1955 and decreasing to 132,164 in 1980 (Scull 1984) and 71,619 in 1994 (Torrey 1997). However, this could be perceived as *transinstitutionalisation* because of the expansion in the number of beds in other sectors, which may have absorbed a significant proportion of the psychiatric population. These include beds in private hospitals as well as nursing and board-and-care facilities:

> General hospital psychiatric beds increased from 7,000 to more than 48,000, with many additional patients admitted to medical services. Private free-standing psychiatric hospitals, recently the fastest growing inpatient programs, currently account for 79,000 beds, and the Veteran Affairs hospitals provide more than 21,000 beds. There are a total of 252,000 psychiatric beds in the USA, 988 per

100,000 population. In addition, more than 750,000 psychiatric patients are estimated to be in non-psychiatric facilities – nursing homes and homes for the aged.
(Elpers, in Kaplan and Sadock 1995: 2666)

If we take the psychiatric figure alone, this means that, even
with the increase in private and general hospital beds, the number of
beds is still less than half what it was in the mid-1950s. The figure for
non-psychiatric nursing and care facilities is difficult to evaluate
because of the impact of an ageing population on the current use of
residential services.

One of the estimates of the number of people with chronic mental
disorder living in the community can be derived from numbers on
social security disability insurance. In 1983, this was estimated as
being between 1.7 and 2.4 million people, of whom 116,000 were in
state mental hospitals (Thornicroft and Bebbington 1989: 742). Other
estimates put the number at between 2.8 and 3.5 million living inde-
pendently, 250,000 in residential facilities and over 1 million in nursing
homes (Liberman *et al.*, in Kaplan and Sadock 1995: 2696). Although
the estimates vary, it is clear that the health needs of a large number of
people and their families require resources and innovative thinking to
support them on a long-term basis. Current government policy is
outlined in the *National Plan for the Chronically Mentally Ill* (US
Government *c.* 1996), which had its origins in the President's Commission on Mental Health and in the Americans with Disabilities Act, both
of which will affect not only the health system, but also the social environment within with people with mental disorder will live and work.
These strong policy statements, together with the increasing size and
power of the consumer movement, especially NAMI, should ensure a
much better deal for people in the future.

Community care

Early approaches to community care were put in place through the
Community Mental Health Centres Act of US President J.F. Kennedy
in 1963. In spite of the great enthusiasm of the time, the psychotherapeutic approaches then dominant did little for people with chronic
and serious mental disorders. It was not until the advent of case
management in the late 1970s that there were noticeable strides made
in community-based interventions with this group. The main strengths
of case management are that there is one person responsible for the

planning and delivery of a specially tailored package of services and that, ideally, the case manager's commitment transcends time and agency. Other initiatives from various parts of the mental health service provider network were also introduced during the late 1970s and early 1980s. The NIMH set up a number of community support projects, and the Robert Wood Johnson Foundation initiated projects in a number of cities that integrated housing services with community mental health centres. Some of the difficulties that have arisen in these and other community-based projects for people with chronic mental disorder have been related to general policy trends rather than to any specific characteristic of mental health care. This is the shift of responsibility for those with chronic mental disorders from federal to state level. This trend, towards the localisation of all kinds of health and welfare services for the poorest members of society (regardless of disability), is one which is not confined to the USA. However, because of the exclusionary nature of American health insurance schemes, it has resulted in more widespread experiences of economic disadvantage among those with mental disorders than in European countries such as the UK, France and Italy.

Hard evidence on modes of survival by people who might have been in hospital in an earlier era is not widely available, but some studies have been carried out. In California in the early 1980s, Leavitt estimated that:

> for the 55,000 patients who would have been in state hospital beds, had deinstitutionalisation not occurred in California... 45 per cent were in board and care residential homes, 22 per cent were independent or with their families, 7 per cent were in locked facilities, and 9 per cent were inpatients. The remaining 9 per cent were untreated and mostly homeless. (Thornicroft and Bebbington 1989: 745)

Other studies on discharged long-stay patients in Los Angeles support findings in British, Irish and German studies that people who were relocated to sheltered housing on discharge from hospital perceived their living situation more favourably than they had done in hospital. This was true even if there had been little change in their employment status (most remaining unemployed), their social circle (mostly former patients and mental health staff) or their psychiatric symptomatology (Donnelly *et al.* 1994; Knapp *et al.* 1995; Thornicroft and Bebbington 1989). What these studies show is that a great many people with chronic mental disorder require continuing, if varying, levels of support and that this can be delivered most effectively through protective housing schemes.

However, some of the greatest economic and social problems are experienced by people who have never been hospitalised, people for whom the providers of mental health services feel no responsibility because of their low use of services. These people are not on any rehabilitation list but show up in homelessness and crime statistics. The debate in the USA on homelessness and chronic mental disorder has been ongoing for a number of years. In 1983, the National Coalition for the Homeless estimated that 2.5 million people were without accommodation in the USA, and studies from the NIMH found that at least 30 per cent of this population suffered from serious mental disorder (Thornicroft and Bebbington 1989: 747). These people (usually men) do not use psychiatric facilities and tend to rely on emergency night shelters for accommodation and help. The Robert Johnson Foundation housing profects offer examples of how housing, therapy and economic support can be combined, but these are only a drop in the ocean. Because of an increase in the number of people who suffer from the double disadvantage of mental disorder and lack of a home, the American Psychiatric Association set up a Task Force on the Homeless Mentally Ill and recommended the expansion of supervised housing schemes and of crisis intervention services, also pleading for a simplified and secure benefit system that would ensure a basic income for all.

The problem of maintaining a basic income is experienced by most people with chronic mental disorder. For some, this may mean holding on to an existing job in spite of absences from work, a situation that is more difficult for those in manual and skilled occupations than for those higher up the occupational ladder. For others, employment projects such as those developed in Europe (co-operatives), as well as those based on the Club House model of occupation and social interaction, offer a stable connection to the market economy. As the consumer movement has become increasingly interested in facilitating supported employment projects, these are not only expanding, but also gaining credibility as commercially viable enterprises. However, not everyone wants to work in a supported environment, either because it is too stigmatising or because it might interfere with benefit payments. A study carried out in Colorado with 100 seriously mentally ill people found that there is a need for rates of pay higher than the minimum wage and incentives towards employment within the benefit system if people are to be encouraged into work (Polak and Warner 1996). This would require a more integrated approach to helping people with disabilities than that which currently operates, but it would, if successful, solve the most basic problem suffered by people with mental disorder – that of poverty.

The impact of 'managed care' on psychiatric services

Although the evidence for a positive link between diagnosed mental disorder and low income is substantial, it must not be forgotten that there are also people on adequate incomes who require mental health care. Recent changes in health insurance legislation have had a significant impact on how services are used by this large sector of the population. In the introduction to the most recent edition of their textbook on psychiatry, Kaplan and Sadock talk about 'the crisis in the future of psychiatry' caused by the introduction of the American Health Security Bill (the Clinton Plan) in 1993 (Kaplan and Sadock 1995: ix). This bill was the catalyst for changes in approach in health insurance companies, HMOs and PPOs. Systems of 'managed care' put in place by these companies dictate the way in which the insured person (the 'patient') gains access to a mental health specialist (usually through a primary care physician), limit the patient's choice to a number of listed psychiatrists and other mental health professionals (either those employed by the HMO or on the list of the PPO) and limit the length of treatment periods (including psychotherapy sessions and days in hospital).

Although one could be sceptical about opposition from the medical profession for systems of money management that may reduce its income, it has to be conceded that this system has problems for consumers. Americans, accustomed to paying health insurance, accept it as part of life but find the current behaviour of their insurers unreasonable and irritating. Until now, they have been able to go directly to the specialist (in this case a psychiatrist) of their choice. However, they are now asked to rely on the choice of the insurance company or HMO not only for the specialist chosen, but also for the initial referral. From the policy perspective of the world outside the USA, this aspect of 'managed care' is not a problem as it seems perfectly reasonable that a primary care physician (general practitioner) be the first port of call for what may turn out to be a minor health problem. However, there are aspects of the 'managed care' package that seem problematic. Decisions on the length and type of treatment are professional decisions, which, it is felt by consumers and professionals alike, cannot be determined solely by financial considerations, and there are fears that financial considerations will skew the kinds of treatment on offer and will not necessarily lead to better outcomes. For example, if there are financial incentives to maintain a patient on a regime of medication without referral to a mental health specialist and without the opportunity for psychotherapeutic treatment, it is probable that this will be the preferred choice of the primary care practitioner. Even when psychotherapy is sanctioned by the insurer, the number of visits is usually limited to between 5 and 20 per year, and each new set of sessions has to be justified by the therapist (for a further discussion, see Carson 1993; Kavanagh 1997).

We have already seen in an earlier section of this chapter that medication dominates the treatment spectrum already present in mental health care. What hope is there for the future development of alternative treatment packages that are neither tidy nor easy to carry through? Recent discussions by mental health economists in the UK (who are very interested in learning any lessons on cost-effectiveness from the American experience) acknowledge some of the negative effects of recent market-driven care systems in operation in HMOs:

> Although most HMOs include some mental health benefits, coverage for chronic serious mental illness is rare. Evidence suggests that HMOs provide less services with poorer patient outcomes compared with fee-for-service care. Furthermore, the role of primary care clinicians (within HMOs) as both service providers and gatekeepers for mental illness has been questioned. (Kavanagh 1997: 155)

These are sobering words. For people with mental health problems, the use of existing services is already problematic, and it is probable that any further difficulty will act as a barrier and will reduce the percentage of people using these services.

Gender and the use of services

Although it has been generally accepted that women appear more often than men in the psychiatric statistics, it is surprising how few studies on the use of services include gender as a variable. Fortunately, however, recent research is beginning to address this issue in a systematic way. From the available evidence, which is not in any way comprehensive, there are patterns emerging that are sometimes in line with our expectations and sometimes not. We have already seen in the literature on the diagnosis of mental disorder that, if substance dependence and personality disorder are included, both women and men are at the same risk of having a current mental disorder, with a 20 per cent 1-year prevalence, although men are at a higher risk of developing a mental disorder in their lifetime – a 36 per cent lifetime prevalence for men against 30 per cent for women (Robins and Regier 1991) – and are at a higher risk of suicide (Paykel 1991). We have also seen that the disorders to which women are more prone are anxiety disorders and depression, and those to which men are more prone are substance dependence and personality disorder. The diagnosis of schizophrenia is equally prevalent among men and women, although some recent cross-national studies, carried out by the WHO, indicate that it is decreasing as a worldwide phenomenon (Edgerton and Cohen 1994) and that this is more so for women than for men (Kendler and Walsh 1995). If we take as our starting point that both men and women need an equal share of mental health services, it is interesting to find that the take-up of services appears anything but equal.

In statistics on medication and the use of other health services, women predominate. Women throughout Europe and North America are prescribed approximately twice as many psychotropic drugs per head as men (Ashton 1991). For example, in a study of 133,081 patients of general practitioners in the UK in the early 1970s, the prescription rate was 20 per cent for women and 10 per cent for men, with the prescription rates rising with age but maintaining the same gender pattern. In a study of 24,633 similar patients in Boston during the same era, the findings were even more startling, with 25 per cent of women and 15 per cent of men receiving psychotropic drugs. A cross-national study in 1980–81 of the use of sedatives (the most commonly prescribed of this group of drugs) confirmed the general pattern. In all of the countries, the female:male ratio was approximately 2:1, the highest ratio occurring in Belgium (21 per cent for women and 13 per cent for men) and the lowest in the Netherlands (9 per cent for women and 6 per cent for men) (Ashton 1991: 31).

Explanations for the differential prescription rates for men and women are to a large extent conjectural, as there are few studies to analyse the doctors' prescription decisions. Some evidence points to the fact that male doctors are more likely to perceive a physical illness as a psychological one when the patient is a woman (Brozovic 1989, in Ashton 1991), that medical advertising more often shows women in advertisements of psychoactive drugs, in contrast to the case with non-psychoactive drugs, where more men are shown (Prather and Fidell 1975, in Ashton 1991), and finally that this type of medication is more socially acceptable for women than for men. All of these explanations support the feminist arguments on the social construction of 'illness behaviour', which made the discourse of mental distress and medical treatment for this condition an acceptable vehicle for women but not for men (Chesler 1972; Showalter 1987; Shorter 1990). This has undoubtedly been the case in the past, but there are signs that this is changing, the new social construction of mental disorder fitting male patterns of behaviour.

For example, the gender balance is completely reversed when illegal drug dependence and alcohol addiction are considered. Young men are the group most likely to show symptoms of both of these dependencies (Kessler *et al.* 1994; Robins and Regier 1991). This means that there seems to be an increase in the experience of this particular type of mental health problem by men. However, is this reflected in the use of services? Has the social construction of mental disorder changed sufficiently for mental health professionals to extend the kind of diagnosis and treatment available to women in the past to men in the present? The answer to this question is based on what we know of the current use of psychiatric services by men and by information given in community studies. It is clear from studies of hospital bed usage in most countries that men have lower admission rates and form a lower proportion of that population than do women. In relation to the ECA and the NCS findings on psychiatric morbidity, this means that, although young men especially are experiencing higher rates of disorder, they are not accessing inpatient services in the same way as women. This is not universally true, however, a fact which may merit more attention and research in the future. Ireland, for example, has always had a higher use of psychiatric beds by men than by women in both the nineteenth and twentieth centuries (Cleary and Treacy 1997; Finnane 1981). This has been related to landlessness (economic disadvantage) in the nineteenth century and patterns of treatment for alcoholism in the twentieth, both interesting connections now being discussed again in relation to changing gender trends in the use of psychiatric hospital beds elsewhere. Recent work by Payne (1995, 1996) in the UK has shown that the trend in admission rate (female dominance) is beginning to change in the younger age group (18–35 years), the male admission rate catching up with and sometimes surpassing the female rate. This finding has been supported by research on census data on Northern Ireland, which clearly shows that, while the total population in residential psychiatric facilities (including health and social care) is dominated by women, there has been a significant increase in the number of younger men (aged 18–35) in these beds between 1981 and 1991 (Prior and Hayes 1998).

The historical pattern of a low usage of psychiatric services by men fits into a pattern of a low service use of general health services. As one of the main purposes of the first ECA surveys was to estimate the level of unmet mental health need in the general population, those judged to have active (within 12 months) symptoms of a psychiatric disorder were asked if they had sought or received help. The answers were startling not only in terms of the population in general, but also because of the patterns that emerged in relation to gender, education and race. As we have already seen in Chapter 4, only 19 per cent of these people had received any form of treatment in the previous year – 2.4 per cent had received inpatient treatment in the previous year and 16.4 per cent received outpatient treatment in the previous 6 months (Robins and Regier 1991: Table 13-5). Women received more treatment than men – 23 per cent as against 14 per cent – and both men and women who had a high-school education were slightly more likely to receive treatment than those who had not, married men without a high school education being those least likely to use services. According to these findings, most people (three out of four) do not receive medical services at all, and there are great variations by gender, and indeed by race, in how services are accessed. In an in-depth analysis of what happened to those who did seek and receive treatment, Shapiro *et al.* (1984) found that there were two major gender differences. In each ECA, more women than men made mental health visits, but these men were more likely to be seen by a mental health specialist than were the women. Whether this was because of the number of women who presented, or because of a perception of women as being not quite as ill as they thought they were, is not clear.

Studies carried out in Europe start from a slightly different baseline as the majority of people in the first instance consult their general practitioner (rather than a specialist, as in the USA). The evidence points to more powerful filters between the general practitioner and the psychiatric services than are seen with any other medical specialty. Everyone does *not* have an equal chance of being referred onwards. As one would expect, those with more serious psychiatric complaints or a previous diagnosis are referred on fairly consistently. As in the USA, men are more likely to be referred than women, and younger patients more than older people (Wilkinson 1989). The finding about older people is worrying as it indicates that there is a tendency to attribute mental distress in older people to the ageing process rather than to seek a thorough assessment of the symptoms independent of age. In a study in the Netherlands in the late 1980s, the patterns of referral to mental health specialists and the reasons for these referrals were tracked (Verhaak 1993). This study indeed found age and gender variations in diagnoses and referrals. The diagnosis of mental disorder was most common in women aged 40 years or more and least common in men under 40, but younger men were overrepresented among referrals to non-residential (ambulatory) mental health services (multidisciplinary teams), while young women were most likely to be among referrals to social workers:

> Although psychiatric morbidity was less frequently identified among younger men, this group was most frequently referred. It might be that this group of patients is over-represented in the 'hidden psychiatric category', and that as a result the illness of the identified sample is on average more severe. (Verhaak 1993: 207)

Other international studies on service use show similar gender trends in patterns of service use – women presenting more often with symptoms of mental disorder, but men more often being referred on to psychiatric services from primary care teams. A study of heavy users of psychiatric services in southern Australia in 1990 came up with some interesting conclusions on the need for more attention to this group. In an extensive literature review, Kent *et al.* (1995a, 1995b) reminded us that readmission rates continue to be used as the main criterion of heavy service use in spite of the debate surrounding the validity of this approach in the light of de-institutionalisation policies throughout most of the Western world. With this limitation in mind, the research findings are fairly consistent:

> [Earlier studies] described a population with a mean age in the mid-thirties; 60–70 per cent were male and white; 70 per cent or more never married; and more than 40 per cent abused alcohol or drugs or both. From 30 to 60 per cent of these patients had a history of suicide attempts, violence and involvement with the criminal justice system. Medication and program non compliance and chronic denial of illness was seen in more than 75 per cent of cases. (Kent *et al.* 1995b: 1254)

The Australian study found nothing which contradicted any of these earlier findings, but it threw up some additional characteristics of this group of people. All of the 50 patients in the sample were on low incomes – 82 per cent had been unemployed for all or most of the 3-year study period, 68 per cent were on a disability pension, and the remainder were on sickness or unemployment benefit for some of the time (Kent *et al.* 1995b: 1255). Schizophrenia was the most common diagnosis, and there was a high incidence of personality disorder as well as a higher incidence of substance abuse than had been clinically indicated. Although these patients had been transferred to community mental health teams, their patterns of emergency service use continued to be outside the team's operating hours (7.30 am to

7.30 pm), which confirms the need for a 24-hour crisis mental health service. As the authors of this study suggest, inpatient services, which are highly expensive, will continue to be used by this group of people until a more comprehensive community service takes its place.

So far, all of the evidence points to the need for an analysis of service use in gender terms. Women more often seek help for mental disorder but are often prescribed drugs by their general practitioner rather than being referred to the psychiatric services; men find it difficult to seek help and are often seriously ill before they come to the notice of the medical services. Having accessed the services, women are more likely to recover from severe mental disorder (Pfeiffer *et al.* 1996), and men are more likely to be heavy users of psychiatric services and to be housed in the new long-stay hospital populations (Lelliot *et al.* 1994). Within this broad framework, there is overwhelming evidence of an underprovision of services for substance dependence, which is now being recognised as a mental health problem. Even where services are provided, women find them hard to use (El-Guebaly 1995; Schober and Annis 1996) because of the sexism inherent in our notions of acceptable gender roles.

Finally, there must be an acknowledgement of the fact that the burgeoning literature on informal care shows the continuing commitment of women to the long-term care of the sick or disabled members of their families. Research on care-givers, self-help organisations and family members of people with serious mental disorders points to the increasing burden, especially on older women, imposed by policies that cause any shrinkage in existing services or remove services without replacing them with others (Benson 1994; Biegal *et al.* 1995; Hatfield *et al.* 1996a; Kuipers 1993; Mueser *et al.* 1996; Solomon and Draine 1995). For example, in a American survey of over 3,000 families in NAMI in 1993, the majority of respondents were female (83 per cent), and the mean age was 60 years (Hatfield *et al.* 1996a: 826). Most of the consumers (relatives with a mental disorder) were male (68 per cent), most were adult children of the respondent (83 per cent), and a large proportion had a diagnosis of schizophrenia (57 per cent). Similar characteristics were found in a study of 225 families in Philadelphia (Solomon and Draine 1995). Most of the participants (usually the main carer) were female (88 per cent) and white (84 per cent), their mean age being 56 years, and most were the parents of an adult child with a mental disorder (76 per cent). Notwithstanding the fact that there is probably a bias inherent in the manner of conducting these studies (a postal questionnaire to people known to the service providers), the pattern of older women taking responsibility for caring for young adults with a chronic mental disorder is indisputable. The policy implications of this fact taken in the context of an ageing population are far reaching. Because of the increasing difficulties being experienced by 'family care-givers', we now see the growth of advocacy organisations devoted to mental health and illness issues, trying to combat the apathy among policy-makers on the plight of people with chronic mental disorder. It is to be hoped that Paul Benson (1994: 133) is right when he says that 'this dismal situation may be improving somewhat with the increased visibility of the National Alliance for the Mentally Ill'. Otherwise, the future is very bleak for these people and their families – or should we say, the female members of their families.

8

The Law and Mental Disorder

Mental health professionals have always needed to have some knowledge of the law as it relates to mental disorder. However, this knowledge is often narrow in scope, extending only to legislation dealing with the compulsory hospitalisation and treatment of individuals with a psychiatric diagnosis. As we shall see in the following discussion, the interaction between law and mental disorder is much more complex than that and covers many situations that have little or nothing to do with hospitalisation or treatment.

The scope of mental health law

One of the most comprehensive overviews on the scope of mental health law was contained in a special section of the *American Journal of Orthopsychiatry* in 1994. In their introduction to the section:

> Mental health law is defined as that field of inquiry that is concerned with the intersection of the law with the mental health status of individuals: the operation of the mental health system and of other public or private systems in their provision of services to mentally ill persons (e.g., education and child welfare systems and private psychiatric hospitals); and the roles, functions, and responsibilities of mental health professionals (MHPs). (Sales and Shuman 1994: 172)

Not surprisingly, this broad definition of mental health law encompasses more than 100 legal topics. These fall into six categories:

1. the licensing and regulation of mental health facilities and professionals;
2. organisational structures for the delivery of mental health services;

3. the financing of mental health services;
4. privacy of professional information;
5. practice relating to the law (including civil commitment and competence to stand trial);
6. limitations on and liability for services (including informed consent and malpractice).

Every country that has a public mental health care system has legislation relating to all of these spheres, most of which have roots in eighteenth- and nineteenth-century lunacy laws. Historically speaking, the first wave of legislation in most countries gave power to a local authority (usually the police) to 'commit' people involuntarily to a secure place if they were found to be causing a nuisance (vagrancy laws). The second wave was usually concerned with the establishment of public asylums, with clauses on financing, managing, staffing and monitoring asylums, and procedures for admitting insane people (lunatic asylum laws). In addition, because people were being deprived of their freedom, another set of laws was necessary to ensure the proper protection of property and safeguards against unnecessary confinement. Finally, because insanity was accepted as a defence in criminal prosecutions, a separate set of laws was necessary for use in the justice system (criminal lunacy legislation). Of the six categories outlined by Sales and Shuman, only two – privacy of professional information and limitations on and liability for services – are of recent origin.

To focus the discussion, we will ask the question, what are the issues of most importance to the consumers of mental health services? This brings us directly into the current literature on mental health law. A leading legal academic, Michael Moore, sees mental disorder as a condition that affects all aspects of the individual's legal life:

> Not only is mental illness relevant to responsibility in the law of crimes and torts, but mentally ill human beings also may not be regarded as sufficiently responsible to manage their own property, to make their own contracts, wills, or marriages, to be granted custody of their children in a divorce, or even to make fundamental decisions such as those concerning their liberty or whether they wish to be medically treated in one way as opposed to another. (Moore 1984: 217)

In other words, the law can be used to show that people with mental disorder are different, that they do not have the same rights or responsibilities as an ordinary citizen. However, this use of the law is not universally accepted. The debate revolves around arguments about the link between mental disorder and moral responsibility. On one side of the argument are those who contend that, if certain behaviours can be attributed to a disease or disorder, the individual can be relieved of legal responsibility for the action. This action, therefore, ought not be punished in the same way as if the individual had full control of the behaviour. On the other hand, it could be argued that the presence or absence of a disease should make no difference to the attribution of blame (Greenberg and Bailey 1994).

This issue is often debated in relation to alcoholism, which is regarded by some as a disease and by others as bad behaviour. For example, in 1988, the USA Supreme Court was asked to consider a verdict of the Veterans Administration that alcoholism constituted 'wilful misconduct' and therefore warranted the removal of benefits from former veterans (Greenberg and Bailey 1994: 153). The Court ruled that the particular case did not require it to decide whether or not alcoholism is a disease and did not interfere in the Veterans Administration decision. Many found this ruling extremely unsatisfactory as they had hoped for one which could be used in future cases. It also left the door open for further debate on the link between alcoholism and disease, and between disease and moral responsibility. Greenberg and Bailey (1994: 154) agree with the Supreme Court ruling and argue that 'the propriety of classifying mental disorders as illnesses has no legitimate implications for questions of social and legal policy such as criminal responsibility and involuntary commitment'. A disease model that implies that individuals have no control over certain behaviours is of no consequence legally as all behaviour is 'caused' by either biological or social influences. They suggest that the basis for legal decisions has to be much broader than this narrow focus on culpability.

Criminal responsibility

In the area of crime, the question of culpability is basic to sentencing decisions. Countries have different approaches to the establishment of grounds for the removal of responsibility for crimes, and this is clearly shown in different legal systems relating to crime and mental disorder. In the Western world, some notion of criminal insanity has been recognised since the thirteenth century. Although current laws are quite different in the USA and the UK, both systems are based on a common intellectual tradition. While there were laws prior to the nineteenth century, one of the legal landmarks occurred only in 1800, when King George III was shot at in London by an ex-army officer, James

Hadfield. Hadfield had been discharged from the army on the grounds of insanity and suffered from the delusion that God was going to destroy the world. In an effort to have himself killed (by execution) without committing suicide (which he regarded as a mortal sin leading to damnation), Hadfield attempted to kill the king. Hadfield was not executed as his defence lawyer won the case, thus creating a new set of rules for pleading 'not guilty on the grounds of insanity' and introducing the practice of presenting medical evidence to the court.

The next legal landmark was the case of Daniel McNaughten, who killed Edward Drummond, Private Secretary to the British Prime Minister, Robert Peel, in 1843. He had meant to kill Peel as he suffered under the delusion that he was being persecuted by the Tory Party. The public at large were not pleased when McNaughten was acquitted on the grounds of insanity, and this prompted the development by the Law Lords of what became known as the McNaughten Rules:

> It must be clearly proved that at the time of committing the act, the party accused was labouring under such a defective reason, from disease of the mind, as not to know the nature and quality of the act he was doing, or if he did know it, that he did not know that what he was doing was wrong. (Quon 1981, in Green *et al.* 1991: 47)

These rules have been enforced in many countries until very recently, when changes have usually resulted from public outrage against a particular crime. For example, in the USA throughout most of this century, the McNaughten Rules were used as the basis for further developments in case law, culminating in the revised American Law Institute Test of 1962 (Kaplan and Sadock 1995: 2763–6):

> A person is not responsible for criminal conduct if at the time of such conduct if, as the result of mental disease and defect, he lacks substantial capacity to appreciate the criminality of his conduct or to conform his conduct to the requirements of law. (in Green *et al.* 1991: 51)

Although there were different interpretations of this test throughout the USA, it was nonetheless accepted by the public as well as the judiciary as being just. This was all changed, however, by the attempted assassination of President Ronald Reagan in 1981 and the subsequent acquittal of John Hinkley (his attacker) on the grounds of insanity. The outcry from the public gave a new impetus to the move for the reform of the insanity law initiated by President Nixon. The result was the complete abolition of the insanity defence in a number of states and a

revision of the insanity test at federal level, making it much more difficult for the offender to avoid responsibility for the crime (La Fond
1994: 217).

The laws in the UK and other countries in Europe are now quite
different from those in the USA because of procedures to ensure
psychiatric treatment for the offender regardless of the level of responsibility for crime. In England, where the McNaughten Rules remain as
the legal definition of criminal insanity, they are rarely used as it is no
longer necessary to prove insanity to access treatment (Green *et al.*
1991: 48). Since 1959, the Court has the power to make a Hospital
Order for a person who has a mental disorder and who has already been
convicted of a crime punishable by imprisonment. The only evidence
required is that of two psychiatrists, which is quite different from the
case in America, where the legal system requires a higher level of legal
representation on behalf of the offender. This Order is renewable every
6 months until the patient is ready for discharge, and it may or may not
be accompanied by a Restriction Order, which will make treatment in
the community compulsory for discharged patients.

Other aspects of criminal law affecting offenders who might have a
mental disorder have been changed quite radically by the Criminal
Procedure Law of 1991, which covers 'fitness to plead' and the insanity
defence. Before 1991, lawyers rarely argued that their clients were
'unfit to plead' as this led to involuntary commitment to a psychiatric
hospital for an indefinite period, with criminal charges pending (Beck
1995). The 1991 law has opened the number of options available to the
Court, allowing for time limits on commitment and community (rather
than hospital) treatment. It is probable that this will lead to a greater use
of this aspect of the law. On the question of the insanity defence, the
new law also allows for more flexibility. The most important change is
the introduction of a time-limited sentence – in contrast to the traditional indefinite commitment for psychiatric treatment.

In these changes, we see trends similar to those appearing
elsewhere – that if psychiatric treatment is seen as necessary, it should
be made as easy as possible for the offender to receive it, and an
offender with a mental disorder should not be confined for longer than
a prison sentence for that particular offence. In other words, the legal
system should not be anti-therapeutic or unjust in relation to offenders
with a mental disorder. This debate on the potential for therapy within
the legal system is one which is now appearing on the legal agenda in
the USA as 'therapeutic jurisprudence'.

Therapeutic jurisprudence

This new school of thought in the USA has emerged from what Sales and Shuman (1994: 174) call the 'utilitarian, consequentialist perspective that espouses legal rules as important to achieve some end'. The proponents of this approach engage in empirical research to see whether laws are actually achieving their explicit and implicit goals. When this perspective is applied to mental health law, it means that the goal of the legal process must be to advance therapeutic outcomes for the individual in question. This is not to say that therapeutic considerations must dominate all others but instead that the consequences of legal decisions should be taken into account when these decisions are being taken. This school of thought is in complete contrast to the deontological perspective prevalent in the USA in the 1970s and early 1980s:

> The deontological perspective... conceives of the law as advancing important values, often ensconced within normative constitutional principles (e.g., the right to an attorney, right to a hearing, privilege against self-incrimination)... From the deontological perspective, recognition of a right to a judicial hearing preceding civil commitment should turn on whether commitment is a deprivation of liberty under the Fourteenth Amendment to the US constitution; from the utilitarian perspective, the right to a hearing should turn on its consequences, such as the accuracy of the hearing's results or patient compliance with the hearing's decision. (Sales and Shuman 1994: 174)

The deontological approach has been supported by the mental health advocacy movement but criticised by many others in the USA. The criticism, voiced by prominent psychiatrists, is that the aggressive advocacy movement of the 1970s and 80s, aimed at protecting people from treatment (including hospitalisation) against their will, has been anti-therapeutic. Unfortunately, it has led to a contraction of services and an increase in homelessness among people with mental disorders. Expressed more graphically, the critics claims that patients now 'die with their rights on' (Treffert 1975, in Perlin 1994: 195).

It is clear from these developments in the USA that all mental health law must include not only protection from inappropriate or unnecessary treatment, but also a protection of rights to treatment. This focus on rights to treatment is likely to become the most controversial issue as we enter a new century in a world in which public expenditure on health is an increasingly visible burden on the tax-payer. How this issue will be resolved will depend on society's view of mental disorder. Professor Michael Perlin argues, in his seminal article on 'sanism', that the battle will be uphill as discrimination against people with mental disabilities is just as rife as any other 'ism' in our society:

> We must confront our systems's sanist biases, identify sanist practices, and artic-
> ulate the roots of sanist behavior. We must enter into a dialogue with the final
> group of unempowered clients, those individuals institutionalized because of
> mental disability, and those individuals in the community who have been subject
> to sanist prejudices. (Perlin 1992: 376)

Like institutionalised sexism and racism, prejudicial approaches are difficult to spot because they are so deeply embedded not only in our institutions, but also in our psyche. For Perlin, they are obvious, and he leaves few stones unturned in his exposition of sanism in the legal system. He reminds legislators that they frequently enact laws that confirm and extend the isolation of people with mental disorder by treating them differently 'in matters of public participation, interpersonal relationships, economic freedom and other civil rights' (Perlin 1992: 308). He argues that the courts reflect the ordinary morality of society because judges often rely on ordinary common sense and biased stereotypes to come to decisions – relying on concrete visual notions of 'craziness', linking mental illness to dangerousness, confusing different types of mental disability (the most obvious being a confusion between learning disability and mental illness) and sometimes going so far as to sanction the death penalty for people with acknowledged mental disorders. Perlin also finds lawyers who represent people with mental disorders to be substandard in terms of their representational skills and the outcomes for their clients. This he attributes to the lack of status that the work merits within the legal academy. For those of us who do not live in the USA, Perlin's critique comes as a surprise because we see the very real efforts that have been made there on behalf of people with mental disorders during the past three decades. His challenge has to be taken up by those in other countries as it is highly unlikely that any European country can proclaim its legal system as free from sanism.

Mental health law in Europe

From a European perspective, the seeming obsession in the American literature with commitment and rights to refuse treatment is difficult to incorporate into a general discussion on the role of the law in the development of good-quality mental health services. This is because, in most countries in Europe, those who are committed involuntarily (compulsory admissions) for hospital treatment form a minority of the hospitalised psychiatric population, and also because the majority of mental health services are either provided or funded by the state. Together, these factors lead to a very different population in publicly funded psychiatric services – both hospital and community.

In a review of compulsory admissions to European psychiatric hospitals, Reicher-Rossler and Rossler (1993) found that they varied (as a proportion of total hospital admissions) from 1 per cent in Spain to 50 per cent in parts of Austria and in Switzerland. These comparisons are not entirely comparable because of the different criteria used in gathering the statistics. For example, in some countries mentally ill offenders were counted, and in others only those who were committed on the grounds of dangerousness were included. However, the point can be made that, for 14 countries, compulsory admissions formed less than 20 per cent of the total number of admissions, which is an indication that people receiving services on a voluntary basis form the majority of the hospitalised psychiatric population in Europe. Northern Ireland, which is part of the UK, can be taken as an example of how the trends in compulsory hospitalisation have changed in the nineteenth and twentieth century, thus providing the background for the debate on the law, a background that seems quite different from that which has characterised the services in the USA.

When Northern Ireland came into existence as a political entity in 1921, its services were based on laws enacted for the whole of Ireland by the British government during the nineteenth century. Although the system was somewhat different from that in the rest of the UK, the outcomes for people with mental disorder were similar. The public asylum system financed by local and central government housed 4,277 people (3.4 per 1,000 of the population), all of whom were classified as paupers and all of whom were certified patients; in other words, compulsory admissions (or involuntary commitments) constituted 100 per cent of the patient population (Prior 1993: 14–25). Almost half of these patients (42 per cent) had been admitted as 'dangerous lunatics' under the auspices of the Lunacy (Ireland) Act 1867: 30 and 31 Vict. C. 118, and the remainder were admitted as persons 'of unsound mind' under the Local Government (Ireland) Act 1898, s. 9(6). During the twentieth century, the law has changed a number of times, and with each new change in the law, the proportion of those admitted to psychiatric hospitals on a compulsory basis has declined. In the 1990s, it stands at approximately 8 per cent of all admissions. The change in patient population, to one in which voluntary patients are overwhelmingly in the majority, has happened within the context of an increase in the number of psychiatric beds in the first half of the century to a peak of 6,486 and a consequent decrease to a planned level of 1,500 in the late 1990s (Prior 1993: 134). As there are no private psychiatric hospital beds in Northern Ireland, it is evident that the laws underpin a very different mental health system from that which prevails in the USA and other countries where there is a significant private sector health input. The current law, the Mental Health (NI) Order 1986 (similar to the British Mental Health Act 1983) is concerned mainly with the civil liberty issues involved in the compulsory hospitalisation and treatment of fewer than 10 per cent of the inpatient population in a public mental health care system. For the other 90 per cent of inpatients and for all mental health service users in the community, the current mental health legislation offers little in the way of protection of their rights to high-quality services, although it is true that the code of practice accompanying the law includes a discussion on issues relating to the care and treatment of voluntary patients and that general health legislation covers all other aspects of the funding, staffing and monitoring of services. Neither provides adequate protection against poor services.

The situation in Northern Ireland is almost identical to that in other parts of the UK and is very similar to countries in Europe that have a publicly funded health care system. The positive aspects are that the public mental health care system is not separated from the general health care system in terms of access and that questions of remuneration (by insurance companies or individuals) have no influence on service development. The negative aspects are related to the lack of resources for community mental health services because of the lack of debate on patients' rights to treatment. For some people, the question of the need to legislate for high-quality services may seem outside the scope of the law, but for the WHO (Regional Office for Europe), these are central to future developments in European legislation for people with mental disorder (Jensen 1995). In a survey carried out in 1992, information on mental health law from 33 countries was collated in an effort to draw together some common strands that might form the basis for future developments in the law. The following discussion draws on this information.

Criteria for involuntary admission to hospital

Most countries have three major criteria for involuntary admission and treatment:

1. the presence of a mental disorder;
2. that the absence of treatment would lead to a deterioration in the person's mental state;
3. that the person presents a serious danger to self or others.

Countries that have all of these criteria include Finland, Sweden, Norway, Denmark, the UK, Russia, Austria and France (for a full discussion, see Jensen 1995). For example, in Finland, new legislation in 1990 contained these criteria, but the patient is admitted in the first instance for 4 days' observation, after which time the chief psychiatrist makes a decision about compulsory treatment conditional on the court's approval. Sweden passed new legislation in 1992, which allows admission for compulsory care for 4 weeks only, after which time a new court decision has to be requested. Norway, which revised its legislation in 1988, allows for 3 weeks of observation by a physician without recourse to the courts, while Denmark, which updated its law in 1989, requires certification by a physician but the carrying out of the commitment by the police and the immediate appointment of a guardian.

Some countries employ only the 'dangerousness' criterion. For example, Belgium, in its 1990 legislation, ruled that 'undesirable behaviour in the ethical, social religious or political sphere cannot be considered as mental illness' and allows involuntary commitment only if the person with a mental disorder presents a danger to self or to the life or integrity of others (Jensen 1995: 9). Similarly, Germany and the Netherlands are very strict about this criterion, and the decision remains with a judge. Legislation in the Netherlands was passed in 1992 after many years of preparation, and the civil rights of patients are highly protected. Admission in the first instance is for 1 week only, after which a judicial review must take place and during which time the patient has the right to refuse treatment. All patients are given an advocate and have the right to submit a request for discharge to the court at any time. Italy is one of the only countries that specifically excludes dangerousness as a criterion for commitment. Based on the original legislation of 1978 (Law 180), the only permitted criterion is that a patient is mentally disordered and needs treatment that he rejects (Jensen 1995: 11).

The authority to authorise an involuntary commitment

Countries in Europe are divided on the question of responsibility for commitment. Recent legislation seems to indicate that there is a trend away from overreliance on the medical profession and back towards the involvement of the judiciary. As we have seen already, Finland, Sweden and Austria allow for initial admission by a doctor but require a judicial decision within a week, while France and Norway allow up to a month for this process. Denmark, Belgium, Italy, the Netherlands, Portugal and Greece all place responsibility for the decision at the judicial level, which can be the chief of police, the mayor or a member of the juridical system. Very few countries leave the responsibility entirely with health and social work professionals. Ireland, Britain, Russia and Israel are among the most prominent of these. Russia, which revised its legislation in 1993, allows for the presentation of a complaint to the court within the first 10 days. In Britain, with legislation dating from 1959 but revised in 1983, the decision to authorise an involuntary admission to hospital treatment is shared jointly by the medical profession (a psychiatrist) and the social work profession (the ASW). There is no involvement of the judiciary in this process, but the rights of the patient are protected through the work of the Mental Health Review Tribunal and the Mental Health Commission (for a discussion, see Barnes *et al.* 1990; Curran and Bingley 1994). Likewise, Israel gives a great deal of authority to health professionals, particularly doctors. Not only is the judiciary *not* involved in ordinary involuntary commitments, but also a patient can be committed for refusing to be examined by a psychiatrist, and in the 6 months following discharge treatment may be given on an outpatient basis without consent (involuntary commitment to community treatment). Surprisingly, this is based not on a old law but on one that was revised in 1991.

Future European legislation

There is a clear trend in most countries in Europe towards an increasing involvement of the judiciary in decisions about involuntary treatment and towards the inclusion of procedures for the review of treatment decisions, including, in some countries, the immediate appointment of patient advocates. Dr Knud Jensen, who carried out the review of legislation for the WHO, is concerned that the criterion of dangerousness, which is also becoming more pronounced in recent legislation, may reflect a social attitude of self-protection rather than patient-centredness. He is also concerned with the absence in most laws of any clause requiring hospital services to be of high quality (similar to general medicine, for example). The third concern, which comes through in his review and which is strikingly obvious when one examines the mental health legislation of many countries, is the lack of protection for the patient who wishes to complain, refuse treatment or ask for a second opinion or a review of the treatment decisions. His final concern is with the underuse of some form of guardianship that is independent of the hospital and the patient's family. Although there are procedures for the use of guardianship in some countries – for example, France and the UK – the role of such a person as an advocate on behalf of the patient is not clear and is not mandatory.

Mental health law in the USA

> Modern mental health law was conceived when courts and commentators recognized that psychiatrists and other mental health professionals often promised society – and the legal system – far more than they were able to deliver. (Wexler 1990: 3)

Wexler is referring to the American system of mental health law, which changed quite significantly during the 1980s. By not deferring to the therapeutic superiority of psychiatry, the laws in most states by 1990 reflected the trend towards civil libertarianism of the 1970s, which was in itself a rejection of an overemphasis on the power of psychiatry during the 1950s. Mental health laws in most states during the 1980s included procedural mechanisms to ensure that people facing civil commitment had adequate legal protection. The promise of therapeutic gain was no longer sufficient to justify the omission of such protection. However, during the 1990s, we have seen a swing back to a reduction in these protective mechanisms and an increase in the power of mental health professionals.

The impact of these ideological changes in the legal system on the lives of people with mental disorders can be charted in the two main areas of mental health care:

1. the delivery of involuntary (compulsory) mental health services (including hospitalisation), which raises the question of treatment rights and the refusal of treatment rights;
2. the delivery of community mental health services.

Involuntary mental health services and the law

Whereas, in most countries, involuntary mental health treatment is synonymous with treatment within a hospital setting, this is not true in the USA. By 1985, 26 states had legislation authorising outpatient commitment (La Fond 1994: 218), and by 1995 this number had risen to 35 (Torrey and Kaplan 1995). As in Europe, the practice of involuntary civil commitment to a mental hospital has its origins in nineteenth-century laws ostensibly aimed at helping individuals with mental disorder – mostly people abandoned by their friends and relatives – who were unable to look after themselves and did not recognise their own need for treatment. Throughout the Western world, hospital treatment was accepted as the best alternative for people with mental disorder, and the hospitalised population in the USA increased from approximately 150,000 in 1900 to 445,000 in 1940 (Grob 1983). It continued to increase until the mid-1950s, reaching a peak of approximately 559,000 patients in state and country mental hospitals in 1955 (La Fond 1994: 209). Most of these patients were legally committed – they were involuntary patients.

With the civil rights movement of the 1960s came a new interest in people confined in substandard psychiatric institutions against their will. The combination of the antipsychiatry movement, a new breed of civil rights lawyers and the arrival of antipsychotic drugs all served to support policy-makers in their decision to lower the mental hospital population by discharging large numbers of patients and supporting more restrictive commitment laws (see Scull 1984). A very important characteristic of this period (the late 1960s and 70s) was the willingness of the courts to 'take on' government agencies and staff, demanding that, if commitment were found necessary, services be geared to the needs of the individual. This led to developments such as the 'least restrictive alternative', which required the state to provide community placements for those who could cope outside hospital. It also led to an expansion of patients' rights within hospital – to more privacy, to less seclusion or restriction of movement, and to an increase in civil and legal rights. Perhaps the most important legal change was to alter the public view on the authority that had previously been held by health professionals. All states limited the authority of mental health professionals to commit people involuntarily to hospital, and many took this power away completely, moving it to judges or juries (La Fond 1994: 212). They also introduced legal procedures for the resolution of cases in which a patient's refusal to take medication could be resolved (Appelbaum and Hoge 1986). Mental health professionals not only found themselves having to justify their professional decisions, but were also increasingly open to lawsuits for the wrongful confinement of a patient and, in some cases, for not fulfilling their 'duty to protect' other citizens from violence by their patients (following the case of *Tarasoff* v. *Regents* [1976], cited in La Fond 1994: 215).

The positive results from this period included a decrease in hospital admission rate for 2–3 years, a greater drive among mental health professionals to find alternative, less restrictive placements for patients, an expansion of resources to community-based services and a recognition of the civil rights of people with serious mental disorder. The negative results included unplanned discharges of large numbers of highly institutionalised people, longer periods in hospital for patients considered dangerous, even if the treatment was not of benefit, an increasing focus on and interest by staff in crisis intervention work rather than long-term treatment, and an increase in psychological stress among mental health professionals, leading to the loss of many good staff in state hospitals.

The civil libertarian ideology of the 1970s, however, soon gave way to the conservatism of the 1980s and 90s. The emphasis now is on community security and the free market economy. The American public have become increasingly intolerant of the dependent poor (including those disabled by physical or mental illness), and they no longer regard government intervention as a threat to individual rights. This has led to a number of changes in mental health law:

> Congress revised the federal insanity test to make it more difficult for criminal defendants to escape criminal responsibility by use of the insanity defense. Eight states changed their insanity test to the same end. Idaho, Montana and Utah abolished the insanity defence entirely... Courts, including federal courts, once the mainstay of the Liberal Era reform, retreated from judicial activism. (La Fond 1994: 217)

In addition to changes in criminal law, many states revised their laws on involuntary commitment during the 1980s, making it easier to admit mentally ill people to hospital. In contrast to the civil libertarianism of the 1970s, the criterion of dangerousness was no longer required. Most states introduced a criterion of 'grave disability', which, although it does not require dangerous behaviour to justify the committal, does imply that, if not treated, the person's mental condition may deteriorate and the person may become dangerous. Outpatient committal runs on parallel lines to inpatient committal. Patients are required to take medication or to attend for therapy at mental health centres. Failure to comply will result in hospitalisation.

The evidence so far is that the number of involuntary hospital admissions has increased in most states, squeezing out voluntary admissions in the state mental health sector. For example, a study carried out in Washington under the auspices of the NIMH showed the immediate impact of a revision in the law in 1979. This change in the law came as a result of the murder by Angus McFarlane of a wealthy Seattle couple in 1978. Angus, their neighbour, had been refused voluntary treatment for his mental disorder at a state mental hospital. The study showed that, between 1977 and 1980, the total number of admissions increased from 959 to 1,511, and the proportion of involuntary admissions increased from 40 per cent to 75 per cent (Durham and La Fond, in Wexler 1990: 126). Similarly, there was a surge in involuntary commitments in New York after Juan Gonzalez killed two passengers and wounded nine others on the Staten Island Ferry in 1986 (La Fond and Durham 1992: 114). This led to severe overcrowding in the state mental hospital sector and reduced the numbers of voluntary admissions.

It is clear that the USA is now back to a situation similar to that in the 1950s, and the public is once again placing its trust in mental health professionals not only to treat people with mental disorders, but also to keep them off the streets and out of sight. Sadly, without the aggressive pro-patient thrust of the courts in the 1970s, it is unlikely that this responsibility will be accompanied by sufficient resources to ensure a good-quality service.

Community mental health services and the law

According to Torrey and Kaplan (1995: 778), if the proportion of state mental hospital patients had remained unchanged since 1966, there would have been 869,000 inpatients in 1992. They estimate that, if one includes the number of patients currently in the psychiatric wards of general hospitals and those in all types of psychiatric facility, there are approximately 750,000 living in the community who would have been likely to be in hospital 40 years ago. Outpatient commitment is one way of ensuring that these people receive support from community mental health services. However, in their national survey of the use of outpatient commitment in those states which have legislation (35 states and the district of Columbia), Torrey and Kaplan found that it remains widely underutilised. This is in spite of the fact that research suggests that it improves treatment outcomes and decreases re-hospitalisation. The main problem seems to be that enforcement of this legislation imposes a level of responsibility not only on the patient to comply, but also on the mental health provider to be accountable and to be interested in the patient's welfare. Unless adequate services are already in place, this level of responsibility cannot be undertaken by the state mental health services.

As outpatient commitment applies only to involuntary patients, the question also has to be asked, how do those who seek treatment on a voluntary basis fare in the community? In other words, do people have a 'right' to voluntary mental health services in the community? Perlin (1994), in his review of the legal literature, laments the lack of interest in this area of law in spite of some good initiatives in the late 1970s. Early 'rights' cases had focused on the 'right to deinstitutionalisation' or the 'right to services in the community' (*Dixon* v. *Weinberger* [1975]; *Halderman* v. *Pennhurst State School and Hospital* [1978], cited in Perlin 1994: 207). Although these cases resulted in some states revising their legislation to include rights to community-based services, there has in general been little further development. Perlin attributes the lack of interest by lawyers, scholars and legislators to a reduction in funding for social programmes during the Reagan and Bush administration years and to an increase in negative public attitudes towards people with mental disorder. Another reason is the anti-therapeutic effect of the patients' rights movement in the 1970s, which was skewed by the 'right to refuse treatment' thrust of many of the cases. Also, litigation taken on behalf of people claiming rights to services has unfortunately not always been successful. For example, in *Arnold* v. *Department of Health Services* [1989], the Arizona Supreme Court ruled that the county and the state were both under statutory obligation to provide mental health care to chronically mentally ill community patients. However, the outcome was quite different in the case of *Rhode Island Department of Mental Health* v. *R.B.* [1988], which found that a mental health facility was under no obligation to accept a patient with a mental disability if the staff did not wish to offer the service to this specific individual (case references cited in Perlin 1994: 205–7).

New legal avenues

The two rays of hope for mental health law lie in the new perspective offered by therapeutic jurisprudence and in the implementation of the

Americans with Disabilities Act 1990 (ADA). If the test of a legal decision is the effect it has on the individual with a mental disorder, the
question of rights then becomes one of a right to an improved life
supported by whatever services are necessary, rather than a right not to
use services and to deteriorate. The kind of issue raised by Professor
Wexler and his colleagues, the champions of therapeutic jurisprudence,
suggest that, at present, many legal decisions do not necessarily benefit
the patient. The law itself can contribute or cause psychological
dysfunction by discouraging needed treatment, by encouraging unnecessary treatment and claims of dysfunction (the compensation
syndrome) and by labelling people so that it may result in people
regarding themselves as lacking in control. According to Wexler
(1990: 5), 'the concept of law-related psychological dysfunction
(juridical psychopathology?) is somewhat similar to the concept of
iatrogenic disease in medicine'. There are many examples of the
process. Therapy may be delayed or rendered futile because laws
restricting confidentiality may cause the patient not to divulge important feelings or behaviours to the therapist. On the other hand, treatment may be lengthened and a 'sick role' maintained for longer than
necessary by the use of the incompetence to stand trial principle. More
seriously perhaps, the use of the insanity defence may backfire and,
instead of leading to the individual receiving treatment, it may result in
irresponsible behaviour in the future.

Used positively, the law can have therapeutic outcomes. For example
the 'right to treatment' case of *Wyatt* v. *Stickney* [1972] led to improve-
ments in staffing levels and mental health facilities (cited in Wexler
1990: 9). Research on the outcomes of involuntary commitment and
treatment has shown that there is little evidence of the efficacy of any
treatment mode under conditions of compulsion (La Fond and Durham
1992), evidence that provides justification for the reluctance of many
lawyers to regard commitment as a positive step for their clients. La
Fond argues that the only justifiable reason for commitment is, therefore, that of dangerousness. In his vision for the future, Wexler suggests
that law students should be part of the psychiatric team, that the court
hearing could be therapeutic for the client, and that all legal professionals involved in these cases should view themselves as part of the
therapeutic process.

It is to be hoped that this new legal perspective will make an impact
on policy-makers and providers of mental health services. Mental
health activists and advocates are encouraged by this new legal interest
and also by the impetus coming from the ADA. By moving mental

disorders into the conceptual framework of disability, the issues are further clarified. If all disabled people have a right to participate equally in the social and civil opportunities available to others, their increasing marginalisation cannot be justified (for a discussion see Haimowitz 1991). At best, the ADA will be used as a 'powerful weapon for litigators seeking to advance the cause of mentally disabled individuals in community settings' (Perlin 1994: 204). At worst, it will make no impact at all on the lives of people with a mental disorder.

A gendered impact?

Although only a small proportion of the total population of those in contact with psychiatric services are receiving treatment on a compulsory basis, recent research in both the UK and the USA points to the fact that certain sections of the population are more at risk than others. As in other areas of public policy, the impact has clear gender patterns. Unfortunately, it is rare in the UK for a researcher to distinguish between those who were admitted on a voluntary basis and those who were not. This is probably due to the fact that voluntary patients constitute the majority of the inpatient population and little attention has been paid to the minority, except when specific cases are brought to the attention of the Mental Health Review Tribunal or Mental Health Commission, both of which have special responsibility for 'detained' patients (involuntary commitments). In the USA, the situation is different, and the proportion of commitments has increased in the state mental health sector. The trends, in terms of gender and race, are similar. Women may use psychiatric services more often than men, but they are much less likely than men to be admitted on a compulsory basis. A national audit of new long-stay patients in the UK in 1992 revealed that the proportion of men in this population has increased since 1972 (from 48 per cent to 57 per cent) and that the proportion of the total NLS population who were 'detained' at the time of the audit has also increased (from 9 per cent in 1972 to 29 per cent in 1992):

> Young NLS patients (aged 18–34) were predominantly single males, often with a history of violence or criminality, and much more likely to be formally detained (35 per cent) than either the older NLS patients (16 per cent) or the proportion of all psychiatric patients admitted on a Section (about 6 per cent). (Lelliot *et al.* 1994: 167)

The authors of the audit suggest a number of reasons for the increase in involuntary commitments among this NLS population, including the probability that less disturbed patients are now more likely to be discharged than they were 20 years ago and that smaller psychiatric units, geared towards short-term admissions, are less able to control the more troublesome patients without the backing of the law than were the older, larger mental hospitals. These reasons are based on their findings that 'legally detained patients differed from voluntary patients in being more violent, having more positive symptoms, more often abusing alcohol and drugs, and being more sexually assaultive' (p. 166).

In another study, an audit of psychiatric admissions in two deprived London districts, the focus was on gender and race (Bebbington *et al.* 1994; Flannigan *et al.* 1994a, 1994b). Of the total number of admissions, 26 per cent were involuntary. When compared with voluntary admissions, these were more likely to be young, male and from the black Caribbean community. Among the Afro-Caribbean admissions, there were gender differences. For Afro-Caribbean men, the involuntary admission rate was almost 13 per cent higher than for white men in Hammersmith and Fulham, and seven times higher in south Southwark. For Afro-Caribbean women, the rate was five times the rate for white women, although overall admission rates were no higher for black women than for white women. Finally, nearly half of all admissions from the black Caribbean community were involuntary, compared with only one-fifth for admissions from the white community (Bebbington *et al.* 1994: 747). This may be only one study in a small area in England, but it confirms the findings of other studies (see Barnes *et al.* 1990: 170; Rogers and Pilgrim 1996: 138) and underlines the need for further analysis of the use of compulsory clauses in mental health legislation in respect of minority populations. These studies are indeed taking place, but the issue of gender is not always adequately addressed. For example, in a study of 439 patients with psychotic disorders in London, the higher level of risk of compulsory admissions among black patients was confirmed – 'nearly half of the white patients were detained under the act compared with 70 per cent and 69 per cent of black Caribbean and black African respectively'(Davies *et al.* 1996: 533). Although females formed over half of the research population (53 per cent), none of the findings in relation to gender difference in the rate of committal was reported. This was also true in a study of all acute psychiatric admissions (a total of 1,534 patients) to the central district of Manchester during a 4-year period from 1984 to 1987 (Thomas *et al.* 1993). The admissions were divided into three ethnic groups – European, Afro-Caribbean and Asian – among whom there were almost equal numbers of males and females except for the Afro-Caribbean group, in which there were twice as many males as females. As with other studies, the findings showed a significantly higher proportion of Afro-Caribbeans and Asians admitted with psychosis, but the Afro-Caribbean patients had the highest risk of being admitted on a compulsory basis (involuntary commitment). Although information was gathered on gender, the numbers were considered too small to include in the discussion. Hopefully, this will not happen in future research as American studies show that there are important differences in male:female patterns of admission.

In a Philadelphia study of 2,200 patients admitted on an involuntary basis, most of whom were between 25 and 34 years of age, men were in the majority (58 per cent). Most of the admissions (69 per cent) were of African Americans, and the most frequent diagnosis was schizophrenia (Sanguineti *et al.* 1996). The predominance of the diagnosis of schizophrenia (which was also found in the Inner London study of Bebbington *et al.* 1994) surprised the authors, who expected alcohol and drug dependence to be a major consideration in emergency admissions. They suggest that allocating resources to substance abuse services may not necessarily reduce these admissions. Other studies in the USA, which are beginning to explore the interaction effect of gender and race in relation to psychiatric treatment, indicate that, as men are more prone to treatments based on risk of dangerousness, they are more at risk of involuntary commitment than women and that, within this gender category, certain ethnic groups are considered more at risk of this than others.

Although we have only discussed a few studies here, they are sufficient to show the importance of examining not only the gendered nature of policy itself, but also gender as a variable in analysing the impact of all aspects of mental health policy. There is no doubt that the use of legal powers to admit people involuntarily to treatment disproportionately affects those groups of people in the community who are the most disenfranchised. Among the poor, men are seen to be more dangerous than women, younger men more dangerous than older men, and black men more dangerous than white men. The law is being used not just to ensure that these people receive treatment, but rather to protect the public from perceived risk. It is hoped that, in the future, it will be again be used more effectively to protect the individual with a mental disorder.

9

Crime and Mental Disorder

> Literature and art have historically reflected the view that the mentally disordered are violent. Both civil and criminal law around the world recognize that some mentally disordered persons must be restrained because they pose threats to themselves and/or to others. (Hodgins 1993a: 3)

Is there a link?

Studies on the relationship between mental disorder and crime range through those which compare psychiatric patients with their counterparts in the community, follow-up studies of discharged psychiatric patients, studies of psychiatric inpatients and studies of individuals who have been exempted from criminal responsibility on the grounds of a mental disorder, to studies on the mental health of prison populations and, finally, birth cohort studies. The results have been as wide ranging as the research topics. For example, research in New York in the early 1990s, comparing psychiatric patients with a control group in the community, found that there was evidence of a higher level of arrests among most patients – 7 per cent of the community cohort were arrested, as against 6 per cent of first contact patients, 12 per cent of former patients and 12 per cent of repeat treatment patients (Hodgins 1993a: 5). There was also evidence that the arrests of patients were more often for violent behaviour and felonies than was the case for those in the community group. In other words, they found evidence that people with a psychiatric history were more likely to commit a violent crime than were their counterparts in the community. However, although the validity of this study is not in question, it is clear that it would be foolish to extrapolate from it to other countries and other police forces. This is especially true now as the police in New York operate a policy of zero-tolerance towards crime and vagrancy and as grounds for the commitment of people with a mental disorder have been broadened.

Follow-up studies of people discharged from psychiatric hospitals are numerous, although they present similar problems about the generalisability of the findings. These studies (mostly carried out in the 1970s) have consistently shown that discharged males are at greater risk of offending than are males in the general population, that differences in the rates of offending are greater for violent than non-violent crime, and that those with schizophrenia are at a higher risk of crime (Hodgins 1993a). Further research to explore the link between current disorder and future violence has concentrated on psychiatric inpatients, focusing on patterns of aggressive behaviour and assessments of potential dangerousness after discharge. There are numerous debates in the American literature on the possibility of predicting dangerousness because this prediction can have a significant impact on legal decisions. For example, in spite of arguments to the contrary, the Supreme Court in the case of *Schall* v. *Martin* [1984] rejected 'the contention that it is impossible to predict future violent behavior' (cited in Litwack *et al.* 1993: 246). In their review of a number of studies on clinical and other evaluations of dangerousness, Thomas Litwack and his colleagues did not totally agree with this judgement and concluded that these evaluations 'should be viewed as assessments of risk rather than as predictions of violence'. As such, they are useful to clinicians and policy-makers because they provide information on which decisions not to discharge patients can be based. However, as predictors of future crime, they cannot be fully tested as this would involve discharging or releasing people who are deemed highly dangerous into the community. There are some long-term research projects in the USA, such as the MacArthur Risk Assessment Study being carried out by H.J. Steadman and colleagues, which aim to measure the accuracy of predictions in terms of later arrests and re-hospitalisations (Litwack *et al.* 1993: 268; Monahan and Steadman 1994). The situation at present is that, until there are some more convincing arguments from these studies, the prediction of dangerousness still remains open to question.

We are alerted to the gendered nature of some of the assessments of dangerousness by Coontz *et al.* (1994), who studied the assessment process in a psychiatric emergency room of a large urban hospital in the USA (see also Newhill *et al.* 1995). The research question arose from earlier studies, which found that clinicians could predict the involvement of a male patient in a violent incident over a specific period with a certain level of accuracy, but that predictions of female involvement in violent crime were not significantly better than a random prediction. Based on the knowledge that gender affects both lay and professional judgements and that violence is stereotypically more closely associated with males than females, the researchers hypothesised that there would be more references to violence in inter- actions between clinicians and males (than in those with females) in the assessment interviews. Their findings clearly support their hypoth- esis. Not only were there more references to violence in interviews with male patients, but also, as clinicians initiated discussions on violence twice as many times as did patients, the gendered assump- tions about violent behaviour were clearly part of the clinician's cultural belief system:

> Gender norms act as a framework for organizing and assessing information, deciding what information should be asked about, presented, followed up, and discussed. As our findings show, an assumption is made throughout the assess- ment process by clinicians and patients alike that violence is a male character- istic... Even among the patients who came to the emergency room following a violent incident, there is evidence showing that clinicians pursue the topic of violence in somewhat greater detail with men than with women. (Coontz *et al.* 1994: 375)

As a result of this gendered perception of violent behaviour, assess- ments of dangerousness are likely to underestimate the potential involvement of women in violent acts, even in situations where the individuals have a mental disorder and a history of violent behaviour.

Another major focus of research on the link between offending or dangerousness and mental disorder is the mental health of people in prison. Studies from the USA suggest that there is a higher level of psychiatric morbidity and a higher prevalence of major mental disor- ders in the prison population than in the community at large (Coid 1984: 79; Hodgins 1993a: 7). However, the definitions used in many of these studies are not universally validated and leave the findings open to question in terms of their generalisability. In contrast, in other studies in Missouri, Perth (Australia) and southern England, which used standardised assessment procedures (such as the DSM or ICD), the levels of psychotic illness were not found to be any higher than in the general population (Coid 1984: 79). Although women form only a small proportion of the prison population (between 3 and 4 per cent in Britain), they are the subject of a great deal of research. Early studies found a high degree of economic and social disadvantage in the female prison population in both the UK and the USA and ruled out a high level of serious mental disorder. Three psychiatric surveys, carried out at Holloway women's prison in England between 1962 and 1990, found a high level of psychiatric morbidity but not of major mental disorder. They suggest that 'about half the population suffers from some degree of psychiatric disorder, [and] it appears that the nature of this disturbance is largely in the field of personality disorder, drug and alcohol abuse and self harm' (d'Orban, in Gunn and Taylor 1993: 615). In both the USA and Canada, research also found high rates of psychiatric disorder, and this was again explained by personality disorder, alcoholism and drug dependence. In studies that compared male with female prisoners, females were found to have a higher level of psychiatric disorder. One excellent example is the study carried out by Maden *et al.* (1994) on 25 per cent of all women serving a prison sentence in Britain. This study found high levels of psychiatric disorder but a low rate of psychosis among women in prison. The authors explain this latter finding in terms of a criminal justice system that favours a 'psychiatric disposal' for women and thus diverts as many as possible from the criminal justice system. Allen (1987) argues that there was a consistent trend in court decisions on female offenders in Britain between 1950 and 1985 – the rate at which women were dealt with under sections of the law on mental disorder was twice that for men. Perhaps society expects women to be more prone to mental disorder than men, resulting in a situation in the criminal justice system (as in the medical system) of an overestimation of psychiatric conditions among women and an underestimation among men.

Jeremy Coid, in his review of 11 surveys of psychiatric morbidity in both male and female prisons carried out in the 1970s and 80s, offers another explanation for the higher level of mental disorder in the prison population than in the population in general. He suggests that certain groups of people may be more at risk of imprisonment than others because of the lack of community support services rather than any inherent predisposition to crime:

> Criminal populations do show high levels of psychopathology as compared with the general population, but this excess is based primarily on the finding of alcoholism, drug dependence and personality disorder... the strong suggestion that the mentally handicapped and epileptics may be more likely to be imprisoned than the general population is clearly a disconcerting finding, which questions the adequacy of their care and supervision in the community. (Coid 1984: 81)

Coid goes on to suggest not only that some people in the community (such as people with a learning disability) are more vulnerable to imprisonment, but also that the higher level of psychiatric morbidity in the prison population might be the result of the negative effects of imprisonment rather than any inherent predisposition in prisoners. In other words, we do not know which comes first, the mental disorder or the crime and consequent imprisonment. In general, it seems to be accepted that major psychiatric disorder is no more common in the prison population than in the general population, but many prisoners have personality and behavioural problems, substance dependence and neurotic disorders (Gelder *et al*. 1989: 876).

More focused studies on specific groups of offenders are more useful to mental health professionals (see Hodgins 1993: 6). In Scandinavia, where all individuals who are arrested for homicide are assessed by a psychiatric team, researchers found that, among homicide offenders in Copenhagen, over a 25-year period, 20 per cent of the men and 44 per cent of the women were diagnosed as psychotic. Among those found to be psychotic, 41 per cent of the men and 13 per cent of the women were substance abusers, and 89 per cent of the men and 21 per cent of women were intoxicated at the time of the homicide (Hodgins 1993a: 9). This finding is supported by evidence from other studies of a higher prevalence of substance abuse and major mental disorder among homicide offenders than in the rest of the prison population.

One of the early birth cohort studies, also carried out in Scandinavia, assessed 11,540 men born in Copenhagen in 1953 and still alive in 1975. Information on the diagnoses of mental disorder was taken from the central psychiatric register in Denmark. Of the men with no mental disorder, 35 per cent had been convicted of at least one offence. Higher rates of conviction were recorded for all those with a record of psychiatric admission: 44 per cent of those with a major mental disorder, 83 per cent of those admitted for substance abuse and 51 per cent of those with other diagnoses (study by Ortmann 1981, in Hodgins 1993a). Sheilagh Hodgins carried out a second study, using information from the Swedish Metropolitan Project, which followed 15,117 men and women born in Stockholm in 1953, in combination with data from criminal records held on the National Policy Register in 1983. The findings point to great differences in rates of crime when gender, age and type of mental disorder are considered. Whereas 29 per cent of men with no disorder committed a crime, 48 per cent of those with a major mental disorder, 90 per cent of those with a diagnosis of substance dependence and 34 per cent of those with other mental disorders had done so. The figures for women were much lower, but the patterns were similar. Among women with no mental disorder, 5 per cent committed a crime, whereas 18 per cent of those with a major mental disorder, 64 per cent of those with a diagnosis of substance abuse and 10 per cent of those with other mental disorders had done so (Hodgins 1993a: 10–11). The findings with regard to violent crime showed that men with a major mental disorder were more than twice as likely (15 per cent) to have committed a violent crime than those with no disorder (6 per cent), and that those with substance dependence diagnoses were represented over eight times as often (49 per cent) as those with no disorder. Among women, those with a major mental disorder were 12 times more likely (6 per cent) to commit a violent crime that those with no disorder (0.5 per cent), and those with a diagnosis of substance abuse were 50 times more likely (25 per cent) to do so than those who had no disorder. The contrast between women with and without mental disorder or with a substance dependence diagnosis show that some women are indeed at a high risk of committing a violent crime.

However, a word of caution is necessary about the research carried out in Scandinavia. It is unlikely that the findings can be applied to countries with different legal systems and crime profiles. In countries where there are higher levels of crime and/or more substance abuse, for example the USA, the correlation between major mental disorder and offending becomes insignificant. In 1993, the number of prisoners in state and federal prisons in the USA was estimated to be nearly one million – almost three times the number in 1980. In the same year, a report from the National Coalition on the Mentally Ill in the Criminal Justice System estimated that 15–30 per cent of the prison population suffered from a mental disorder and that 5–10 per cent had a learning or developmental disability (Watkins and Callicutt 1997: 298). In other words, the majority of prisoners in the USA do *not* have a mental disorder.

Gender and crime

Any conclusions drawn on the link between crime and mental disorder have to be placed within the wider context of the level of crime in the community and the gender patterns among offenders. In contrast to psychiatric statistics, criminal statistics have long shown a predominance of men – 'one of the most striking features of crime is that it is overwhelmingly a male activity' (d'Orban, in Gunn and Taylor 1993: 599). In his review of gender differences in crime statistics in the UK, d'Orban suggests that there are not only numerical differences, but also differences in the kinds of crime that women and men commit. In

England and Wales in 1986, men were arrested for 83 per cent of indictable offences and for 76 per cent of summary offences (excluding motoring offences). The male:female ratio for indictable offences has remained pretty consistent over the past decade at 5:1.

The predominance of men over women in crime statistics has been a feature of many countries during the past two centuries (Daly 1994; Heidensohn 1996; Morris 1987; Naffine 1987). However, the ratio is not static over time, and the indications are that, in Europe, female crime has declined, probably because of the fact that certain crimes associated with women have either been decriminalised (prostitution) or are not as common (infanticide) in the twentieth century. An examination of the offences committed by women in Britain shows also that it would be wrong to assume a constant ratio between men and women in relation to different crimes. Some offences (such as soliciting and infanticide) can only be committed by women, and others (for example, sexual offences) are rarely committed by women. Women form the majority of offenders in some crimes – offences that are related to children, such as cruelty or neglect, or failure to send children to school. In addition, there are some offences in which women feature frequently, for example, shoplifting and child abduction. In his analysis of the 1986 statistics d'orban found that:

> The male:female ratio for the various groups of indictable offences was, in decreasing order – 82:1 for sex offences, 25.5:1 for burglary, 21:1 for robbery, 12:1 for criminal damage, approximately 9:1 for violence against the person, just over 7:1 for drug offences, 3.5:1 for fraud and forgery, and just over 3:1 for theft and handling stolen goods. (d'Orban, in Gunn and Taylor 1993: 600)

One of the interesting features of women's crimes, in the context of our discussion on mental disorder, is that the age profile is different from that of men. Adolescence is the peak time for crime for both sexes, but a higher proportion of women appear in the crime statistics in the over 50-year-old group. For both men and women in the 'older' category, alcoholism and affective disorders are found to be characteristic. Men are likely to have offended previously, while for women it is often their first conviction. Although the menopause has been put forward as a cause of midlife female offending, there is no evidence that this is the case. The debate on a possible link between the menstrual cycle and female crime, which had a high level of credibility in the nineteenth century, is no longer a popular one. Although premenstrual syndrome is often used as a defence in modern courts, the evidence is that other diagnoses of disturbed affect could be used in the same cases. However, there are some examples in the current literature of the kind of attitude that prevailed in the not too distant past:

> It is accepted that some women become unaccountably argumentative and aggressive during their paramenstruum and violent activity is well recorded. The consequences may be serious, ranging from assault and non accidental injury to children... to homicidal acts. (Vanezis 1991: 12)

In his favour, it has to be said that Dr Vanezis is merely reviewing the literature on menstruation and crime, and he does acknowledge in his conclusion that it may be used as an excuse by women offenders and is still open to question as a cause. However, what is most interesting about his words are that they clearly show how powerful the stereotypical pictures of male and female conduct are and how they might affect the legal process.

As Heidensohn (1996) and Walklate (1995) have shown, stereotypical notions of gender-appropriate behaviour apply at all levels of the judicial system. As we have already seen, predictions of violent behaviour are often inaccurate for women because it is not judged to be as probable as for men. There is also evidence that women are treated more leniently within the justice system. In Britain in 1992, of the males arrested for indictable offences, 36 per cent were cautioned compared with 61 per cent of females (Hedderman and Hough 1994). The same study of statistics showed that women are far less likely than men to receive a custodial sentence for almost all offences, that prison sentences are shorter than those for men and that, even in cases of domestic homicide, women are at lower risk of imprisonment than men. For example, between 1984 and 1992, only 4 per cent of males as against 23 per cent of females indicted for homicide were acquitted on all charges:

> Of those found guilty, 80 per cent of the women, compared with 61 per cent of the men, were found guilty of the lesser charge of manslaughter; and more than two-thirds of the men convicted of manslaughter received a prison sentence compared with less than half the women. (Hedderman and Hough 1994: 3)

This brings us neatly to a discussion of one of the crimes in which the differences in both the nature of the crime and the sentencing are greatest – that of homicide.

Homicide

In his classic study of homicide in Philadelphia in the 1950s, Wolfgang found that the female murder rate was a little over one-tenth of that for males, and that the differential was constant for both white and non-white ethnic groups. There are also a number of differences in the victims of the homicide and in the factors that lead up to the crime. Homicides by women more often involve friends or relatives, alcohol consumption is not involved as often as for men, and the presence of a mental disorder is more common for women than men. The most striking feature of homicide by women is how often it involves either a partner or a child. Studies in both Scotland and England during the 1970s showed that approximately 80 per cent of charges of murder for women related to a family member, whereas for men it was around 30 per cent (d'Orban, in Gunn and Taylor 1993).

The killing of a child by a mother has always been treated with leniency in the courts as it assumed that the instinct to preserve one's child's life is stronger than that to destroy it, even in dire circum-stances. Historically, abnormality of female behaviour was often linked to the reproductive system so it was not difficult for legislators to make the decision to excuse a woman from her crime on the grounds of mental disorder. In my own research on the Central Criminal Lunatic Asylum in Dundrum, Ireland, in the nineteenth century, I found that great sympathy was expressed for women who were sent there for infanticide and they were, in general, released fairly quickly (Prior 1997). An example of the rhetoric of the time comes from the report of the Inspector of Lunacy, Dr Francis White, who was a specialist in mental disorder:

> A young woman, of respectable condition, and the mother of three children, who, from fright at her last confinement, was attacked by puerperal mania, and destroyed her infant. She is now, and has been for about eighteen months, restored to reason, her husband and family are urgent for her liberation. (6th Report of the Inspectors of Lunacy 1852–3: 16)

The majority of the women committed to Dundrum for homicide during the nineteenth century had killed children. Similarly, in Britain at the time, the killing of children was the most common form of homi-cide among women, and it was a common occurrence. In the middle of the nineteenth century, 61 per cent of all homicide victims in England were under 1 year old (Bluglass and Bowden 1990: 524). In modern times, children still continue to be at a high risk of being the victims of homicide, and women continue to be the main perpetrators of the crime. Between 1977 and 1986, children under 16 years of age constituted 15 per cent of all homicides in Britain, and the majority of these were killed by their mothers (d'Orban, in Gunn and Taylor 1993: 610). International studies confirm that children under 1 year old are still at the highest risk (Bourget and Labelle 1992). Current research refutes the nineteenth-century belief that mental disorder associated with childbirth was almost always present in these cases. Although many women who kill their children have psychiatric problems, puerperal psychotic illness accounts for fewer than 10 per cent of cases. Low intelligence and severe social and economic problems outweigh psychiatric symptoms in most of the remaining cases.

Research on assessments of the psychological state of both men and women who have committed homicide fail to prove that mental disorder is the main causal factor. However, there are some consistent trends. As we already know, males predominate in homicide statistics, outnumbering women in proportions varying between 6:1 and 9:1. The majority are between 20 and 40 years of age, and their profile is consistent:

> In adolescent offenders, the emerging profile consists of a personal background of addiction, psychiatric contact, forensic involvement, and developmental problems. Studies on adult, adolescent, and child murderers almost unanimously report a background of serious family disorganization or maladjustment. (Bourget and Labelle 1992: 662)

This profile of adolescent murderers could equally be applied to older male perpetrators, who are often from the most disadvantaged sections of society. Nevertheless, although mental disorder cannot be said to be the most significant cause of homicide or other violent crime, neither can it be dismissed as a cause as it is clear that it does play a part in a certain percentage of those crimes.

How to deal with the offender with a mental disorder during his or her confinement to prison and how to prevent this person from offending in the future are problems to which most countries find different solutions. These solutions depend on a number of factors, including the size of the problem population, the adequacy of the prison system to cope with criminals with or without mental disorder, the relationship between mainstream psychiatric services and the prison service, and lastly public attitude to both crime and mental disorder.

Services for offenders with mental disorders

When lunatic asylums were set up in Europe in the eighteenth and nineteenth centuries, it was often in response to demands within the prison system and the hospital system that people with mental disorders were disruptive in both settings. In England, the earliest attempt to cater specifically for 'criminal lunatics' was the opening of two criminal wings at Bethlem Hospital in 1816 (Bluglass and Bowden 1990: 61–101; Walker 1968). This was followed by the opening of Fisherton House, near Salisbury, in 1848, but this did not solve the problem of the growing population of people defined as criminally insane. In Ireland, during the same period, there was a strong lobby from the prison system for the establishment of one central criminal lunatic asylum. In his evidence to the Select Committee on the State of the Lunatic Poor in Ireland 1843, Dr Francis White, Inspector of Prisons (who subsequently became the first Inspector of Lunacy in Ireland), showed his support for a central institution:

> Solid Objections exist to Criminal Lunatics being received into District Asylums which never were intended for Prisons. As there is a Want of Room for Pauper Lunatics, it would save expense to remove all the Criminal Lunatics to one Spot... The Advantages of bringing together all the Criminal Lunatics under the immediate Eye of the Governor is obvious; their Security could readily be provided for, and Strangers could be prohibited from visiting that Department from Motives of Curiosity. (Select Committee on the State of the Lunatic Poor in Ireland, 1843: xxv)

The building of a central facility for all offenders with mental disorder was seen then, as it is still today, as one possible solution to the problem. This was the chosen solution in Ireland, where a Central Criminal Lunatic Asylum was built at Dundrum in 1850 with accommodation for 150 patients (Prior 1997). The centralised solution was also chosen in England, and Broadmoor Central Criminal Lunatic Asylum was opened in 1863, with accommodation for 500 patients. Ireland continues to uphold this policy, and the institution at Dundrum has been renamed the Central Mental Hospital, housing offenders who have committed serious crimes and have been found to have a mental disorder, as well as offenders from the ordinary prison system who are deemed to be in need of secure psychiatric treatment. In Britain, in spite of a number of reports advocating the expansion of regional secure units, the centralised option is still the model of treatment, most of the available beds being in the three 'special hospitals' – Broadmoor, Ashworth and

Rampton. In 1996, there were 1,506 patients in these three hospitals, each of which has a capacity of around 500. Of the total number, only 238 (16 per cent) were women (Eaton and Humphries 1996: 36).

One of the problems of having separate specialist hospitals is that they can become isolated from mainstream psychiatry and suffer a lowering of service quality as a result. Reports on the British secure 'special hospitals' 'have demonstrated fairly unremitting evidence of, to say the least, custodial patient care which sometimes lacked therapy and, at worst, cruelty' (Eastman 1993: 5). As the aim of any intervention with people who are assessed as having psychiatric problems must be to help them to improve their mental state, services that are professionally isolated are of questionable value. To reduce this isolation, the Butler Interim Report of 1974 recommended the establishment of medium secure units (RSUs) on a regional basis to cater for patients who were 'persistent absconders and represented a risk to the public, or who were seriously disruptive to hospital regimes, or who exhibited persistent and impulsive violence (Eastman 1993: 6). However, the development of these units has been slow and fraught with difficulties. In 1991, only 597 permanent beds existed in this kind of unit, a figure that was 1,400 beds short of the Butler target and 900 beds short of the Reed Committee target of 30 beds per million (Eastman 1993: 8). Since then, there has been some expansion of beds in medium secure units that operate under contractual arrangements with the NHS (Bartlett 1993; Fernando *et al.* 1998). These are seen as a partial answer to the problem caused by the decrease in the number of ordinary psychiatric beds (which often included locked wards in large secure hospitals), a problem that is highlighted each time the court looks for a secure environment within easy reach of an offender's own home. In the Netherlands, the move towards a fully decentralised system of treatment of offenders with mental disorders has already taken place. There are eight hospitals for TBS patients (*Ter Beschikking Stelling* – detention at the government's pleasure) with a total capacity of approximately 450 beds (Derks *et al.* 1993). The system of treating offenders has to be understood within the context of Dutch law in which the question of responsibility for a crime is central to understanding decisions on punishment. As in other countries, a person may commit a crime without being held fully responsible for it. However, what is different about the Netherlands is that degrees of responsibility for the crime are distinguished and that certain conditions (including mental illness) may be accepted as reasons for its absence. Another feature of Dutch law is that, unlike the situation in other countries, the purpose of the 'Insanity Law' of

1841 was to prevent the 'criminal lunatic' from having to be put on trial or imprisoned in the first place (Derks *et al.* 1993: 218). Because this law did not empower courts to prevent the discharge from an ordinary mental hospital of someone who might be dangerous, another law for the treatment of 'psychopaths' was passed in 1928. Even in this law, it was clear that retaliation by society against the offender could not be the reason for locking him up. All of these ideological strands are clear in the current legislation, which was revised in 1986 and under which current TBS patients are held. Offenders are sent to one of the six secure units, and their length of stay is determined, to a large extent, by the seriousness of the crime. In cases that do not involve violence against persons or against the integrity of others, the maximum duration of treatment is 4 years. For all other (serious) crimes, detention is legal as long as treatment is not complete, which can be for life. However, every case has to be reviewed by the court every 1–2 years, and the decision of the court is not always that of the mental health professionals who have been conducting the treatment programme. These differences of opinion often reflect the public attitude, which, according to Derks *et al.* (1993), has become increasingly negative towards any kind of coercive treatment. This attitude is being demonstrated in a movement from some consumer groups for the introduction of an advocacy system into forensic psychiatric hospitals similar to that which is already in place in ordinary psychiatric hospitals.

The Dutch system is extremely manageable when one considers that all their hospitals have what many mental health professionals would regard as the luxury of relatively small numbers of patients – approximately 60–100. Countries with larger populations claim that they cannot afford to fund this kind of approach. Germany is an example of a large country that gives a great deal of autonomy to local government in all areas of public policy. In common with other aspects of health policy, the kind of care varies from state to state and depends on both the population patterns of the local area and the political ideology of local policy-makers:

> Both the urban states like Berlin, Bremen, and Hamburg, and the more centralistic oriented states like Hesse, Lower Saxony, and parts of North Rhine-Westfalia, have opted for a central institution for the treatment of mentally ill offenders; whereas states like Bavaria, Baden-Wurttemberg, and Rhineland-Pfalz created regional departments of forensic psychiatry within their state hospitals. (Nedopil and Ottermann 1993: 246)

As one would expect, the central institutions are larger (200–350 patients) than the regional units (40–180 patients). Each has the advantages and disadvantages of its size – the large central institutions can offer specialist programmes of education and therapy, and regional units offer the advantage of maintaining links between the offender and his family, making future integration easier. The major problem in the smaller regional unit is that of security, a problem that led to the building of the central maximum security hospital in Bavaria in 1973 (Nedopil and Ottermann 1993). As in other countries, the numbers of offenders requiring psychiatric treatment is increasing slowly but steadily, and among them, the proportion of offenders with substance dependence has been the most significant. Because of perceived increases in violent crime, public opinion is in favour of high-security environments for dangerous offenders, but there is resistance to the building of such a facility in most areas. It will be interesting to see whether the trend in Bavaria, towards a new centralisation of offenders, requiring maximum security, will spread to other parts of Germany.

The USA

Anyone who is looking for a range of solutions to the problem of how to treat offenders with mental disorder (referred to as 'mentally disordered offenders' in the American literature) has only to travel through the USA. Because of the vastness of the territory, different state laws and the involvement of the private sector in the provision of health and correctional services, the services can be quite different from one part of the country to another. In his review of services, Norman Poythress found 189 agencies listed in a 1986 directory of facilities providing treatment for mentally disordered offenders (Poythress 1993: 53). At that time, almost all of the agencies were publicly funded and operated, and included hospitals, clinics, detention centres and assessment centres. Since then, there has been a trend towards privatisation in some states, although the bulk of facilities are still state run. The general context within which the services operate has also been changed by two other factors, the reintroduction of the death penalty in an increasing number of states, and the abolition of the insanity defence (not guilty by reason of mental disease or defect) in some states, including Idaho and Utah.

The services vary in a number of ways, including types of service provided, budgets and organisational structures, and target populations for service provision. All states have some kind of correctional facility but only some offer pre-trial assessments. Alabama, Michigan and Virginia are among those which provide extensive pre-trial and pre-sentencing assessments, while Florida relies on private mental health practitioners for these assessments (Poythress 1993). Mental health services for mentally disordered offenders can be jointly provided by a department of correction and a department of mental health, or transferred directly from the courts to the responsibility of a department of mental health. Among the targeted groups are mentally disordered sex offenders, for whom special treatment programmes are provided in some states, including Florida and Massachusetts.

As we saw in relation to Germany, the question of centralising or regionalising services often has to do with population density and patterns of urbanisation. Small states or states with small populations, such as Mississippi, Alabama and Georgia, have single high-security hospitals for adult male mentally disordered offenders. Larger states and those with large urban centres (such as California and New York) are less centralised, and a number of institutions provide services either as a specialist service or as part of a large general psychiatric hospital. However, even in states where services look similar from an organisational point of view, the financial resources devoted to them is often quite different:

> Kirby Forensic Psychiatric Center, a hospital in the New York system, currently has approximately 330 staff positions for 160 inpatient beds with a budget between 12–13 million dollars. Alabama's Taylor Hardin Secure Medical Facility, on the other hand, has approximately 220 staff positions for a slightly smaller capacity of 137 beds, but a budget of only 5.5 million dollars. (Poythress 1993: 54)

Because of the differences in financial resources devoted to these two facilities, the kinds of programme on offer must be substantively different. We will look later at some of the services in one of the large special institutions for mentally disordered offenders in California. At the federal level, there has been an increase in the number of staff with mental health training, and these are used in assessments of the mental health of prisoners, in their treatment and, more recently, in planning the prison environment to reduce risk factors (Watkins and Callicutt 1997: 299). One of the additional strains on the federal system is the cultural diversity among the prisoners – one-third of them are foreign nationals. This has led to special cultural programmes for certain population groups, such as the long-term Cuban Units housing people who are awaiting repatriation to their own countries. These programmes are in addition to specialist programmes for women and for issues including substance dependence, suicide prevention, sex offending and HIV/AIDS. For all prisoners with mental health problems, management at a local level is the first option. It is only if the mental disorder is chronic or difficult to manage that prisoners are sent to one of five modern mental health centres run by the Federal Bureau of Prisons. Once stabilised, the prisoner is returned to his own local unit. On a positive note, the authorities claim that, in spite of the increasing level of substance dependence and violence among the prison population, fewer than 2 per cent are prescribed any form of psychotropic drug and fewer than 1 per cent are prescribed major antipsychotic medication (Watkins and Callicutt 1997: 300).

Inside 'special hospitals'

Just to give the reader a flavour of what happens inside some of the hospitals specially designated for the care and treatment of offenders with mental disorders, we will look briefly a the specific situation of women in the 'special hospitals' in the UK and at the men in Atascadero State Hospital (ASH) in the USA.

The insight into women in 'special prisons' in the UK comes from recent research by Eaton and Humphries (1996). Women are in the minority in the three 'special hospitals' in Britain. In August 1996, there were 97 in Broadmoor (20 per cent of the total population), 59 in Ashworth (11 per cent of the total) and 82 in Rampton (17 per cent of the total). The study's aim was to gain some insight into the women's perceptions of their problems and of the hospital. Interviews with 15 women (five from each hospital) provide a vivid picture of lives perceived as gaining little benefit from the 'special hospital' system. As general research on prisons show, these women have high levels of substance dependence and involvement in violent crime and are known for high levels of violence towards staff. The women explained this behaviour in two ways – violence directed towards themselves was an antidote to memories of abuse and violence that were too painful to bear, while violence to staff was often the result of frustration and anger. Although it is not possible in any communal setting to avoid situations in which certain individuals will experience frustration, it is possible to avoid deliberate provocation of anger, an allegation made about the staff by many of the women interviewed. These women are no strangers to abuse as the majority had experienced some form of violence, isolation and abuse in their childhood. For many, prison was perceived as providing an opportunity for safety:

> Institutional care and prison... were initially seen as an escape from the intolerable home situation. But these were 'escapes' which proved illusory, and which frequently became the sites of further abuse and isolation. (Eaton and Humphries 1996: 41)

The attitude of the women towards psychiatric labels and treatment was overwhelmingly negative. Almost all of the women admitted that they needed help with their problems but rejected their specific psychiatric diagnoses and viewed the 'special hospital' as a punitive environment. Over half of them felt that they had not benefited from the psychiatric treatment they had received, and the label of 'psychopathy' was seen as the most questionable and the most damaging. Any psychiatric label was viewed as stigmatising by the women, and the rationale for their committal to a 'special hospital' was rejected by all. Negative attitudes towards the hospital extended to medical and nursing staff, although there were one or two who were perceived as helpful. The feelings of discomfort and unease among the women was especially related to the presence of male prisoners in many of the programmes in which the women participated. The majority of women experienced male prisoners as sexually and physically threatening and said that they would feel 'safer and happier in a woman-only environment'. The words of the women are especially horrifying when placed against the background of a childhood of abuse and violence:

> I don't like it because I keep being asked for sex the whole time. On Monday I was asked by three separate men if I would go and have sex in the toilets with them... this was in the space of two hours... I don't like going to education this morning. It's spoiling it. (Eaton and Humphries 1996: 37)

The questions raised by this kind of research are very fundamental. Does a prison environment, even if it is a hospital unit, offer anything except a holding situation for women with mental health problems? If it is legally necessary to have some form of secure environment for women who are too disturbed for the ordinary prison system, would a small unit (for females only) be more successful in helping these women to move on in their lives?

Atascadero State Hospital

We now turn to quite a different scenario. One of the solutions to the problem of large numbers of male offenders is to designate certain services for specific groups of offenders. ASH, a maximum security facility, in California was one such solution. Opened in 1954, with a specific mandate to treat sex offenders, ASH promised therapy based on the concept of a therapeutic community (Marques *et al.* 1993: 58). Since its opening, a number a changes have occurred in the patient population as well as in psychiatric treatment methods and the public's perception of crime. In 1989, ASH had a patient population of 875, a bed capacity of 927 and a staff of 1,650. The staffing level has constantly increased since the hospital was opened, and the trend in treatments has been away from insight-orientated therapies, to cognitive behaviour treatment and social skills training programmes.

The patient population has changed a great deal since the facility was first opened, when nearly half were sex offenders. The law under which these offenders were sentenced was repealed in 1981, so the proportion of people in this category continues to decrease. In 1989, the patient population, in terms of the legal basis for their commitment was as follows: mentally ill prisoners – 346 patients (39 per cent); incompetent to stand trial – 230 patients (26 per cent); not guilty by reason of insanity – 173 patients (19.5 per cent); mentally disordered sex offenders – 33 patients (3.7 per cent); mentally disordered offender (new category) – 15 patients (1.7 per cent) (for a full discussion, see Marques *et al.* 1993: 59–60).

When viewed in terms of the mental health problems experienced by the patient population, the difference between this and an ordinary prison becomes obvious. More than three-quarters of patients were diagnosed as having major mental disorders, the largest proportion being diagnosed as having schizophrenia (44 per cent) and the next two largest groups having diagnoses of affective disorders (14 per cent) and other psychoses (14 per cent). Also, personality disorder was either the primary or secondary diagnosis for 21 per cent of patients. The demographic characteristics of the patient population are similar to those in other prison populations in some respects but not others. Most patients are young – over 75 per cent are between 20 and 40 years of age. Only 11 per cent of the patients define themselves as currently married; two-thirds have never married, and 20 per cent are separated or divorced. In contrast to the prison population, where the proportions are almost one-third for each ethnic group, more than half of the ASH patients are white, almost 30 per cent are black, and 16 per cent are Hispanic. It is not clear what these differences in the ethnic composition of the patient population mean. Perhaps the intensive substance dependence programmes now available in state and federal prisons have an impact on referrals.

Because of its large size, there are many different kinds of treatment programmes in ASH, all run by members of the mental health teams, who come from different disciplinary and therapeutic backgrounds. However, although this hospital started off with a commitment to non-medical approaches to therapy, this has now virtually disappeared. This is probably partly because of the increase in the proportion of psychotic patients and partly because the state has become more proactive in advocating the medical approach. The result has been an increase in medication and cognitive behavioural programmes. In 1988, 73 per cent of patients were taking antipsychotic drugs (Marques *et al.* 1993: 63). This is indeed an extremely high level of pharmacological control by any reckoning, especially in the light of the 'right to refuse treatment' movement in the USA and the claim by the Bureau of Prisons that fewer than 1 per cent of the general prison population receives antipsychotic medication. The other main way of controlling and guiding patients towards a level of functioning that will enable them to return to society at large is the five-level Patient Privileging System. All patients are assigned to one level and are reviewed by their treatment team on a monthly basis. If they achieve their therapeutic objectives, patients can progress through the system, which is as transparent as possible, gaining more privileges at each level.

In spite of being a large facility with an increasingly difficult patient population, ASH has maintained its commitment to high-quality services, and there have been a number of outcome studies on discharged patients, the results of which have been incorporated into the programmes. However, what it is like to live in an institution such as ASH is difficult to imagine. What is even more difficult to imagine is what it is like to leave a highly structured environment such as ASH and return to live in a society that has become more punitive about crime and more negative about mental disorder. To add to these disadvantages, community psychiatric services are not receiving the resources required to replace hospital services in order to provide the high level of support needed by these very needy men. Those who work in hospitals like ASH are concerned that these pressures will lead to a further criminalisation of people with mental disabilities and a greater demand for secure services, which would change the current system into something completely different.

10

A Final Word

Definitions of mental disorder are undergoing significant change as we enter a new century. These definitions, as we have seen, are highly gendered. In the past, symptoms and behaviour associated with women were more easily defined as mental illness than those which were associated with men. This led not only to a higher level of diagnosis and treatment among women, but also to service planning and development based on deeply rooted stereotypical notions of male and female mental health experiences and behaviours associated with these experiences. As a result, women were overrepresented and men underrepresented in psychiatric statistics, trends that have had a negative effect on the lives of both men and women. One result has been the medicalisation of certain aspects of womens' lives, aspects that require changes in social structures and individual circumstances to remove the causes of the particular stresses, rather than medical intervention of any kind. Other results have been the overuse of medication by women to help them to cope with their 'problems of living' (Szasz 1961, 1971) and the clouding of issues relating to the oppressive or unhappy life conditions under which many of these women have lived. This is not to deny that a proportion of women have genuine mental health problems, some of which need medical treatment, but instead to suggest that an approach that overmedicalised women's lives has not restored a great many of these women to full mental health.

Similarly, men have not benefited from the fact that their mental health problems have often been ignored and underresourced within health service structures. Because the behaviour exhibited by men has often been interpreted as 'bad' rather than 'mad', they have not been as successful as women in accessing mental health services. In the nineteenth century, when the criterion of potential dangerousness was used to justify admissions to asylums, men did indeed find themselves inside the mental health care system, but in this century, because the focus has been on 'illness' and on community treatment, men increasingly found themselves outside this system. Until very recently, the accepted construct of 'mental illness' excluded substance dependence and personality disorder (disorders diagnosed more often in men than women) as both were regarded as untreatable. The current change to a different construct of 'mental disorder' allows for the inclusion of these two categories, not because a new form of medical treatment has been found, but because the concept now incorporates notions of risk to the public. As we have seen in the chapter on crime, research on the link between diagnosed mental illness and violent behaviour is inconclusive, but this has not prevented the media perpetrating the myth of the dangerous 'psychopath'. This myth feeds on public fears of assault and murder by an unknown stranger and is partly to blame for the current pressure on mental health professionals to institutionalise those who are seen as presenting a risk to others. Because the number of psychiatric beds has been decreasing in most Western countries, this has translated into higher levels of imprisonment and compulsory hospitalisation for sections of the population who are viewed as the most dangerous – usually men, the majority of whom are likely to be young and black. The kind of treatment offered to these men in prison and during compulsory hospital admission varies greatly, but it is highly unlikely that they receive the care they need. However, now that it is recognised that men have higher lifetime rates of psychiatric morbidity than women and that only one in five of these receives help from the mental health care system (Robins and Regier 1991), it is to be hoped that a wide range of community-based services with a genuine interest in men's mental health problems will develop in the future.

It is clear from our discussion that mental health service alone will not solve the problems associated with mental disorder. As psychiatric morbidity and psychiatric hospitalisation are both inversely related to low income, wider socio-economic programmes (for example, to improve housing and employment) will undoubtedly have a positive impact on mental health. Because of the complexity of the relationship between gender, mental health and other factors, such as race and income, very few generalisations can be made about the best way forward for mental health policy. However, it can be said that service development must be based on the needs of all sections of the population and must take into account all the socio-economic factors that cause mental distress and impede recovery. If, as is happening in the USA, the service splits into a private system for the rich and a public system for the poor, there is a danger that the public sector will return to the institutional answer, not only because the community option is too difficult to manage, but also because many innovative staff will leave the public system. The institutional solution is also very attractive to the commercial sector, a sector that is becoming increasingly visible in hospital and prison services in the USA, the UK and other European countries.

The diversification of service providers and other similar developments are the result not only of changes in attitudes to mental disorder, but also of changes in social policy directions at national and international levels. Many of the current trends in mental health policy merely reflect the changes in government policy in relation to public spending in general, and health service expenditure in particular. As we saw in the second part of this book, many factors contribute to the final decision on policy direction and service development, factors that have little or nothing to do with mental health issues. For example, in many European countries, including the UK, the trend towards the withdrawal of the state from the direct provision of health and welfare services, and the development of a 'mixed economy of care' approach, has slowed the expansion of community services. Similarly, in the USA, the devolvement of many health services (including those for people with chronic mental disorders) from federal to state level, and the expansion of the insurance-based system of 'managed care' to mental health services, has meant that the quality of service delivery is highly dependent on the area of the country in which a person lives and the willingness of insurance companies to underwrite psychiatric treatment plans. Because many of the people requiring mental health services come from the disadvantaged sections of society, the reduction in both public and private funding for mental health services is of grave concern. It will inevitably lead to more and higher barriers to service use. It will also lead to an increase in the number of people with mental disability coming into contact with the criminal justice system as behaviour associated with substance dependence and personality disorder will undoubtedly be noticed and reported.

This trend is already appearing as the 'care' option is increasingly replaced by the 'control' option in many areas of government policy in Europe and in the USA. Let us hope it does not herald a return to the dark days of the early nineteenth century, when those who were already marginalised by poverty and class position were further isolated for any display of mental disturbance. Kate Millett, who experienced the worst and the best of what is on offer from the psychiatric sector, articulates the call from mental health service users for new attitudes to sanity and madness:

Let there be no more forced hospitalization, drugging, electroshock, no more definitions of insanity as a crime to be treated with savage methods. No more state intervention into grief or ecstasy. Let sanity be understood to be a spectrum that runs the full course between balancing one's checkbook on the one hand and fantasy on the other... A spectrum. A rainbow. All human. All good or at least morally indifferent... None to be punished. None to be feared. If we go mad – so what? We would come back again if not chased away, exiled, isolated, confined. (Millett 1991: 314)

Bibliography

Abas, M., Phillips, C., Carter, J., Walter, J., Banerjee, S. and Levy, R. 1998. 'Culturally Sensitive Validation of Screening for Depression in Older African Caribbean People Living in South London', *British Journal of Psychiatry*, **173**: 249–54.

Abraham, G.W. 1886. *Law and Practice of Lunacy in Ireland*, Dublin, Ponsonby.

Allen, H. 1986. 'Psychiatry and the Construction of the Feminine', in *The Power of Psychiatry* (eds P. Miller and N. Rose), Cambridge, Polity Press.

Allen, H. 1987. *Justice Unbalanced: Gender, Psychiatry and Judicial Decisions*, Milton Keynes, Open University Press.

American Psychiatric Association. 1987 *DSM-III-R: Diagnostic and Statistical Manual of Mental Disorders, Ed. 3-Revised*, Washington D.C., American Psychiatric Association.

American Psychiatric Association. 1994 *DSM-IV: Diagnostic and Statistical Manual of Mental Disorders, Ed. 4*, Washington D.C., American Psychiatric Association.

Anderson, J. 1994. *Public Policymaking: An Introduction* (2nd edn), Boston, Houghton Mifflin.

Angst, J. 1988. 'European Long-term Follow-up Studies of Schizophrenia', *Schizophrenia Bulletin*, **14**: 501–13.

Anson, O., Paran, E., Neumann, L. and Chernichovsky, D. 1993. 'Gender Differences in Health Perceptions and their Predictors', *Social Science and Medicine*, **36**(4): 419–27.

Appelbaum, P.S. and Hoge, S.K. 1986. 'The Right to Refuse Treatment: What the Research Reveals', *Behavioural Sciences and the Law*, **4**: 279–92.

Ashton, H. 1991. 'Psychotropic-drug Prescribing for Women', *British Journal of Psychiatry*, **158** (Suppl. 10): 30–5.

Bakker, A., Van Kersteren, P., Gooren, L. and Bezemer, P. 1993. 'The Prevalence of Transsexualism in the Netherlands', *Acta Psychiatrica Scandinavica*, **87**: 237–8.

Bancroft, J. 1983. *Human Sexuality and its Problems*, Edinburgh, Churchill Livingstone.

Barnes, M. and Maple, N. 1992. *Women and Mental Health: Challenging the Stereotypes*, Birmingham, Venture Press.

Barnes, M. and Shardlow, P. 1997. 'From Passive Recipient to Active Citizen: Participation in Mental Health User Groups', *Journal of Mental Health*, **6**(3): 289–300.

Barnes, M., Bowl, R. and Fisher, M. 1990. *Sectioned: Social Services and the 1983 Mental Health Act*, London, Routledge.

Barnett, R., Biener, L. and Baruch, G. (eds). 1987. *Gender and Stress*, New York, Free Press.

Bartlett, A. 1993. 'Rhetoric and Reality: What do We Know about the English Special Hospitals?', *International Journal of Law and Psychiatry*, **16**(1–2): 27–51.

Bebbington, P., Dean, C., Der, G., Hurry, J. and Tennant, C. 1991. 'Gender, Parity and the Prevalence of Minor Affective Disorder', *British Journal of Psychiatry*, **158**: 40–5.

Bebbington, P., Feeney, S., Flannigan, C., Glover, G., Lewis, S. and Wing, J. 1994. 'Inner London Collaborative Audit of Admissions in Two Health Districts. II: Ethnicity and the Use of the Mental Health Act', *British Journal of Psychiatry*, **165**: 743–9.

Beck, J. 1995. 'Forensic Psychiatry in Britain', *Bulletin of the American Academy of Psychiatry and Law*, **23**(2): 249–60.

Belle, D. 1990. 'Poverty and Women's Mental Health', *American Psychologist*, **45**(3): 385–9.

Benson, P. 1994. 'Deinstitutionalization and Family Caretaking of the Seriously Mentally Ill: The Policy Context', *International Journal of Law and Psychiatry*, **17**(2): 19–38.

Bhui, K., Christie, Y. and Bhugra, D. 1995. 'The Essential Elements of Culturally Sensitive Psychiatric Services', *International Journal of Social Psychiatry*, **41**(4): 242–56.

Biegal, D., Song, L. and Milligan, S. 1995. 'A Comparative Analysis of Family Caregivers' Perceived Relationships with Mental Health Professionals', *Psychiatric Services*, **46**(5): 477–82.

Bille-Brahe, U. 1993. 'The Role of Sex and Age in Suicidal Behavior', *Acta Psychiatrica Scandinavica*, Suppl., **371**: 21–7.

Blaxter, M. 1990. *Health and Lifestyles*, London, Tavistock/Routledge.

Bluglass, R. and Bowden, P. (eds). 1990. *Principles and Practice of Forensic Psychiatry*, Edinburgh, Churchill Livingstone.

Bourget, D. and Labelle, A. 1992. 'Homicide, Infanticide and Filicide', *Clinical Forensic Psychiatry*, **15**(3): 661–73.

Braybrooke, D. and Lindblom, C. 1963. *A Strategy of Decision Making*, New York, Free Press.

Brown, G., Wise, T., Costa, P., Herbst, J., Fagan, P. and Schmidt, C. 1996. 'Personality Characteristics and Sexual Functioning of 188 Cross-Dressing Men', *Journal of Nervous and Mental Disease*, **184**(5): 265–73.

Busfield, J. 1989. *Managing Madness: Changing Ideas and Practice*, London, Hutchinson.

Busfield, J. 1996. *Men, Women and Madness: Understanding Gender and Mental Disorder*, London, Macmillan.

Carson, D. 1993. 'Managed Care: A Provider Perspective', *New Directions for Mental Health Services*, **59**: 81–7.

Castel, T., Castel, F. and Lovell, A. 1982. *The Psychiatric Society*, New York, Columbia University Press (first published in French in 1979).

Chesler, P. 1972. *Women and Madness*, New York, Doubleday.

Chew, R. 1992. *OHE Compendium of Health Statistics* (8th edn), London, Office of Health Economics.

Chodoff, P. and Lyons, H. 1958. 'Hysteria, the Hysterical Personality and "Hysterical" Conversion', *American Journal of Psychiatry*, **114**: 734–40.

Chung, H., Mahler, J. and Kakuma, T. 1995. 'Racial Differences in Treatment of Psychiatric Inpatients', *Psychiatric Services*, **46**(6): 586–91.

Clare, A. 1976. *Psychiatry in Dissent*, London, Tavistock.

Clatterbaugh, K. 1990. *Contemporary Perspectives on Masculinity: Men, Women and Politics in Modern Society*, Oxford, Westview Press.

Cleary, A. and Treacy, M. (eds). 1997. *The Sociology of Health and Illness in Ireland*, Dublin, University College Dublin Press.

Cohen, S. and Scull, A. (eds). 1983. *Social Control and the State: Historical and Comparative Essays*, Oxford, Martin Robertson.

Coid, J. 1984. 'How Many Psychiatric Patients in Prison', *British Journal of Psychiatry*, **145**: 78–86.

Compton, W., Helzer, J., Hwu, H. *et al.* 1991. 'New Methods in Cross-Cultural Psychiatry: Psychiatric Illness in Taiwan and the United States', *American Journal of Psychiatry*, **148**(12): 1697–704.

Connell, R. 1992. 'A Very Straight Gay: Masculinity, Homosexual Experience, and the Dynamics of Gender', *American Sociological Review*, **57**: 735–51.

Connell, R. 1995. *Masculinities*, Oxford, Polity Press.

Coontz, P., Lidz, C. and Mulvey, E. 1994. 'Gender and the Assessment of Dangerousness in the Psychiatric Emergency Room', *International Journal of Law and Psychiatry*, **17**(4): 369–76.

Corin, E. and Bibeau, G. 1988. 'H.B.M. Murphy (1915–87): A Key Figure in Transcultural Psychiatry', *Cultural Medicine and Psychiatry*, **12**(3); 397–415.

Costa-Santos, J. and Madeira, R. 1996. 'Transsexualism in Portugal: The Legal Framework and Procedure and its Consequences for Transsexuals', *Medicine Science and Law*, **36**(3): 221–5.

Cox, B.D., Huppert, F.A. and Whichelow, M.J. (eds). 1993. *The Health and Lifestyle Survey: Seven Years On*, Aldershot, Dartmouth.

Curran, C. and Bingley, W. 1994. 'The Mental Health Act Commission', *Psychiatric Bulletin*, **18**: 328–32.

Daly, K. 1994. *Gender Crime and Punishment* New Haven, Yale University Press

David, D. and Brannon, R. (eds). 1976. *The Forty Nine Percent Majority: The Male Sex Role*, Reading, MA, Addison-Wesley.

Davies, S., Thornicroft, G., Leese, M., Higginbotham, A. and Phelan, M. 1996. 'Ethnic Differences in Risk of Compulsory Psychiatric Admission Among Representative Cases of Psychosis in London', *British Medical Journal*, **312**: 533–7.

Dear, M. and Wolch, J. 1987. *Landscapes of Despair: From Deinstitutionalisation to Homelessness*, Cambridge, Polity Press.

De Cecco, J. and Parker, D. 1995. 'The Biology of Homosexuality: Sexual Orientation or Sexual Preference', *Journal of Homosexuality*, **28**(1–2): 1–27.

Dennerstein, L. 1993. 'Psychosocial and Mental Health Aspects of Women's Health', *World Health Statistics Quarterly*, **46**(4): 234–6.

Dennerstein, L. 1995. 'Mental Health, Work and Gender', *International Journal of Health Services*, **25**(3): 503–9.

Department of Health. 1992. *The Health of the Nation: A Strategy for Health in England*, Cm. 1986, London, HMSO.

Department of Health and Social Security. 1975. *Better Services for the Mentally Ill*, London, HMSO.

Derks, F., Blankstein, J. and Hendricks, J. 1993. 'Treatment and Security: The Dual Nature of Forensic Psychiatry, *International Journal of Law and Psychiatry*, **16**(1–2): 217–40.

Dohrenwend, B. 1975. 'Sociocultural and Social Psychological Factors in the Genesis of Mental Disorders', *Journal of Health and Social Behaviour*, **16**: 365–92.

Donnelly, M., McGilloway, S., Mays, N., Perry, S., Knapp, M., Kavanagh, S., Beecham, J., Fenyo, A. and Astin, J. 1994. *Opening New Doors: An Evaluation of Community Care for People Discharged from Psychiatric and Mental Handicap Hospitals*, London, HMSO.

Eastman, N.L. 1993. 'Forensic Psychiatric Services in Britain: A Current Review', *International Journal of Law and Psychiatry*, **16**: 1–26.

Easton, D. 1965. *A Systems Analysis of Political Life*, New York, Wiley.

Eaton, M. and Humphries, J. 1996. *Listening to Women in Special Hospitals: The Report of a Pilot Study*, London, St Mary's University College.

Edgerton, R. 1980. 'Traditional Treatment for Mental Illness in Africa: A Review', *Culture, Medicine and Psychiatry*, **4**: 167–89.

Edgerton, R. and Cohen, A. 1994. 'Culture and Schizophrenia: The DOSMD Challenge', *British Journal of Psychiatry*, **164**: 222–31.

Edley, N. and Wetherell, M. 1995. *Men in Perspective: Practice, Power and Identity*, London, Prentice Hall/Harvester Wheatsheaf.

El-Guebaly, N. 1995. 'Alcohol and Polysubstance Abuse Among Women', *Canadian Journal of Psychiatry*, **40**(2): 73–9.

Erikson, E. 1950. *Childhood and Society*, London, Imago.

Erwin, K. 1993. 'Interpreting the Evidence: Competing Paradigms and the Emergence of Lesbian and Gay Suicide as a Social Fact', *International Journal of Health Services*, **23**(3): 437–53.

Ezzy, D. 1993. 'Unemployment and Mental Health: A Critical Review', *Social Science and Medicine*, **37**(1): 41–52.

Fennell, P. 1992. 'Balancing Care and Control: Guardianship, Community Treatment Orders and Patient Safeguards', *International Journal of Law and Psychiatry*, **15**(2): 205–35.

Fernando, S. 1988. *Race and Culture in Psychiatry*, London, Tavistock/Routledge.

Fernando, S., Ndegwa, D. and Wilson, M. 1998. 'Forensic Psychiatry, Race and Culture', London, Routledge.

Figert, A. 1996. *Women and the Ownership of PMS: The Structuring of Psychiatric Disorder*, New York, Aldine de Gruyter.

Finnane, M. 1981. *Insanity and the Insane in Post Famine Ireland*, London, Croom Helm.

Flannigan, C., Glover, G., Wing, J., Lewis, S., Bebbington, P. and Feeney, S. 1994a. 'Inner London Collaborative Audit of Admissions in Two Health Districts. III: Reasons for Acute Admission to Psychiatric Wards', *British Journal of Psychiatry*, **165**: 750–9.

Flannigan, C., Glover, G., Feeney, S., Wing, J., Bebbington, P. and Lewis, S. 1994b. 'Inner London Collaborative Audit of Admissions in Two Health Districts. I: Introduction, Methods and Preliminary Findings', *British Journal of Psychiatry*, **165**: 734–42.

Foulds, G. 1965. *Personality and Personal Illness*, London, Tavistock.

Freeman, H., Fryers, T. and Henderson, J. 1985. *Mental Health Services in Europe: 10 Years On* (Public Health in Europe 25), Copenhagan, World Health Organization.

Gelder, M., Gath, D. and Mayou, R. (eds). 1989. *Oxford Textbook of Psychiatry* (2nd edn), Oxford, Oxford University Press.

Goffman, E. 1961. *Asylums*, Harmondsworth, Penguin.

Goldberg, D. 1972. *The Detection of Psychiatric Illness by Questionnaire*, London, Oxford University Press.

Gomez, J. 1993. *Psychological and Psychiatric Problems in Men*, London, Routledge.

Gove, W. and Tudor, J. 1973. 'Adult Sex Roles and Mental Illness', *American Journal of Sociology*, **78**: 813–35.

Green, C., Naismith, L. and Menzies, R. 1991. 'Criminal Responsibility and Mental Disorder in Britain and North America: A Comparative Study', *Medicine, Science and the Law*, **31**(1): 45–54.

Greenberg, A. and Bailey, J. 1994. 'The Irrelevance of the Medical Model of Mental Illness to Law and Ethics', *International Journal of Law and Psychiatry*, **17**(2): 153–73.

Greene, B. 1994. 'Ethnic-Minority Lesbians and Gay Men: Mental Health and Treatment Issues', *Journal of Consulting and Clinical Psychology*, **62**(2): 243–51.

Grob, G. 1983. *Mental Illness and American Society 1875–1940*, New Jersey, Princetown University Press.

Gromb, S., Chanseau, B. and Lazarini, H. 1997. 'Judicial Problems Related to Transsexualism in France', *Medicine Science and Law*, **37**(1): 27–31.

Gunn, J. and Taylor, P.J. (eds). 1993. *Forensic Psychiatry: Clinical, Legal and Ethical Issues*, London, Butterworth Heinemann.

Hafner, J. and An der Heiden, W. 1989. 'The Evaluation of Mental Health Care Systems', *British Journal of Psychiatry*, **155**: 12–17.

Haimowitz. S. 1991. 'Americans with Disabilities Act 1990: Its Significance for Persons with Mental Illness', *Hospital and Community Psychiatry*, **42**: 23–4.

Hall, P. L. and H. and Webb, A. (eds). 1975. *Change, Choice and Conflict in Social Policy*, London, Heinnmann.

Halpern, D. 1993. 'Minorities and Mental Health', *Social Science and Medicine*, **36**(5): 597–607.

Ham, C. 1992. *Health Policy in Britain*, London, Macmillan.

Ham, C. and Hill, M. 1988. *The Policy Process in the Modern Capitalist State*, Sussex, Wheatsheaf.

Hatfield, A. and Lefley, H. 1993. *Surviving Mental Illness: Stress, Coping and Adaptation*, New York, Guildford Press.

Hatfield, A., Gearon, J. and Coursey, R. 1996a. 'Family Members' Ratings of the Use and Value of Mental Health Services: Results of a National NAMI Survey', *Psychiatric Services*, **47**(8): 825–31.

Hatfield, B., Mohamad, H., Rahim, Z. and Tanweer, H. 1996b. 'Mental Health and the Asian Communities: A Local Survey', *British Journal of Social Work*, **26**: 315–36.

Hayes, B.C. and Prior, P.M. 1998a. 'The Changing Impact of Gender and Marital Status on Use of Health and Social Care Services: What is Happening to the Single Woman?', Paper presented at the Annual Conference of the Social Policy Association, Lincoln, England.

Hayes, B.C. and Prior, P.M. 1998b. 'Changing Places: Men Replace Women in Psychiatric Beds in Britain', Paper presented at the World Congress of the International Sociological Association, Montreal, Canada.

Hedderman, C. and Hough, M. 1994. 'Does the Criminal Justice System Treat Men and Women Differently', Research Findings No. 10, London, Home Office RSD.

Heidensohn, F. 1996. *Women and Crime* (2nd edn), London, Macmillan.

Heller, T., Reynolds, J., Gomm, R., Muston, R. and Pattison, S. (eds). 1996. *Mental Health Matters: A Reader*, London, Macmillan/Open University.

Hellman, R. 1996. 'Issues in the Treatment of Lesbian Women and Gay Men with Chronic Mental Illness', *Psychiatric Services*, **47**(10): 1093–7.

Hickman, R. 1995. 'Madness: Citizenship's Awkward Interrogator', Paper presented to the British Sociological Association, Medical Sociology Conference, held in York.

Hill, M. 1997a. *The Policy Process in the Modern State* (3rd edn), London, Prentice Hall/Harvester Wheatsheaf.

Hill, M. (ed.). 1997b. *The Policy Process: A Reader* (2nd edn), London, Prentice Hall/Harvester Wheatsheaf.

Hill, P., Murray, R. and Thorley, A. (eds). 1986. *Essentials of Postgraduate Psychiatry* (2nd edn), London, Grune & Stratton.

Hodgins, S. 1993a. *Mental Disorder and Crime*, London, Sage.

Hodgins, S. 1993b. 'Mental Treatment Services in Quebec for Persons Accused or Convicted of Criminal Offences', *International Journal of Law and Psychiatry*, **16**(1–2): 179–94.

Hopper, K. 1991. 'Some Old Questions for the New Cross Cultural Psychiatry', *Medical Anthropoligy Quarterly*, **5**: 299–329.

Hopton, J. and Hunt, S. 1995. 'Housing Conditions and Mental Health in a Disadvantaged Area in Scotland', *Journal of Epidemiology and Community Health*, **50**: 56–61.

Jablensky, A. 1986. 'Epidemiology of Schizophrenia: A European Perspective', *Schizophrenia Bulletin*, **12**: 52–73.

Jebali, C. 1995. 'Working with Women in Mental Health: A Feminist Perspective', *British Journal of Nursing*, **4**(3): 137–40.

Jenkins, R. 1994. 'The Health of the Nation: Recent Government Policy and Legislation', *Psychiatric Bulletin*, **18**: 324–327.

Jenkins, R. and Meltzer, H. 1995. 'The National Survey of Psychiatric Morbidity in Great Britain', *Social Psychiatry and Psychiatric Epidemiology*, **30**: 1–4.

Jensen, K. 1995. *Mental Health Legislation in Europe*, Paper presented at the World Congress on Mental Health in Dublin, Ireland (survey for the World Health Organization, Regional Office for Europe).

Jones, K. 1972. *A History of the Mental Health Services 1744–1971*, London, Routledge & Kegan Paul.

Kaplan, H. and Sadock, B. 1995. *Comprehensive Textbook of Psychiatry,* Vols 1 & 2 (6th edn), Baltimore, Williams & Wilkins.

Katz, M., Marsella, A., Dube, K. *et al.* 1988. 'On the Expression of Psychosis in Different Cultures', *Culture, Medicine and Psychiatry*, **12**: 331–55.

Kavanagh, S. 1997. 'Purchasers, Providers and Managed Care: Developments in the Mental Health Market Place', *Current Opinion in Psychiatry*, **10**: 153–9.

Kavanagh, S., Opit, L., Knapp, M. and Beecham, J. 1995. 'Schizophrenia: Shifting the Balance of Care', *Social Psychiatry and Psychiatric Epidemiology*, **30**: 206–12.

Kelleher, M. 1998. 'Youth Suicide in the Republic of Ireland', *British Journal of Psychiatry*, **173**: 194–7.

Kendall, R. and Zealey, A. (eds). 1988. *Companion to Psychiatric Studies* (4th edn), Edinburgh, Churchill Livingstone.

Kendler, K. and Walsh, D. 1995. 'Gender and Schizophrenia: Results of an Epidemiologically-based Family Study', *British Journal of Psychiatry*, **167**: 184–92.

Kent, D., Fogarty, M. and Yellowless, P. 1995a. 'A Review of Studies of Heavy Users of Psychiatric Services', *Psychiatric Services*, **46**(12): 1247–53.

Kent, D., Fogarty, M. and Yellowless, P. 1995b. 'Heavy Utilization of Inpatient and Outpatient Services in a Public Mental Health Service', *Psychiatric Services*, **46**(12): 1254–7.

Kessler, R., McGonigle, K., Zhao, S. *et al.* 1994. 'Lifetime and 12 Month Prevalence of DSM-III-R Psychiatric Disorders in the United States. Results from the National Comorbidity Survey', *Archives of General Psychiatry*, **51**: 8–19.

Kimble, O. 1900 'Mental Health Policy as a Field of Inquiry for Psychology', *American Psychologist*, **35**(12): 1066–80.

Knapp, M., Beecham, J., Fenyo, A. and Hallam, A. 1995. 'Community Mental Health Care for Former Hospital In-patients: Predicting Costs from Needs and Diagnoses', *British Journal of Psychiatry*, **166** (Suppl. 27): 10–18.

Kuipers, L. 1993. 'Family Burden in Schizophrenia' (Review and Editorial), *Social Psychiatry and Psychiatric Epidemiology*, **28**(5): 207–10.

La Fond, J. 1994. 'Law and Delivery of Involuntary Mental Health Services', *American Journal of Orthopsychiatry*, **64**(2): 209–22.

La Fond, J. and Durham, M. 1992. *Back to the Asylum: The Future of Mental Health Law and Policy in the United States*, Oxford, Oxford University Press.

Laing, R. 1960. *The Divided Self: An Existential Study in Sanity and Madness*, London, Tavistock.

Le Grand, J. 1982. *The Strategy of Equality: Redistribution and the Social Services*, London, Allen & Unwin.

Leibenluft, E. 1996. 'Women with Bipolar Illness: Clinical and Research Issues', *American Journal of Psychiatry*, **153**(2): 163–73.

Lelliot, P., Wing, J. and Clifford, P. 1994. 'A National Audit of New Long-Stay Psychiatric Patients. 1: Method and Description of the Cohort', *British Journal of Psychiatry*, **165**: 160–9.

Lesage, A., Boyer, R., Grunberg, F. *et al.* 1994. 'Suicide and Mental Disorders: A Case-control Study of Young Men', *American Journal of Psychiatry*, **151**(7): 1063–8.

Lister, R. 1998. *Citizenship: Feminist Perspectives*, London, Macmillan.

Litwack, T., Kirschner, S. and Wack, R. 1993. 'The Assessment of Dangerousness and Predictions of Violence: Recent Research and Future Prospects', *Psychiatric Quarterly*, **64**(3): 245–73.

Louzoun, C. (ed.). 1993. *Santé Mentale: Réalités Européennes*, Paris, ERES.

Lukes, S. 1974. *Power: A Radical View*, London, Macmillan.

Maden, T., Swinton, M. and Gunn, J. 1994. 'Psychiatric Disorder in Women Serving a Prison Sentence', *British Journal of Psychiatry*, **164**: 44–54.

Malcolm, E. 1989. *Swift's Hospital*. Dublin, Gill & Macmillan.

March, J. and Olsen, J. 1989. *Rediscovering Institutions*, New York, Free Press.

Marques, J., Haynes, R. and Nelson, C. 1993. 'Forensic Treatment at Atascadero State Hospital', *International Journal of Law and Psychiatry*, **16**: 57–70.

Marshall, T. 1981. *The Right to Welfare and Other Essays*, London, Heinemann Educational Books.

Mason, P. and Wilkinson, G. 1996. 'The Prevalence of Psychiatric Morbidity: OPCS Survey of Psychiatric Morbidity in Great Britain', *British Journal of Psychiatry*, **168**: 1–3.

Meltzer, H., Gill, B., Petticrew, M. and Hinds, K. 1995. *OPCS Surveys of Psychiatric Morbidity in Great Britain: Report No. 1: The Prevalence of Psychiatric Morbidity Among Adults Living in Private Households*, London, HMSO.

Millett, Kate. 1970. *Sexual Politics*, New York, Ballantine Books.

Millett, Kate, 1991. *The Loony Bin Trip*, New York, Virago Press.

MIRE. 1995. *Comparing Social Welfare Systems*, Vol. 1: *The Oxford Conference*, Paris, Ministry of Social Affairs.

Mitchell, J. 1975. *Psychoanalysis and Feminism*, Harmondsworth, Penguin.

Monahan, J. and Steadman, H. (eds). 1994. *Violence and Mental Disorder: Developments in Risk Assessment*, Chicago, University of Chicago Press.

Moore, M. 1984. *Law and Psychiatry: Rethinking the Relationship*, Cambridge, Cambridge University Press.

Morris, A. 1987. *Women, Crime and Punishment*, Oxford, Basil Blackwell.

Mueser, K., Webb, M., Pfeiffer, M., Gladis, M. and Levinson, D. 1996. 'Family Burden of Schizophrenia and Bipolar Disorder; Perceptions of Relatives and Professionals', *Psychiatric Services*, **47**(5): 507–11.

Munday, B. and Ely, P. (eds). 1996. *Social Care in Europe*, London, Prentice Hall.

Naffine, N. 1987. *Female Crime: The Construction of Women in Criminology*, Sydney, Allen & Unwin.

Nazroo, J. 1997. *Ethnicity and Mental Health: Findings from a National Community Survey*, London, Policy Studies Institute.

Nedopil, N. and Ottermann, B. 1993. 'Treatment of Mentally Ill Offenders in Germany: With Special Reference to Straubing in Bavaria', *International Journal of Law and Psychiatry*, **16**(1–2): 247–55.

Newhill, C., Mulvey, E. and Lidz, C. 1995. 'Characteristics of Violence in the Community by Female Patients Seen in a Psychiatric Emergency Service', *Psychiatric Services*, **46**(8): 785–9.

Oliver, M. 1990. *The Politics of Disablement*, London, Macmillan.

Paykel, E. 1991. 'Depression in Women', *British Journal of Psychiatry*, **158**(Suppl. 10): 22–9.

Payne, S. 1995. 'The Rationing of Psychiatric Beds: Changing Trends in Sex-ratios in Admission to Psychiatric Hospital', *Health and Social Care in the Community*, **3**(5): 289–300.

Payne, S. 1996. 'Masculinity and the Redundant Male: Explaining the Increasing Incarceration of Young Men', *Social and Legal Studies*, **5**(2): 159–78.

Perkins, R. and Moodley, P. 1993. 'Perception of Problems in Psychiatric Inpatients: Denial, Race and Service Usage', *Social Psychiatry and Psychiatric Epidemiology*, **28**: 189–93.

Perlin, M. 1992. 'On sanism', *Southern Methodist University Law Review*, **46**: 373–407.

Perlin, M. 1993. 'Decoding Right to Refuse Treatment Law', *International Journal of Law and Psychiatry*, **16**(1–2): 151–77.

Perlin, M. 1994. 'Law and the Delivery of Mental Health Services in the Community', *American Journal of Orthopsychiatry*, **64**(2): 194–208.

Pfeiffer, S., O'Malley, D. and Short, S. 1996. 'Factors Associated with the Outcome of Adults Treated in Psychiatric Hospitals: A Synthesis of Findings', *Psychiatric Services*, **47**(3): 263–9.

Phan, T. and Silove, D. 1997. 'The Influence of Culture on Psychiatric Assessment: The Vietnamese Refugee', *Psychiatric Services*, **48**(1): 86–90.

Philo, G. (ed.). 1996. *The Media and Mental Distress*, London, Longman.

Philpot, T. 1989. 'Bringing Home the Bacon', *Community Care*, 16 November: 21–4.

Pilowsky, L., O'Sullivan, G., Ramana, R., Palazidou, E. and Moodley, P. (eds). 1991. 'Women and Mental Health', *British Journal of Psychiatry*, **158**(Suppl. 10): 1–92.

Plath, S. 1963. *The Bell Jar*, London, Heinemann.

Pleck, J. 1981. *The Myth of Masculinity*, Cambridge, MA: MIT Press.

Polak, P. and Warner, R. 1996. 'The Economic Life of Seriously Mentally Ill People in the Community', *Psychiatric Services*, **47**(2): 270–4.

Poythress, N. (ed.) 1993. 'Forensic Treatment in the United States: A Survey of Selected Forensic Hospitals', *International Journal of Law and Psychiatry*, **16**(1–2): 53–132.

Prior, P.M. 1992. 'The Approved Social Worker – Reflections on Origins', *British Journal of Social Work*, **22**(2): 105–19.

Prior, P.M. 1993. *Mental Health and Politics in Northern Ireland*, Aldershot, Avebury.

Prior, P.M. 1995. 'Surviving Psychiatric Institutionalisation: A Case Study', *Sociology of Health and Illness*, **17**(5): 651–67.

Prior, P.M. 1996. 'The Dark Side of Goodness: Women, Social Norms and Mental Health', *Journal of Gender Studies*, **5**(1): 27–37.

Prior, P.M. 1997. 'Mad not Bad: Crime, Mental Disorder and Gender in Nineteenth Century Ireland', *History of Psychiatry*, **8**(4); 501–16.

Prior, P.M. and Hayes, B.C. 1998. 'The Increasing Visibility of Young Men in Psychiatric Beds in Northern Ireland: An Emerging International Trend?', Paper presented at the Annual Conference of the Society for the Study of Social Problems, San Francisco.

Pugliesi, K. 1992. 'Women and Mental Health: Two Traditions of Feminist Research', *Women and Health*, **19**(2/3): 43–68.

Ramon, S. 1995. *Psychiatry in Britain: Meaning and Policy*, London, Croom Helm.

Ramon, S. 1996. *Mental Health in Europe: Ends, Beginnings and Rediscoveries*, London, Macmillan.

Regier, D., Boyd, J., Burke, J. *et al.* 1988. 'One Month of Prevalence of Mental Disorders in the USA', *Archives of General Psychiatry*, **45**: 977–86.

Regier, D., Farmer, M., Rae, D. *et al.* 1993. 'One Month of Prevalence of Mental Disorders in the USA and Sociodemographic Characteristics: The Epidemiologic Catchment Area Study', *Acta Psychiatrica Scandinavica*, **88**: 35–47.

Reicher-Rossler, A. and Rossler, W. 1993. 'Compulsory Admission of Psychiatric Patients – an International Comparison' (Review), *Acta Psychiatrica Scandinavica*, **87**: 231–6.

Reik, T. 1967. *Of Love and Lust: On the Psychoanalysis of Romantic and Sexual Emotions*, New York, Farrar, Strauss & Giroux.

Ripa, Y. 1990. *Women and Madness: The Incarceration of Women in Nineteenth Century France*, Cambridge, Polity Press (published in France as *La Ronde des Folles*).

Robins, L. and Regier, D. (eds). 1991. *Psychiatric Disorders in America: The Epidemiologic Catchment Area Study*, New York, Free Press.

Rogers, A. and Pilgrim, D. 1996. *Mental Health Policy in Britain: A Critical Introduction*, London, Macmillan.

Rogler, L. and Cortes, D. 1993. 'Help-Seeking Pathways: A Unifying Concept in Mental Health Care', *American Journal of Psychiatry*, **150**(4): 554–61.

Roughan, P. 1993. 'Mental Health and Psychiatric Disorders in Older Women', *Clinics in Geriatric Medicine,* **9**(1): 173–90.

Rudnick, A. and Levy, A. 1994. 'Personality Disorders and Criminal Responsibility: A Second Opinion', *International Journal of Law and Psychiatry*, **17**(4): 409–20.

Russell, D. 1995. *Women, Madness and Medicine*, Cambridge, Polity Press.

Sales, B. and Shuman, D. 1994. 'Mental Health Law and Mental Health Care: Introduction', *American Journal of Orthopsychiatry*, **64**(2): 172–9.

Salize, H. and Rossler, W. 1996. 'The Cost of Comprehensive Care of People with Schizophrenia Living in the Community', *British Journal of Psychiatry*, **169**: 42–8.

Sanguineti, V., Samuel, S., Schwartz, S. and Robeson, M. 1996. 'Retrospective Study of 2,200 Involuntary Psychiatric Admissions and Re-admissions', *American Journal of Psychiatry*, **153**(3): 392–6.

Sargent, C. and Brettell, C. 1996. *Gender and Health: An International Perspective*, Upper Saddle River, New Jersey, Prentice Hall.

Saris, A. 1994. 'The Return of the Repressed: Bringing Culture Back to Psychiatry', *Culture, Medicine and Psychiatry*, **18**: 115–33.

Sartorius, N. 1986. 'Cross-cultural Research on Depression', *Psychopathology*, **19**(Suppl. 2): 6–11.

Sartorius, N., Nielson, J. and Stomgren, E. 1989. 'Changes in Frequency of Mental Disorder over Time: Results of Repeated Surveys of Mental Disorders in the General Population', *Acta Psychiatrica Scandinavica*, **79**(Suppl. 348): 1–187.

Scheff, T. 1966. *Being Mentally Ill*, London, Weidenfeld & Nicholson.

Schober, R. and Annis, H. 1996. 'Barriers to Help-seeking for Change in Drinking: A Gender-focused Review of the Literature', *Addictive Behaviour*, **21**(1): 81–92.

Scull, A. 1984. *Decarceration: Community Treatment and the Deviant – A Radical View*, New Jersey, Polity Press.

Scull, A. (ed.). 1991. *The Asylum as Utopia: W.A.F. Browne and the Mid Nineteenth Century Consolidation of Psychiatry*, London, Tavistock/Routledge.

Shapiro, S., Skinner, E., Kessler, L. *et al.* 1984. 'Utilization of Health and Mental Health Services: Three Epidemiologic Catchment Area Sites', *Archives of General Psychiatry*, **41**: 971–8.

Shepherd, G., Muijen, M., Hadley, T. and Goldman, H. 1996. 'Effects of Mental Health Sevices Reform on Clinical Practice in the United Kingdom', *Psychiatric Services*, **47**(12): 1351–5.

Shorter, E. 1990. 'Mania, Hysteria and Gender in Lower Austria 1891–1905', *History of Psychiatry*, **i**: 3–31.

Showalter, E. 1987. *The Female Malady: Women, Madness and English Culture 1830–1980*, London, Virago Press (first published 1985).

Sims, A. and Owens, D. 1993. *Psychiatry* (6th edn), London, Baillière Tindall.

Skultans, V. 1979. *English Madness: Ideas on Insanity 1530–1890*, London, Routledge & Kegan Paul.

Smith, R. 1981 *Trial by Medicine: Insanity and Responsibility in Victorian Trials*, Edinburgh, Edinburgh University Press.

Solomon, P. and Draine, J. (1995) 'Adaptive Coping among Family Members of Persons with Serious Mental Illness', *Psychiatric Services*, **46**(11): 1156–60.

Sommers, I. and Baskin, D. 1992. 'Sex, Race, Age, and Violent Offending', *Violence and Victims*, **7**(3): 191–201.

Stevenson, C. 1996. 'Robert Hooke's Bethlem', *Journal of the Society of Architectural History*, **55**(3): 254–75.

Stoller, R.J. 1984. *Sex and Gender: The Development of Masculinity and Femininity* London, Karnac (first published 1968)

Subotsky, F. 1991. 'Issues for Women in the Development of Mental Health Services', *British Journal of Psychiatry*, **158**(Suppl. 10): 17–21.

Sugarman, P. and Craufurd, A. 1994. 'Schizophrenia in the Afro-Caribbean Community', *British Journal of Psychiatry*, **64**: 474–80.

Sundram, C. 1995. 'Implementation and Activities of Protection and Advocacy Programs for Persons with Mental Illness', *Psychiatric Services*, **46**(7): 702–6.

Szasz, T. 1961. *The Myth of Mental Illness*, New York, Harper & Row.

Szasz, T. 1970. *Manufacture of Madness*, New York, Harper & Row.

Szasz, T. 1971. *The Manufacture of Madness: A Comparative Study of the Inquisition and the Mental Health Movement*, London, Routledge & Kegan Paul.

Thomas, C., Stone, K., Osborn, M., Thomas, P. and Fisher, M. 1993. 'Psychiatric Morbidity and Compulsory Admission Among UK-born Europeans, Afro-Caribbeans and Asians in Central Manchester', *British Journal of Psychiatry*, **163**: 91–9.

Thornicroft, G. and Bebbington, P. 1989. 'Deinstitutionalisation – from Hospital Closure to Service Development', *British Journal of Psychiatry*, **155**: 739–53.

Thornley, C., Walton, V., Romans-Clarkson, S., Herbison, G. and Mullen, P. 1991. 'Screening for Psychiatric Morbidity in Men and Women', *New Zealand Medical Journal*, **104**(925): 505–7.

Tooth, G. and Brooke, E. 1961. 'Trends in Mental Hospital Population and their Effect on Future Planning', *Lancet,* I: 710–13.

Torrey, E. 1997. *Out of the Shadows: Confronting America's Mental Illness Crisis*, New York, Wiley.

Torrey, E. and Kaplan, R. 1995. 'A National Survey of the Use of Outpatient Commitment', *Psychiatric Services*, **46**(12): 1291.

Uffing, H., Ceha, M. and Saenger, G. 1992. 'The Development of De-institutionalization in Europe', *Psychiatric Quarterly*, **63**(3): 265–79.

US Government. circa 1996. *National Plan for the Chronically Mentally Ill*, Department of Health and Human Services, Center for Mental Health Services, Washington, D.C., Government Printing Office.

Ussher, J. 1991. *Women's Madness: Mysogyny or Mental Illness?*, London, Harvester Wheatsheaf.

Vanezis, P. 1991. 'Women, Violent Crime and Menstrual Cycle: A Review', *Medicine, Science and Law,* **31**(1): 11–14.

Verhaak, P. 1993. 'Analysis of Referrals of Mental Health Problems by General Practitioners', *British Journal of General Practice*, **43**: 203–8.

Viinamaki, H., Kontula, O., Niskanen, L. and Koskela, K. 1995. 'The Association Between Economic and Social Factors and Mental Health in Finland', *Acta Psychiatrica Scandinavica*, **92**: 208–13.

Wade, J.C. 1993. 'Institutional Racism: An Analysis of the Mental Health System', *American Journal of Orthopsychiatry*, **63**(4): 536–44.

Walker, N. 1968. *Crime and Insanity in England: The Historical Perspective*, Edinburgh, Edinburgh University Press.

Walklate, S. 1995. *Gender and Crime: An Introduction*, London, Prentice Hall/Harvester Wheatsheaf.

Walters, V. 1993. 'Stress, Anxiety and Depression: Women's Accounts of their Health Problems', *Social Science and Medicine*, **36**(4): 393–402.

Watkins, T.R. and Callicutt, J.W. (eds). 1997. *Mental Health Policy and Practice Today*, Thousand Oaks, California, Sage.

Wexler, D.B. 1990. *Therapeutic Jurisprudence: The Law as a Therapeutic Agent'*, Durham: Carolina Academic Press.

Wilkinson, G. 1989. 'Referrals from General Practitioners to Psychiatrists and Paramedical Mental Health Professionals', *British Journal of Psychiatry*, **154**: 72–6.

Wilkinson, R. 1996. *Unhealthy Societies: The Afflictions of Inequality*, London, Routledge.

Williams, F. 1989. *Social Policy: A Critical Introduction*, Cambridge, Polity Press.

World Health Organization. 1992. *International Classification of Diseases* (10th edn), Geneva, World Health Organization.

Young, R. 1996. 'The Household Context for Women's Health Care Decisions: Impacts of UK Policy Changes', *Social Science and Medicine*, **42**(6): 949–63.

Yuval-Davis, N. and Anthias, F. (eds). 1989. *Woman – Nation – State*, London, Macmillan.

Zerbe, K. 1995. 'Anxiety Disorders in Women', *Bulletin of the Menninger Clinic*, **59**(2, Suppl. A): A38–A52.

Zlotnick, C., Shea, T., Pilkonis, P., Elkin, I. and Ryan, C. 1996. 'Gender, Type of Treatment, Dysfunctional Attitudes, Social Support, Life Events and Depressive Symptoms over Naturalistic Follow-Up', *American Journal of Psychiatry*, **153**(8): 1021–7.

Name Index

Subject Index